The Creative Teaching and Learning Toolkit

Brin Best and Will Thomas

continuum

Also available from Continuum

Getting the Buggers to Think – Sue Cowley
Teaching Thinking 2nd Edition – Robert Fisher
100 Ideas for Teaching Creativity – Stephen Bowkett
Psychology and the Teacher – Dennis Child
Coaching Solutions – Will Thomas and Alistair Smith

The Creative Teaching and Learning Toolkit

Brin Best and Will Thomas

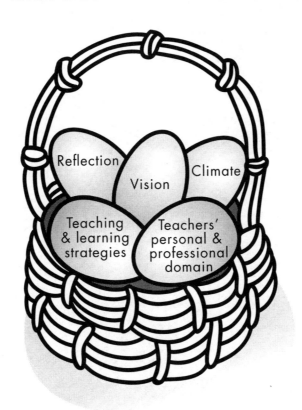

'It's unwise to count your chickens before they've hatched...but it's fun to imagine what they'll look like'

Continuum International Publishing Group
The Tower Building
11 York Road
SE1 7NX

80 Maiden Lane, Suite 704
New York, NY 10038

www.continuumbooks.com

British Library Cataloguing-in-Publication Data
A catalogue record for this book is available from the British Library.

ISBN: 0826485987 (paperback)

Typeset by Fakenham Photosetting Limited, Fakenham, Norfolk
Printed and bound in Great Britain by Athenaeum Press.

"Survivor" by Roger McGough from *Holiday on Death Row*, (© Roger McGough) is reproduced by permission of PFD (www.pfd.co.uk) on behalf of Roger McGough.

Contents

Acknowledgements

The book has benefited from the input of a wide range of people who have helped to improve its content. The following made valuable contributions to the Creative Teaching Framework: Anthony Blake, Sophie Craven, Barry Hymer, Geoff Petty, Dan Varney and Belle Wallace. We are grateful to all those who provided case studies for the book, although some have chosen to remain anonymous.

We are especially grateful to Gill O'Donnell who made several key contributions to the book, proof-read the whole document and generally provided support in a multitude of ways.

Brin Best is very grateful to his wife, mum and dad for many years of unfailing support during his career as a teacher, adviser and consultant. He would also like to place on record how much he has learned from fellow teachers throughout this time.

Will Thomas would like to thank Richard, mum, dad and Sal for their ever-present support and encouragement. He also wishes to thank Nicky Anastasiou, Penny Clayton, Gavin Kewley, Sarah Mook, Tom Hill and Simon Percival for their continuing support, encouragement and innovation. Will also wishes to thank Alistair Smith for the many years of inspiration, from that first in-service training all those years ago, to the present day.

The support and enthusiasm of our editor Alexandra Webster has been very significant. We have been continually inspired by her faith in this project, and buoyed up by her positive approach to shaping the book. It is fitting that we can pay tribute to her and the team at Continuum here.

Finally, we would like to emphasize how important the love and support of our families and friends have been in allowing us to see this project through to completion. They have helped to provide our own effective climate for working, which has contributed to this book immeasurably.

Note: unless attributed all quotes used in the book are our own.

Authors' preface

For some time in our teaching careers, we had found ourselves asking the question, 'What is education *really* for?'. Through re-evaluating the purpose and process of educating young people we rediscovered many approaches which lit the motivational fuses of the young people we worked with. We found that, as fascinated by the knowledge and skills of our students as we were, some youngsters were yet to tap into this level of inspiration.

Steadily, we began experimenting, using our own ideas, building on the pioneering work of people like Eric Jensen, Colin Rose, Alistair Smith and Barry Teare until we had discovered ways of bringing all youngsters into the fold. Some of this was about an unconditional positive belief in their ability to improve, to take steps forward and to succeed. Another part of it was about constructing a *scaffold* for learners, based on the unique experiences they already had, by acknowledging these and building on them. It was underpinned by an important principle, that if learning was going to happen for every child we taught, it was going to need to invoke positive emotional experiences.

Fostering creativity in ourselves and our learners was the key to this happening. The more we thought and read about creativity, the more we realized that it was central to the success of teachers and learners, but had somehow been neglected in previous teaching books. Over the last couple of years the topic has occupied much of our attention as we strived to produce a highly practical book that is still rooted in academic rigour. This book is our attempt to place creativity at the heart of the teaching and learning process.

Brin Best and Will Thomas, January 2007

'In today's world, creativity is fundamentally important for our personal, social, economic and cultural wellbeing. The most important developments in civilization have come about through the creative process.'

Robert Fritz

Read this first!

Read the following primer pages to get a quick five-minute overview of the book. We explain what the book is about and how you can benefit from it. If you're considering buying the book, then this section should answer your basic questions; if you've already bought it, consider this section your route-map through the key ideas in the book.

Essential facts about this book

Here are ten key points that summarize in a nutshell what this book is about:

1. The main aim of the book is to help you become an *even* more effective teacher – this is the essential precursor that will enable your students to become better learners. We wish to build upon what you already know and do, rather than trying to 'reinvent the wheel'.

2. Our belief is that *every* teacher can become more effective if the conditions are created to allow their inner abilities to flourish, while at the same time they learn new skills and techniques.

3. The book is relevant for teachers who work with learners of all ages and abilities, but special emphasis is placed on the secondary school years.

4. Our main motivation in writing the book is to improve the educational opportunities offered to the young people in our schools. This will only happen if their creativity is nurtured.

5. We focus on **creativity** as the principal factor that binds together all effective teachers across the full spectrum of subjects and age ranges – by which we mean the use of new and appropriate methods to get the desired results.

6. We define teachers' creativity as the successful implementation of new or refined teaching and learning approaches which are able to enhance student learning.

7. We believe that **everybody** has the ability to become more creative – there is nothing mystical or special about creativity over and above any other human attribute. This book contains a wealth of strategies to enable you and your students to be more creative.

8. We present a fresh way of thinking about effective teaching, called the **Creative Teaching Framework**, which combines five domains which are critical in teaching excellence, all of which depend on creativity:
   - Vision
   - Climate for learning
   - Teaching and learning strategies
   - Reflection
   - The teacher's professional and personal domain.

9. The book champions the role of the teacher as a highly skilled professional, and as such teachers need to make informed decisions about which teaching strategies they use from the wealth of possibilities on offer. The book provides over 200 strategies and approaches for you to consider.

10. We believe that teachers can gain many useful insights into the teaching and learning process from the world of education psychology – the 'science' that underpins teaching – but teachers themselves have a key role to play in answering the many questions that remain.

What are the key principles of the book?

As you read the book you'll soon become acquainted with the following principles, which we challenge you to embrace:

1. *Change* is essential for us to grow, but that change needs to come from *within* by making appropriate choices.

2. Positive changes can be *challenging* and will require high levels of commitment and much determination.

3. *Values* and *vision* underpin everything we do, but they're frequently not articulated.

4. We possess *within* us the resources to find solutions to many of the questions or problems that we set ourselves – but we sometimes need an external influence to help us to see a situation differently and to find an alternative preferred future.

5. One of the keys to making positive change is the ability and willingness to pose yourself challenging and thought-provoking *questions*.

6. Effective learning is *fun* – for both teachers and students.

7. Effective learning happens when teachers and learners work together in partnership (not when teachers 'deliver' a curriculum to learners).

8. *Be* the change you want to see in your classroom – when we model the behaviours we want in our students we get them more of the time.

9. Taking calculated *risks* leads to invention and growth – encourage this whenever you can.

How will this book make you an even better teacher?

One of the key aims of the book is to help you improve your teaching skills:

1. It will help you to build upon what you *already* do well and identify the areas of your teaching that require further refinement.

2. It will support you to use the Creative Teaching Framework to keep improving in your role.

3. It will help you to use untapped resources to develop further as a teacher.

4. It will encourage you to see that you're never 'the finished article' as a teacher; instead you are continually learning and improving.

5. It will encourage you to adopt an *open but critical* approach to your teaching: embracing new ideas, but being rigorous about how they're applied.

6. It will show you how to develop a robust personal *vision* of the kind of teacher you want to become, which will allow you to survive government initiatives and other external pressures and feel empowered to create a better future.

7. It will provide you with a user-friendly self-evaluation tool that will facilitate a structured path to self-improvement and career development.

8. It will allow you to take advantage of some of the latest research and theories into what is effective in the classroom.

9. It will help you to evaluate what really works in the classroom to aid learning.

10. It will help you to rediscover the joy of teaching by focusing on things that work and the ways of maximizing the life opportunities of the young people you work with.

What questions will this book help you to answer?

Throughout the book we pose challenging questions that will help you to reflect on the role of the teacher. Some of the more fundamental questions underpinning the whole work include the following:

❶ What **values** underpin **your** teaching?

❷ What do you need to do next to develop your expertise as a teacher?

❸ What can **other staff** at your school do to help you improve as a teacher?

❹ How can you create the conditions that will enable **you** and your learners to be in the optimal state **psychologically** to teach?

❺ How can you become more **creative** as a teacher?

❻ How can you facilitate lifelong thinking and learning skills to your students, while at the same time covering the curriculum to ensure their examination success?

❼ What lessons can you learn from educational **research** and how can you put this information into practice in the classroom?

❽ How can so-called **'accelerated learning'** techniques help your students?

❾ What can you do to ensure that your students are **motivated** to learn?

How will this book help your students?

Teachers only exist because of their students, so the book is ultimately aimed at improving *their* life opportunities:

❶ It will allow you to focus on the learning techniques that are most appropriate to students' individual needs, thereby encouraging more **personalized** learning.

❷ It will stimulate you to continually **innovate** in order to present your students with attractive learning opportunities that motivate and inspire.

❸ It will make you a more **reflective** teacher, who is open to the views of students.

❹ It will emphasize the key role of the learner as a **constructor** of knowledge, not a passive receiver of information.

❺ It will support you to focus on the **physical** and **emotional** climate for learning, two often neglected components of effective teaching.

❻ It will help you to see your students as **partners** in the learning process, thereby empowering them to engage more effectively in their lessons.

❼ It will encourage you to deal with any behavioural issues positively, as part of a focus on high quality learning for all.

❽ It will provide you with the tools to design interesting and meaningful learning experiences.

❾ It will encourage you to have the highest expectations for all your students, challenging them to aim even higher.

How is this book creative?

We set out to make this book really useful and to give you more than you might expect of a typical teacher support handbook. Here are some ways that this book is creative:

❶ It places *creativity* and classroom *innovation* at the heart of effective teaching.

❷ It provides four books in one:
  • A simple all-encompassing framework for effective teaching based on rigorous theoretical underpinning and research.
  • Over 200 practical strategies to promote teaching and creative learning.
  • Diverse case studies from real classrooms.
  • A compendium of quotes on creativity and learning to inspire, challenge and motivate, linked to the issues raised in each chapter.

❸ It considers the *personal domain* of the teacher, an area missed out in most popular education texts.

❹ It demystifies the process of creative thinking.

❺ It challenges traditional thinking about what humans find motivating and what promotes great learning.

❻ It provides you with *multiple ways* to access the materials, from reading cover to cover, to dipping into sections, to considering suggested action points to an index-based reference source, to name but a few.

❼ It provides the top six tools for generating creative thoughts for adults and for young people.

❽ It provides a practical *self-evaluation tool* that will enable you to create your own unique professional development plan.

❾ It includes a CD-ROM with classroom-ready materials that can be used straight away.

Why do teachers need to be creative?

Creativity is at the heart of effective teaching and is vital to teaching in every subject area. Creativity has such a central role in teaching because:

❶ It's vital to develop learning experiences that give students a *variety* of different teaching and learning approaches – students thrive on this variety and research shows that novelty maintains motivation and can aid learning.

❷ Learners need rich opportunities to develop their own creative skills, and learners must use innovative approaches to enable this process.

❸ Teachers need to be able to incorporate findings from their own work, and that of others, to develop fresh approaches to education that inspire learners.

❹ Education is constantly changing and there's frequently an imperative to adapt to new government initiatives and other changes imposed on teaching from outside.

❺ Teachers need to be able to model creativity, so their students can be enabled to develop their own creative skills.

❻ Teachers need to be able to move from simply being *flexible* in what they do, to being genuinely *creative*.

❼ To develop as a teacher and move forward with professional development, it's necessary to take creative steps that are beyond your immediate comfort zone.

What principles of teaching and learning are enshrined in this book?

Knowing the foundations upon which you operate ensures you and your students experience consistency of expectation. Here are the essential principles for effective learning which appear in the book:

1. Create a **learning agreement** based on the behaviours required from everyone to allow learning to flourish.

2. Engage learners through a variety of experiences.

3. Balance support with challenge.

4. Create **space** for learners to find and secure connections.

5. Encourage students to reflect on how they learn and how they can improve.

6. **Model** the behaviours that you want to see in your students.

7. Make learning memorable by engaging learners through all of the senses and their emotions.

8. Build-in **choice** at all stages of the learning process.

9. Develop your learners as teachers.

How can you get the best from this book?

This book is packed full of information and ideas, but you need to be prepared to get the most out of it:

1. Open your mind to what might be possible.

2. Be willing to **challenge** your existing beliefs.

3. Be prepared to try new approaches whole-heartedly.

4. Be prepared to **enjoy** the process of experimentation.

5. Banish negative beliefs about your creativity or that of your students.

6. Be willing to share with your students that you're experimenting with new activities and invite their constructive feedback.

7. Buy in to the principle that 'there are no mistakes, only learning' and apply it to yourself as you try different approaches.

8. Set yourself up to **succeed**. Trial new approaches first in situations where you're most likely to get useful feedback. Then move to more challenging situations.

9. Build in 'creative time' (however small the amount) each day for yourself to read, think and enthuse. It's good for your work and it feeds your soul.

10. Don't expect things to change overnight and be prepared to be really determined to see through the changes that stem from reading this book.

Introduction

Imagination is more important than knowledge. Knowledge is limited. Imagination encircles the world.

Albert Einstein (1879–1955)

Message to the reader

We know that people tend to skim over introductions, but we ask you to spend five minutes studying the next few pages as they do contain important ideas which help you to see the big picture of *The Creative Teaching and Learning Toolkit*, get to grips with the point of the book and know why we've written it. The introduction also explains the role of creativity in our book.

Introducing the book

Our main aim in writing *The Creative Teaching and Learning Toolkit* is simple: to help you become a better teacher. Effective teaching will enable your students to reach their potential, giving them the platform to live happy and successful lives. In this way they can play their part in shaping a better world for us all.

The book aims to help you develop as a teacher through a combination of key features:

- **A new way of thinking about effective teaching called *The Creative Teaching Framework***
  The aim is to provide you with the 'big picture' that will enable you to think about the various components that combine to create really good teaching. We've created the framework based on our own teaching experience, and after extensive investigation into education research and successful teaching approaches. We encourage you to reflect on your current practice and make plans for how you can

move your teaching to the next level. *Creativity* is singled out as a vital quality that will help you maintain your effectiveness.

- **Over 200 strategies and tools that you can use to teach more effectively**
  We want to help teaching reclaim its place as a highly-skilled professional role, carried out by discerning practitioners. As such, we wish to avoid simplistic step-by-step approaches that claim to have universal appeal. Teaching and learning are highly complex activities and the role of the teacher is to reflect on the desired learning outcomes of any particular learning experience and select the most appropriate tools to achieve these. The book aims to be your personal toolkit to success in the classroom. Tasks throughout the book require you to reflect on the context and make some personal meaning out of it.

- **Insights into successful approaches from other teachers**
  Much can be gained from the work of other teachers, and an important feature of this book is the case studies which illustrate the success that others have achieved in their classrooms. Though we do not claim these to be scientifically proven teaching approaches, we do feel that they provide helpful information which has relevance to your own classroom.

- **An interactive self-evaluation tool**
  We do not believe that personal growth will happen by accident: we need to actively plan for it and set appropriate goals. A significant feature of the book is a practical tool for self-evaluation that you can use to create a powerful personal action plan. It can be considered a structured path for improving your teaching. If you're serious about making positive changes, then we strongly recommend that you carry out the exercises we've included in this section.

An **accompanying CD-ROM** contains electronic versions of all the key material, with many resources that can be printed off ready for classroom use. These include the quotes that appear at the bottom of each page, which can be printed out poster-size for your classroom or staffroom wall.

Who's the book for?

This book has been written with all types of teacher in mind, as the key principles and competences covered in the book are applicable for *all* phases. However, we've placed special emphasis on the secondary age range, as this is where we have most classroom experience, and where much of our advisory and consultancy work has been carried out.

Whether you're a full- or part-time classroom teacher, teaching assistant, a newly-qualified teacher, a subject leader or a school manager with teaching responsibilities, there are key resources for you in *The Creative Teaching and Learning Toolkit*. The vital message is that we can *all* improve if we *want* to do so and are determined to make the positive changes that are required. The book will also encourage you to think about wider *leadership* issues in your school and classroom.

The book will also be of use to school managers, advisory teachers and consultants working with schools to develop particular aspects of teaching. There's also much that can be used in training sessions with teachers.

Building on what you already do well

While we're sure that there are many things that you *already* do well, we're also sure that you'll find areas that you'd like to work on. Remember, nobody is ever the 'finished article' when it comes to teaching.

The importance of *choice* is a vital message throughout the book. You have choices about everything you do. You can choose to think negatively about teaching and all its pressures, or you can choose and plan for a better future. We believe that by choosing to take action to improve your teaching you'll become a happier, more fulfilled person. And you'll also gain control of your life outside school too.

There's much in our book that focuses on the essential teaching skills and strategies that will bring you success in the classroom – indeed this is major part of the work. You'll find hundreds of ideas, tools, templates and lesson ideas that you can use tomorrow. But unlike many other books for teachers, we try to get to the root of self-improvement by addressing the key area of the *teacher's personal domain*.

For some reason the *feelings* and *emotions* of the teacher are often forgotten in teaching books. Unfortunately in many schools too, these key personal issues are brushed under the carpet. It's wrongly assumed that teachers are completely satisfied in this area and that they're performing at their optimum level. The truth, of course, is that there are often significant barriers which interfere with the teaching process – much as there are for learners when they learn. Teaching is indeed one of the most stressful occupations, and we're currently experiencing record levels of absence in the profession.

We believe passionately that unless we address this issue we cannot claim to be nurturing the next generation of effective teachers. This book confronts it head on and suggests a range of practical strategies focussing on the personal domain, which complement the main content on the day-to-day aspects of the role of the teacher.

A central ingredient in the book is the principle that change happens from *within*, and that we all have it within us to become more creative and effective in our work and private lives. The book is designed to help that change happen within *you*.

How to use the book

We've put a lot of thought in the planning, writing and design of the book. We want it to be the most user-friendly education book you've ever read, and have included several innovations and other special features to make this possible.

Each chapter follows a consistent format, which models the accelerated learning approach and includes:

- Mind maps summarizing the main content.

- Previews which help you to quickly understand what you'll learn.

- Questions to help activate your prior knowledge.

- The main content, with embedded tasks to encourage engagement and actions.

- Information boxes which illuminate the text.

- Case studies to bring the main content to life.

- Summary points reviewing the chapter.

- Suggested action points.

- Recommended further reading.

A special feature of the book is the inclusion of **stories** to illuminate the text. These convey important messages about teaching, working life and life outside school, that aim to enrich your reading and enjoyment of the book. They also help you to make some personal meaning out of the book, through your own unique interpretation of the stories.

We've also included an extensive **glossary** of terms used in the book, allowing you to quickly check any terminology you're not familiar with. There's also a full **bibliography** enabling you to take your study further if you wish.

This means that you can read the book in a number of ways. You could:

- Start at the beginning and work methodically through the book.

- Read the chapter previews first and then dip in.

- Scan the chapter mind maps first.

- Consider the chapter preview questions as a guide.

- Use the book as a reference using the case studies or tools.

- Use Chapter 4 as a source of strategies for lesson planning straight away – or chose another chapter that grabs your attention.

- Use the book as a personal and professional development experience by working through the self-coaching questions and tasks in each chapter.

- Use the self-evaluation tool as an auditing mechanism and then read the parts of the book that most require your attention, based on the outcomes of the tool.

The vital place of creativity

That you have decided to pick this book up is a clear sign of the talented teacher within you. Talent is born of knowledge, skills, tenacity and curiosity, and in *The Creative Teaching and Learning Toolkit* we seek to support you to nurture this talent and to recognize, develop and employ the creative dimension of your teaching. In so doing you model and encourage creativity in your learners.

We're not arguing in this book that creativity is the 'be all and end all' of education, but we *are* asserting that it has three increasingly important roles in the contemporary classroom:

❶ Creativity supports the *motivation* of the increasingly expectant and demanding young people that we meet in our classrooms.

❷ Creativity encourages the development of complex and important *problem-solving skills* which we believe all young people need in order to become proactive and useful citizens, employees and employers.

❸ We believe that creativity is an *innately human* capacity and intensely rewarding experience, which makes it worthy in its own right.

A clear purpose

In the last fifty years, and particularly in the last decade, there's been steady growth in interest and action around the subject of creativity. But for some the concept of creativity still refers only to artistic activities, or is restricted to certain traditional subjects in schools. Our belief is that creativity is for everyone and has key relevance to *all* subject areas.

The Creative Teaching and Learning Toolkit sets out to:

- Characterize creativity.
- Demystify and debunk the myths surrounding it.
- Justify its place in education and in classrooms.
- Distil the pathways by which you can encourage its development in both teaching and in learners themselves.
- Provide the necessary theoretical backdrop.
- Provide a series of effective tools for working creatively and stimulating creativity in others.
- Suggest genuinely creative teaching strategies for your classroom.

The overall purpose of the book is to support you to move your practice from being a talented to an even more creative teacher.

A **talented teacher** makes use of their knowledge, experience and skills to provide stimulating and inclusive learning experiences, taking account of learner preferences, to provide access to the curriculum.

A highly **creative teacher** does all the above but also encourages learners to go beyond the boundaries of the curriculum and to think in innovative and resourceful ways. He or she encourages the highest levels of risk assessment, risk-taking and reflection, and encourages learners to generate understanding of their own approach to learning and improve on their practice. The creative teacher actively nurtures fascination, resourcefulness, curiosity and task-focus in their learners. Above all, the creative teacher uses creative strategies systematically in his/her work to get powerful results, and encourages learners themselves to be highly creative.

If you realize you're already a creative teacher, this book will extend your thinking and challenge you and your learners to go even further into the *creativity zone*.

Whether you tell yourself you're creative or whether you say you're not, you're probably right (to purloin a famous quote from Henry Ford). Throughout the book we wish to support you to challenge any beliefs you may have about the limits of creative practice in yourself, your learners or your systems. We believe everyone has a natural curiosity and freedom to combine ideas to create new entities. You may need to respond differently in order to let it happen and take risks. With the concepts, tools and approaches available within this book we would invite you to challenge any such beliefs and take even more calculated, creative risks!

Curriculum or creativity?

At the 2006 Education Show a lively and polarized debate took place between creativity expert Sir Ken Robinson and former chief inspector of schools Chris Woodhead, entitled 'Curriculum or Creativity?'. Our belief is that it's not helpful to think in terms of one or the other, because creativity only exists in schools in the context of a curriculum which, by its very nature, is largely subscribed. Perhaps the challenge we're currently facing in our schools is how we can provide a 'curriculum of creativity' for young people?

This book is not about creativity for creativity's sake. It's about how to encourage it in classrooms and schools, to enhance learning for better understanding of the curriculum and for success in examinations, but also, vitally, to promote lifelong learning habits. It's about creativity as an essential attribute of human nature and *human excellence*.

Chapter 1

Creativity, teaching and learning

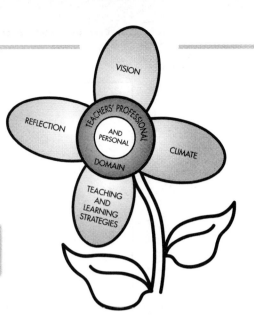

'It is our mind and that alone which chains us or sets us free'

Dilgo Khyentse Rinpoche (1910–1991)

Message to the reader

This first chapter contains some theory and explains the concepts behind *The Creative Teaching and Learning Toolkit*, focusing on creativity and learning. If you're ready to dive straight in to thinking about practical strategies for your classroom, go to Chapter 4, which is the most extensive section of the book. If you want learn more about the key role of 'Vision' in teaching, head for Chapter 2, or if you want to know how to create a better 'Climate for learning', visit Chapter 3. Later, we deal with 'Teachers' personal and professional domain' in Chapter 5. While it's vital that you head first for the material that you find most engaging, do call back to this initial chapter at some point, as it provides essential grounding and definitions of terms used elsewhere, and helps you to see the importance of creativity in teaching and learning. It also introduces the Creative Teaching Framework which underpins the rest of the book.

'One must still have chaos in oneself to be able to give birth to a dancing star.' *Friedrich Nietzsche*

Preview

This chapter defines creativity, focuses on the importance of creative thinking and introduces key models of the creative process and teaching in classrooms.

Key learning points:

▶ What is meant by creativity and creative acts.

▶ The background to the concept of creativity in learning.

▶ Why creativity is so important.

▶ The conditions required for creativity to thrive.

▶ The cyclical process associated with creativity.

▶ The Five Domains of Effective Teaching.

▶ How the Creative Teaching Framework provides the big picture for thinking about effective teaching.

Key questions to ask yourself before beginning this chapter:

1 How do you define creativity?

2 Why is creativity important in education?

3 What are the factors which impact on the creative process?

4 Is creativity learnable? If yes, how? Is it teachable?

5 What is the relationship between creativity and learning?

'Greater than the tread of mighty armies is an idea whose time has come.' *Victor Hugo*

Setting the scene

In 2004, whilst working in Spain, one of the authors visited the Prado Museum, in Madrid. In awe of the collection of grand masters of European painting, he wandered from room to room marvelling at the works of Ribera, Morales, Titian, Goya and so on. In a quiet area of the gallery, nestling among Botticelli and Weyden, was a curious sight.

Most paintings had one or two admiring spectators standing back, moving closer and sharing their thoughts within one another. Others stood in furrowed speculation. One painting was surrounded by a large crowd of excited, energized onlookers. As he approached he heard individuals of all nationalities chatting – in English and French, Spanish and Dutch. Moving closer, he found a small gap in the throng and through it he got his first glimpse of Hieronymus Bosch's famous triptych, *The Garden of Earthly Delights* (you can view the image in all its glory on the web – see link below). Mesmerized by its surreal content and structure he joined the group and chatted to a French lady, Catherine.

View the picture

The Garden of Earthly Delights can be viewed at:

http://www.ibiblio.org/wm/paint/auth/bosch/delight/

The Museo del Prado's website can be found at:

http://museoprado.mcu.es/ihome.html

After being awe-struck for a few moments, he moved on, enchanted not only by the painting itself, but by the rich contrast between this work and that of Bosch's contemporaries of the early 1500s. How could something so starkly different from contemporary works have been created? What exactly was it like for the artist, in that era, to step away from the norm of religious icons, of architectural representations and portraiture? The artist was pushing the boundaries of this pre-photographic age. To what extent was he viewed as creative? To what extent was he viewed as an eccentric or even a madman? It raised some interesting questions about the social construction of creativity and forces us to examine the personal constructs we have about what constitutes creativity.

What is creativity?

Creativity can be defined in a number of ways, and two of our favourites are given opposite, together with examples of how different people can express their creativity.

'If at first the idea is not absurd then there is no hope for it.' *Albert Einstein*

Creativity is...

Most simply:

'The process of finding and implementing new and appropriate ways of doing things'.

More technically:

'The intentional and purposeful search for innovation in problem solving'.

Creativity is expressed through actions, and ultimately outcomes, which themselves are seen as *creative*. Those of us who are able to continually express our creativity successfully are sometimes called *creative* people.

Note that creativity is different to *talent* which is about being able to perform well within a specific domain without necessarily the ability to innovate.

How different people are creative

Artists are creative by making works of art which express themselves and affect how others think or feel.

Car designers are creative by imagining ingenious interior features and novel external car designs that appeal to customers.

Physicists are creative by calculating new ways of understanding the universe.

Athletes are creative by finding new ways to gain a competitive edge.

Teachers are creative by finding effective ways to teach that engage learners.

All the above have a *purpose* in mind for their creativity – what was the purpose of your last creative act?

From science to the arts, the response to *questions* generates thinking and it is this thinking which can lead to creative acts. Examples of questions which have led to, and are still leading to, creative acts include:

- How can I design a quicker and safer way of travelling from one place to another?
- How can I portray this landscape through art or music?
- Why does love feel the way it does?
- How can I help find a cure for cancer?

'Every child is an artist. The problem is how to remain an artist once he grows up.' *Pablo Picasso*

- What is the purpose of balance?

- How can I express myself, my moods and my feelings, through a three dimensional medium such as sculpture?

- How can I solve the mysteries of the universe?

- When is it time to take action?

- How can civilization develop, while still safeguarding the environment?

- How can I teach my students in a way that will enable them to really understand my subject?

- How can I use the laws of nature to change the world for the better?

- What is the purpose of education?

- What is society for?

- What is fundamentally engaging to everyone, no matter who they are?

- How can nuclear research save the world?

- Who is really in charge?

Creative people, behaviours or processes?

Is there such a thing as a creative person, or are there just creative behaviours or a creative process? We believe that creativity is available to anyone who wishes to utilize it, and although it has been traditionally defined within the so-called creative arts of painting, sculpture, music and dance, these are surely just domains in which it is easier to demonstrate creativity for others to see. We believe that creativity relates to every facet of human study and learning.

Clearly, some people seem to be able to be creative much more readily than others – Mozart, Einstein and Picasso are just three examples of exceptionally creative people whose creativity *seems* effortless. But even these legendary figures used a *creative process* to achieve their success that can be used by everyone one of us. Perhaps their trick was to be able to stay in the zone of creativity for longer than most us are able to?

'Impossible is 80% possible.' *Anonymous*

Creative Teachers, Creative Learners

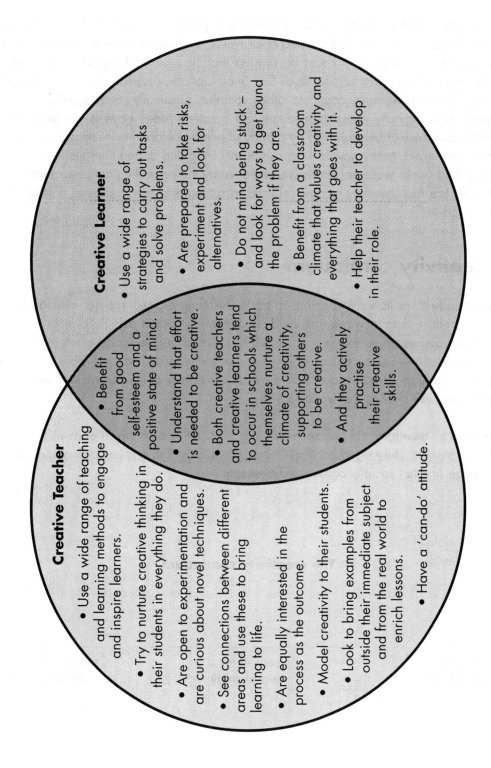

Creative Learner
- Use a wide range of strategies to carry out tasks and solve problems.
- Are prepared to take risks, experiment and look for alternatives.
- Do not mind being stuck – and look for ways to get round the problem if they are.
- Benefit from a classroom climate that values creativity and everything that goes with it.
- Help their teacher to develop in their role.

(overlap)
- Benefit from good self-esteem and a positive state of mind.
- Understand that effort is needed to be creative.
- Both creative teachers and creative learners tend to occur in schools which themselves nurture a climate of creativity, supporting others to be creative.
- And they actively practise their creative skills.

Creative Teacher
- Use a wide range of teaching and learning methods to engage and inspire learners.
- Try to nurture creative thinking in their students in everything they do.
- Are open to experimentation and are curious about novel techniques.
- See connections between different areas and use these to bring learning to life.
- Are equally interested in the process as the outcome.
- Model creativity to their students.
- Look to bring examples from outside their immediate subject and from the real world to enrich lessons.
- Have a 'can-do' attitude.

Questions to consider:
To what extent do you possess the qualities of a creative teacher?
Which area would you like to focus on first as you try to improve your creative abilities?
In what ways are your students creative?

'The principle goal of education is to create men who are capable of doing new things, not simply of repeating what other generations have done – men who are creative, inventive and discoverers.' *Jean Piaget*

Judging creativity

Who decides whether an act, or for that matter a person, is creative? Pieces of modern art, such Tracey Emin's *My Bed* created controversy, as have many other works of art and music throughout the ages. It could be argued that creative thinking has been a part of the successes of such diverse people as Da Vinci, Gandhi, Branson, Beethoven, Roddick, Hoover, The Buddha, and countless other socially, artistically, linguistically, musically, spiritually and logically gifted individuals. But creativity does have a *social* dimension – creative acts have to be approved by a body of people before they're recognized as such by the wider world. Many now-famous composers struggled during their lifetimes precisely because their works were *not* considered creative by the prevailing critics or audiences of their time. The fact that they're now referred to as masterpieces indicates that our ideas have moved on.

A creativity continuum

When a baby takes its first steps, it is an earth-shattering moment for that individual – and a highly creative leap forward. The child is combining thought and actions, in a way not previously possible, to enable him or herself to move about the world much more quickly and easily. But these first steps of children are never recorded in the history of a nation. By contrast, a highly creative act carried out by somebody at the pinnacle of their chosen domain may well change the world forever.

Creative acts, therefore, can be seen as lying on a *continuum* which ends in the world's most creative acts. The judgement about what is or is not creative is complex and dependent on a range of often *socially constructed* elements:

The creativity continuum

| Creativity for an individual | Creative for a field of study | Creative for a nation or the world |

'True creativity often starts where language ends.' *Arthur Koestler*

- The age or maturity of the individual.

- The level of impact of the creative outcomes e.g. impact on the individual through to the entire human race.

- Who's judging it.

- What the criteria for judging creativity are, who was involved in drawing them together and the degree of objectivity of this.

- What people's values and beliefs are as distinct from those criteria.

- The degree to which the creative response is similar to or different from other contemporary questions, solutions, or responses to the same questions.

- Its fitness for the purpose to which it was intended.

- The degree of an individual's familiarity to the subject matter or domain.

Accidental creativity

Are all creative outcomes intended? Surely accidental creativity happens? The example of the Post-It note shows us that what are seen as creative acts are not always intended.

Box 1.1: Spencer Silver's unintended invention

An American named Spencer Silver changed the face of offices across the world by accidentally inventing one of the most simple, yet innovative products of the late 20th century – the humble Post-It note. Employed in the research laboratories of US company 3M in the 1970s, Spencer's mission was to develop a strong adhesive. He successfully developed a new adhesive, but unfortunately it was even *weaker* than the product 3M already produced. It stuck to objects well, but could easily be lifted off – it was super weak instead of super strong.

At the time, no use could be found for Spencer's new adhesive, but he kept the formula rather than discarding it. Four years later, Arthur Fry, another 3M scientist, had a problem. He sang in the church choir, and needed markers for his hymn book that stayed in place, but did not damage the pages. Remembering Spencer's adhesive, he used some to coat his markers – and eureka!

In 1980, ten years after Spencer's initial work on his super weak adhesive, 3M began distributing what became known as Post-It notes, which are today one of the most popular office products.

3M's motto is 'The Spirit of Innovation. That's 3M.' The company's website proudly proclaims: 'Our unstoppable commitment to innovation, creating new technologies and products, places us exactly where our customers need us.'

Read more

A fascinating book, *Mistakes that Worked* by Charlotte Foltz Jones and John O'Brien (Doubleday 1994), tells the amazing stories behind the accidental inventions of forty familiar objects and products.

Task 1.1: The role of unintentional creativity

Try to identify any times when you have been unintentionally creative, or at least when experimentation led you to a helpful outcome. To what extent is experimentation likely to lead to creative outcomes in your role as a teacher? How have your students been unintentionally creative? How can you create the conditions for this unintentional creativity to flourish?

An understudied field

In 1950 eminent psychologist Joy Paul Guilford reported that in the first half of the twentieth century only 0.2 per cent of the articles in *Psychology Abstracts* had a focus on creativity. Despite a small growth in interest in the 1950s the profile of creativity remained low. A further analysis of articles in the same journal over the twenty year period 1975 to 1995 showed that there was still only 0.5 per cent of articles which had a direct concern with creativity (Sternberg and Lubart 1999).

In the annals of psychological research even now, it would seem that creativity is being largely ignored. Despite this there's an increasing professional interest in the development of creative approaches to building vision, and of overcoming challenging problems, in society, business, some areas of science and art. And in schools, creativity has long been valued, though perhaps traditionally linked to artistic activities.

There's some evidence that unconscious cognition (brain processing) is happening at far greater speeds, with far less interference, and considering far greater depth and breadth

'If they give you ruled paper, write the other way.' *Julio Ramon Jiminez*

of data, than conscious processing is capable of. If this is the case, it makes sense to utilize this intuitive cognition. Research suggests that creativity is learned and is learnable. The emphasis on conscious thought processes in contemporary education may be having an effect on the ability of youngsters to be creative in their teens. Perhaps we're stifling an unconscious *metaprocessing* of the data and information in our young people?

Task 1.2: Defining creativity

Reflect on the various definitions and concepts of creativity outlined here. Which definition did you feel most comfortable with before starting this chapter? Has your view been changed by what you have read? How? Try to write your own simple description of what creativity means to you. Notice how this may evolve as you work your way through the book and develop your own ideas on creativity.

Popular myths about creativity

Myths about creativity abound. Included here are some of the popular beliefs collected from teachers interviewed on the subject of creativity in schools, followed by our views gained through studying the literature on creativity and spending many hours thinking about the topic:

'Creativity is an effortless, spontaneous process' – the study of the world's most creative thinkers suggests that a combination of thinking styles, including the imaginative, the intuitive and the logical, is operating to produce innovative and outstanding outcomes. It's far from an effortless and spontaneous process. Although there may be periods of so-called 'flow', bringing creativity to a purposeful and useful conclusion involves effort, determination and focus.

'Genius is 1% inspiration and 99% perspiration'.

Thomas Edison (1847–1931)

'Some people are creative and some are not' – let's set the record straight, it appears that creative processes can be learned, indeed there are a range of models which outline the steps in the process. However, some people *do* seem to have innate predisposition to be more creative than others – but this is *not* the same as people simply being creative or not. The *creativity continuum* illustrates this point very well. Every week, you are likely to carry out creative acts to the left-hand edge of the continuum, like when you combine some ingredients to make a really special dish and your family are very impressed! This won't change the world, but for that meal it changed your family's world.

'Creative inventions find their time. Leonardo da Vinci's drawings for what were considered outrageous designs have only recently been put to the test. His manned flying machine did in fact outfly the craft created by the Wright brothers, his clockwork car actually worked and his mega crossbow really fired.'

'Creative people are outside normality, and might be regarded as unusual, even weird' – firstly we would challenge the notion of a 'creative person'; creativity is not a fixed attribute but a set of thinking and behaviours which lead to purposeful, innovative and expressive outcomes. We're *all* capable of it, however contemporary society places great value on what can be seen and rationalized. The creative process has eluded researchers and it is only relatively recently that we have been able to articulate its process. Creativity is an attribute which is available to everyone, is highly valuable and may be decommissioned by conventional schooling.

'Creativity is just an "arty" thing' – from science to technology, from politics to religion, creativity as a process for producing innovative, workable outcomes has made its mark in every aspect of human endeavour. Its relevance, therefore, to all classrooms cannot be disputed. Perhaps the reason that creativity has traditionally been viewed as the domain of the arts is that it may be more easy to articulate one's creativity through a medium such as art, music or literature. A creative scientist or mathematician, by contrast, may find it much harder to convince the masses of their creativity.

'Creativity is a luxury activity in the overregulated curriculum' – empowering young people to use and develop creative strategies may involve a shift in approach for some teachers. In a changing and challenging world we would argue that it's not knowledge that will endure but the ability to approach problems from different perspectives. If we really think about it, knowledge is superseded every day by new research. What endures is the mind and its capacity to adapt. We encourage you to look for the opportunities to exploit the current curriculum and see it as a platform rather than a cage. Focus on the possibilities and not the constraints. For whatever you focus upon, you will find!

'Creativity is a frivolous and undisciplined activity' – say that in the dark, without the light bulb! Thomas Edison employed his creativity to find solutions to the many problems he encountered in developing the electric light bulb. His tenacity, hard work and methodical approach to experimenting with materials and approaches was anything but frivolous and undisciplined. We provide in this book a cyclical model and a series of stepped strategies for creative acts. It requires a discipline to see it through to completion.

Task 1.3: Exploring the creative myths

Study carefully these 'myths' about creativity. Which are you reluctant to let go of? Why? To what extent do you agree with the authors' position? Can you think of any other 'myths' which need to be dispelled in your own classroom or school? Who could help you to tackle these?

'Creativity often begins with a dumb question.'

Why is creativity important?

Creativity is important on many levels:

- **Individuals:** a human trait which defines the human species and provides a sense of completeness and purpose.

- **Society:** encourages diversity, connection and energy in human culture, through the entire range of endeavour, as well as in human relationships.

- **Economy:** provides the competitive edge in generating wealth, improving standards of living and arguably quality of life.

- **Environment:** preserving and enhancing the natural and built environment, as well as seeking the balance when conflicts of interest arise.

- **Education:** enabling individuals to find solutions, solve problems and develop the resourcefulness that will be required throughout their lives in a world of change.

Are there conditions which encourage creativity?

We believe there are conditions which, when present, encourage creativity. We suggest that there are three key domains required, which are relevant to schools (Figure 1.1):

- Internal state

- External conditions

- Cognitive skills

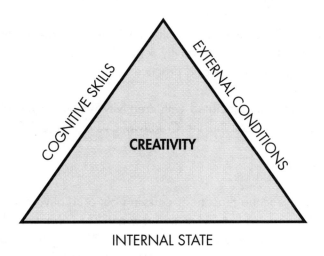

Figure 1.1: Conditions for creativity

'To lose oneself in the moment is to unlock the true power of creativity.'

- **Internal state:** this is about how learners think and respond. It includes a positive state of mind, with high confidence and buoyant self-esteem. It is associated with the willingness to take risks. An understanding that effort, commitment and determination is required to complete a creative act is needed. The ability to free up thinking and allow unfettered unconscious thoughts to surface is key. A willingness to use intuition is crucial. This means a readiness to be aware of and trust unconscious thoughts. A mindset of curiosity is also essential and determination is paramount.

- **External conditions:** this is about the climate the teacher nurtures and defines. It includes a climate where risk-taking is encouraged and supported. External influences (written, verbal, icons, nature and so on) are freely available and the teacher encourages delight in the unexpected, curiosity, sharing goals and dreams, playfulness and flexibility. Encouragement of speculative thinking is important. The nurturing of confidence, as the belief that 'one can improve' is similarly important. This climate is created by the teacher, through what they model and through how they provide direct and indirect permission for such activity. Teachers provide the appropriate structures for learners to develop creativity though a range of individual and group experiences.

- **Cognitive skills:** thinking skills such as analysis, synthesis, evaluation and application are important in generating creative output. Specific thinking strategies and tools such as mind mapping, bisociation, association, LogoVisual Thinking, abstraction to detail, convergent/divergent, fine detail/big picture all play a part in creative generation. These thinking skills and thinking tools may be precursors to some deeper thought processing which takes place beneath the conscious level of awareness.

The creative process

With the above three conditions in place creativity can then begin. But how does creativity work? Is there a process? Creativity appears to be more than a random thought-generation process. It appears that since purpose is an essential part of the definition of creativity, there must therefore be 'lines of enquiry' along which the thinking proceeds for most creative acts. Teachers will only take creativity seriously in the classroom setting if we can indeed stimulate it through conditions and practices.

We believe there is a *process* associated with creativity which is cyclical and this can be modelled and stimulated – we call this the *Creativity Cycle* (Figure 1.2).

The creative cycle explained:

1 **Vision or purpose:** this is the reason for carrying out a creative act and can be defined through questions like 'what do we want?' or 'what would we prefer?'. It gets to the essence of the problem to be solved. It's essential to become clear about the very last step in the vision that makes it clear that the vision has indeed been accomplished. In the classroom context, specific purposes could be:

'Make spaghetti, weed the garden, put sand in your hair, run into the wind, be free; and all your solutions flood in.'

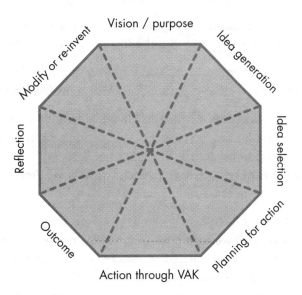

Figure 1.2: The Creativity Cycle

- What technique should I use to teach essay writing?
- How can I engage more boys in classroom debates?
- When should I include more thinking skills approaches into my lessons?
- How do I help Sunita to develop her awareness of the concepts behind the big ideas of the curriculum?

2   Idea generation: this step is actually the most cognitively challenging. It involves utilizing a range of thinking skills and tools including bisociation, association, mind mapping and so on in order to come up with possible responses to the question or problem. There is extensive guidance on idea generation in Chapter 4.

3   Idea selection: this element of the cycle is about picking the most appropriate idea or ideas from the ideas generated. There may be a necessity to recombine ideas to generate further possibilities. Idea selection needs to revisit the original vision or purpose so as to check suitability of ideas, and also to establish if the original purpose or vision still holds. Once we begin to think differently about an issue or problem, the very nature of the problem can shift. Important questions that arise here are:

- Do we still want the same vision?
- Does this idea we're selecting move us closer to or further from that end point of the vision?

4   Planning for action: this step takes care of the practical aspects of resource acquisition and environment. This is where we plan to implement our chosen ideas and devise the steps. Research in the field of Neuro-Linguistic Programming suggests that rigorous planning of the steps to achieving a goal can actually be counter-productive; over-planning limits our awareness of resources and opportunities available to achieve the outcome desired. This step may be better left as a loosely defined process.

5   Action (articulation through the senses): using all the senses, we take the necessary actions to advance towards the vision. Communicating the vision and key

'For truly creative thought, occupy the conscious mind or lose it altogether.'

accomplishment points along the way is essential and this is most effectively done through the phrase: 'show it, say it and encourage others to do it.'

6 **Outcome:** as a result of your actions you'll gain outcomes. They may or may not meet your vision. You need to measure your end points against the vision.

7 **Reflection:** does the outcome of your creative intervention give you the end result you want? If not then it's time to reflect on the actions taken so far and review the ideas used. What's been successful? What's not working? What specifically might need to change? What are the limiting factors just now? Analytical and evaluative thinking is likely to be needed at this stage.

8 **Modify or re-invent:** at this stage if all has gone according to the vision, you'll have your outcome. If however it hasn't, it may be necessary to modify your approach based on your reflections. Modification requires that you use more of the thinking skills and tools utilized in the 'Idea generation' step, but this time factoring in the analysis and evaluation you've done in the reflection stage. As a result of adjusted ideas, recheck with the vision and follow the cycle again. Finally it's important to consider what you've learned from the whole exercise.

This cycle is of course, just a model. It's our best attempt to capture the stages in the creative process. It should be used flexibly, and later in this book we explore in greater detail the kinds of thinking skills and thinking tools which unlock the creative potential of individuals.

It's important to recognize that some people may be skilled at *parts* of the Creativity Cycle, but not necessarily all of them:

- A person may be good at selecting the best idea from a list of possibilities (step 3), but finds it hard to generate that list (step 2).

- Another person may find generating many ideas at stage 2 relatively easy, but selecting the most appropriate one to move forward with tricky (step 3).

- A third person may be highly skilled at using reflection to establish whether the desired outcome has been achieved (step 7), but finds the other aspects of the Creativity Cycle challenging.

Those people that are able to sustain high-quality creative outputs may be those who are skilled at *every stage* of the Creativity Cycle. If this is so, then we need to make sure that as teachers we model to students how they can improve the skills involved at each stage. And of course we need to practise those skills ourselves first, so we're comfortable being the lead learner for creativity.

Task 1.4: Using the Creativity Cycle

The next time you're trying to find a creative solution or work through a problem, actively plan for creativity by using The

'Being creative is not so much about finding the right answers as posing meaningful questions.'

Creativity Cycle as a guide. By considering the creative process step by step, you may find it easier to generate more appropriate responses. This exercise will also improve your understanding of the creative process considerably, as you'll have real experience of creativity in action.

When doing this exercise it's vital to devise a suitably focused question (step 1: 'Vision' – see above). Remember that from step 5 onwards ('Action'), the cycle refers to the actual method(s) you've chosen to tackle the issue you're dealing with. It's important to carry the exercise through to reflect on the outcomes (step 7) and to consider how you might change things (step 8). Finally, do not miss the opportunity to consider what you think you've learned – this can be used the next time you're thinking creatively. If you're eager to try this out straight away, then break off from the book and consider a lesson you'll need to teach next week. If you're finding the process of generating ideas difficult, then you should find the techniques in Chapter 4 helpful.

Putting it all together

Over the last two years, as we worked on this book, we've given a lot of thought to the essential factors that underpin effective teaching. We wanted to provide a new but simple overall framework that would help teachers to think critically about the various key elements in their teaching. Our framework also had to encompass the vital element of creativity which, as we have already stated, we believe is a central element binding together all effective teaching.

Any framework can only be truly effective if teachers are free to interpret it in their own way, bearing in mind their specific circumstances. There's nothing worse than a rigid approach to teaching and learning that prescribes rules, methods and even trademarked approaches. Instead, our approach is to attempt to provide the 'big picture' in order to help you design your own really effective learning experiences. Our framework is rooted in sound educational research on what *really* works in the classroom.

As such we wish to introduce *The Five Domains of Effective Teaching* (Figure 1.3), our simplified model summarizing the factors that combine to influence the quality of teaching and learning. Teaching can, of course, only be effective if desirable (usually the intended) learning outcomes have been achieved. But we feel that some recent attempts to focus simply on the learning taking place in lessons have tended to overlook the fact that, in our schools, such learning occurs through the *mediation* of teachers. As such, teachers can be seen as expert learning facilitators.

'When a low probability line of thought leads to an effective idea, there is a "Eureka" moment and at once the low probability approach acquires the highest probability.' *Edward de Bono*

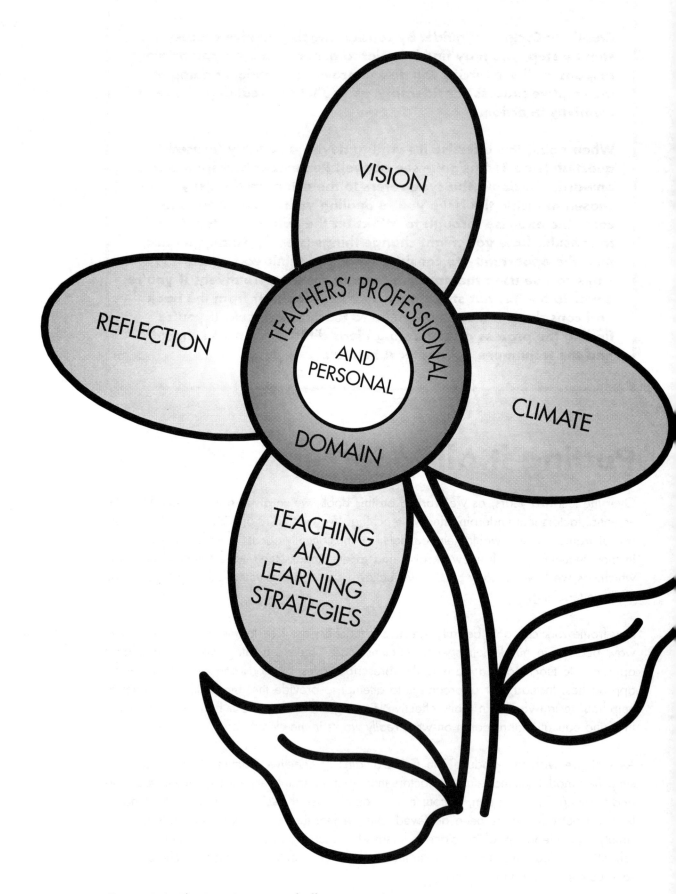

Figure 1.3: The Five Domains of Effective Teaching

'Chaos often breeds life, when order breeds habit.' *Henry Brooks Adams*

The Five Domains of Effective Teaching

Vision: a vision is a dream of the future. It should be the utopia of your classroom, your department, your school, your community and so on. It is closely associated with the values of yourself or the organization driving it and is examined in more detail in Chapter 2. Effective teaching is underpinned by a vision and how that influences students. Vision actually operates on many levels, from the metavision of what education is for, to the more day-to-day reality of learning outcomes. The higher levels of vision are frequently not expressed.

Climate: climate relates to the emotional and physical nature of the classroom. Are your students hydrated, oxygenated or at the right temperature? Do they have positive, supportive relationships with their peers and with their teacher? Is the classroom a stimulating and interactive learning space? Climate has a key role to play in effective teaching and learning and is explored in Chapter 3.

Teaching and learning strategies: a range of teaching strategies are employed to help learners reach their potential, including accelerated learning, thinking skills, assessment for learning and so on. They're at the heart of effective teaching and are discussed in detail in Chapter 4. Extensive research from the field of education psychology has been carried out on a range of teaching and learning strategies, and have helped to highlight the key importance of this domain within the overall model. None of the other domains has been shown, through empirical studies, to have such a direct effect on student achievement.

Reflection: a process of reflecting on what worked and what didn't work should be undertaken with a view to modifying practice. These reflections can be based on feedback from yourself, other teachers, the students, parents, Ofsted and so on. The outcomes of this reflective step feed back into all of the other domains of effective teaching. Reflection has its own section: Chapter 5.

Teachers' professional and personal domain: it's essential that a teacher knows his or her subject or subjects well. But the possession of up-to-date subject knowledge is not enough in its own right. Teachers must understand the major theories about learning, be able to plan learning experiences which scaffold learning appropriately and allow young people to draw their own conclusions, and give helpful feedback and manage behaviour positively – in short they need to display the professional knowledge and skills required of a teacher. Certain key personal attributes are important too, such as having the patience to explain a difficult concept repeatedly, or the good humour to deal with challenging situations. It's also vital to consider that effective and, in particular, creative teaching takes place when teachers are happy, have low levels of negative stress, are fulfilled, healthy, motivated and empowered. Within this book we suggest ways to have more of these positive and resourceful states of mind and body. This is also the domain of values and beliefs. Chapter 6 explores the intrinsically-linked areas of a teacher's professional and personal domain in more detail.

'Confusion is the welcome mat at the door of creativity.' *Michael Gelb*

The way this model differs from many other overviews of effective teaching is that it includes the *personal domain* of the teacher. We felt that it was important to address in detail this hitherto overlooked dimension. Who the teacher is, their values, beliefs and self-esteem, has a key influence on the way that they build relationships and interact with their students. It also has a fundamental bearing on how effective they are as a teacher.

In the remainder of the book we examine these key elements of effective teaching and provide practical and effective strategies to optimize all elements of the model. Additionally, we weave into the book how creativity plays a crucial role in enabling teachers and learners to realize their visions and become more effective.

Task 1.5: What's your big picture like?

It's important to engage with the key ideas in this book as soon as possible, so pause now to consider the Five Domains of Effective Teaching for a few moments. How does this model compare to other 'big picture' models of effective teaching that you've come across? Consider each domain individually. Which ones do you feel most confident about? Which are you not so happy to address? Why is that? In your school and department which domains are given most prominence? Do you agree with this emphasis? Try to redraw the model as a flower with the size of the 'petals' proportional to how important you think each factor is for you as a teacher. When you get the opportunity carry out the exercise with another teacher in your department, from a different department and with a senior manager. What does this reveal about the views of staff at your school?

An holistic model emerges

The Creativity Cycle is an integral part of the education process and as such the cycle and the Five Domains of Effective Teaching interrelate. The Creativity Cycle links in to the vision for effective teaching and acts as an innovations promoter to generate novel and interesting ways to meet the demands of each facet. When we combine the five domains with a creative process of teaching and nurturing creativity in students we have a *Creative Teaching Framework* (Figure 1.4). This is the ultimate expression of creativity in the teaching and learning process, and for us represents the most holistic framework for effective teaching.

In this framework each Domain of Effective Teaching sits within the Creativity Cycle to show that they can only combine to produce truly effective teaching if creativity is injected into every stage. Perhaps most important of all, teachers need to use creativity to select the most appropriate teaching and learning methods to achieve the desired learning outcomes.

'One of the advantages of being disorderly is that one is constantly making exciting discoveries.' *A. A. Milne*

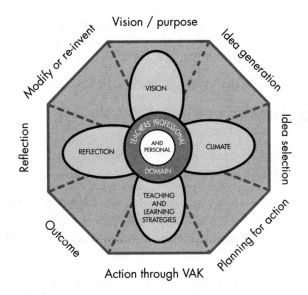

Figure 1.4: The Creative Teaching Framework

The Creative Teaching Framework is not intended simply to represent a cycle. Instead, you can begin at any point and see what happens as you consider moving in any direction. A learning experience may take the form of a sequence from Vision through to Reflection, but equally valid would be to explore an issue with the domains, beginning with Reflection and working the other way. Clearly, each domain interrelates and has an influence on the others in important ways. For example, Vision can refer to the vision for the classroom context for learning, which would come under Climate. Equally, it could refer to the vision for the Teaching and Learning Strategies to be used, or the aims of the reflection to be carried out. Creativity, of course, has a vital bearing on every stage.

- - - - - - - - - - - - - - - - - - -

⟲ Review

This chapter has sought to emphasize the following key points:

- Creativity can be defined in a variety of ways, but all definitions encompass the search for new and appropriate solutions.

- The exact definition of what is and what is not creative is socially constructed and is influenced by time, trends and opinions.

- Relatively little research has been done into creativity and yet it is prized by society as a way of solving problems and remaining competitive.

- Creativity has an essential part to play in preparing young people for a world of challenge and change.

- There are conditions for fostering creativity.

- There is an eight stage Creativity Cycle which encompasses creative, analytical and evaluative thinking skills and strategies.

- There are five domains to effective teaching, and the development of excellent practice

'Chance is always powerful. Let your hook be always cast; in the pool where you least expect it, there will be fish.' *Ovid*

43

in these domains is supported by the Creativity Cycle. When combined they form the Creative Teaching Framework, which has the power to transform your classroom and your school.

⇨ Action points

Consider the following actions in the light of this chapter and using the self-evaluation tool select those that are most appropriate for your needs:

- Examine your own beliefs about creativity. Do you believe that you're personally creative? If yes, what is the benefit to you and your students? If no, what is the basis upon which you have chosen this belief? What is choosing to continue to hold onto this belief costing you?

- Consider the Creativity Cycle. Take steps to examine the degree to which it's already operating in your classroom, your department, your school or your community. What might further promote creative problem-solving?

- Explore with colleagues the relationship between effective teaching and creativity. In what ways is creativity being overlooked or undervalued in your work? What might the next steps be to value it more?

👁 Further reading

Jensen, E (1995) *Super Teaching*. San Diego: The Brain Store Inc.

- A theoretical and practical collection of educational wisdom and strategy.

Rocket, M & Percival, S (2002) *Thinking for Learning*. London: Network Educational Press.

- Provides an excellent overview of thinking skills strategies.

Sternberg, R (ed.) (1999) *Handbook of Creativity*. Cambridge: Cambridge University Press.

- Provides an extensive and detailed survey of a wide range of creativity issues, but is a rather academic read.

Smith, A, Lovatt, M & Wise, D (2004) *Accelerated Learning: a user's guide*. London: Network Educational Press.

- A practical guide to effective teaching strategies within an accelerated learning framework.

'What we imagine is order is merely the prevailing form of chaos.' *Kerry Thornley*

End of chapter metaphor: Read the story and use the questions that follow to consider further aspects of the chapter content.

The secret

You know once upon a time, some way from here, in a land of hunger and pestilence, there was a king. He was a sad king who had little to do with his people, and he shared little with them. Now this king knew a secret, in fact he knew THE secret. The secret was a long held and closely guarded one, which he kept safely in the depths of a pool, right at the very base of his vast royal castle. Each day he would visit the pool and reach into it to pull out a rough hessian bag, waxed and sealed with candle cord. He would untie the cord and peer into the bag to check that the secret was still safe. Some days it was hard to find, and he hardly believed it was true at all. On other days it was easier to find, in fact it floated up towards him. There were days he'd only to think about it and it was there. This secret brought him some small contentment when he believed in it and used it, but there was still a sadness … he was not happy and he was not as good a king as he could be.

Then one day he fell sick. He was so ill that he couldn't get out of his bed. He was terrified that the secret wouldn't be safe, without his checking it. He was scared because he knew the secret was an answer, and that the answer helped him rule his land … what would he do? What might happen? He wrestled with his conscience but his illness overcame him and he gave into the fight. As he yielded to his malaise, he fell into a deep sleep, down and down he went, deeper and deeper, further and further into deep, deep sleep.

And there in his sleep the secret spoke to him from the bag. "I am here, I am safe, but you must realize that the secret is already out, some people who already know it and believe in it, use it everyday," it said.

"But surely that is dangerous?" replied the king in his slumber. "If everyone knows and uses it then there will be chaos," he thought.

"Not so," said the secret. "For if everyone knows then they are free, and freedom brings possibility and independence and your people will prosper and love you for it."

The king dreamed of a bright land bathed in sunshine with happy people full of joy and rich in every way and felt a wave of joy come over him in his dream. He saw himself happy and proud. Eventually he rose from his vivid dream-state and at once knew that he knew … that he must share the secret widely, and that this was good.

'The things we fear most in organizations – fluctuations, disturbances, imbalances – are the primary sources of creativity.'
Margaret J. Wheatley

Slowly at first and then more quickly, he told everyone of the secret and invited people who didn't believe in it to visit the pool and see it for themselves. People came from across the land to look in the bag. Slowly but surely his subjects realized the power of the secret and began to use it; they allowed it to guide their path. Those that found the secret for the first time embraced it and enjoyed its benefits, and those that had always known rejoiced at being able to share its gifts openly. Over the years that followed the kingdom became richer and brighter and its people happier, but the happiest person of them all was ... the king, for he'd realized that there are secrets you have to believe in and there are secrets you have to share.

You might wish to consider:

1 What does the story mean to you?

2 What might the joyful secret be in your own setting and how could it support your work in school?

3 As you reflect back on the first chapter in this book, what questions does the story raise?

For more information about the construction and use of stories in learning, turn to Chapter 4.

'Millions saw the apple fall, but Newton asked why.' *Bernard Mannes Baruch*

Chapter 2

Vision

'Your vision isn't big enough unless people are falling over laughing.'

Elizabeth Jeffries

Message to the reader

If you're not inspired by vision, feel free to skip to another section of *The Creative Teaching and Learning Toolkit* that interests you more. However, do come back to this section at some point — vision is extremely important to effective teaching and learning. If you're not getting the success you want in the classroom, it could be that there is a mismatch between your own vision and that of your students. Take time to study the ideas in this chapter — even if they don't immediately seem relevant — and carry out the tasks. Hopefully if you persevere you'll begin to see why the much-neglected area of vision is so fundamental, and why making time to think about vision is always time well spent. The chapter also tries to demystify the complex area of values which, once understood, provides a fascinating insight into your own and other people's inner worlds.

'The one thing worse than not being able to see is having no vision.' *Helen Keller*

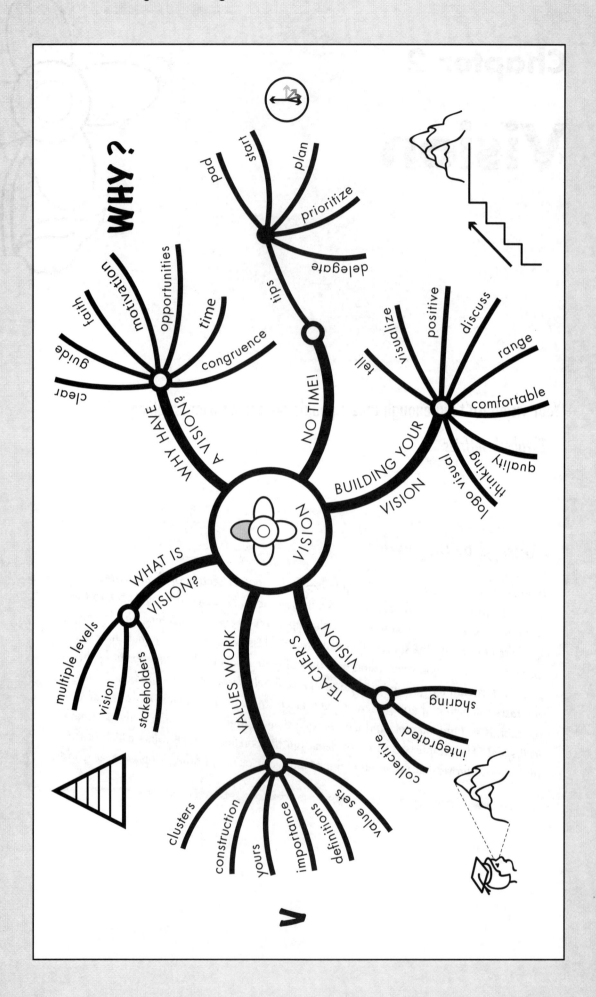

'Where there is no vision the people perish.' *Proverbs 29:18*

Preview

This chapter focuses on the importance of developing a **vision** for everything you do as a teacher.

Key learning points:

▶ Why a robust vision should underpin all your work.

▶ What happens if you don't have a vision.

▶ The various levels at which a vision can operate.

▶ How your vision relates to that of your students and other stakeholders.

▶ Practical ways to develop your vision.

▶ How values and vision relate to one another.

▶ How values are sources of conflict and yet can be used as connectors in schools.

▶ How to make sense of complex value systems in classrooms and schools.

▶ How your vision relates to the other components of the Creative Teaching Framework.

Key questions to ask yourself before beginning this chapter:

1 Do you have a personal vision of:
  • The purpose of education?
  • What you want to achieve as a teacher?
  • What type of classroom teacher you want to be?
  • What type of learners you want to create?

2 Are you aware of your students' vision for what they want to get out of their time in school? How could you gather this kind of information? How would you use it?

3 Are you aware of other stakeholders' views on their vision for education? Who might these stakeholders be and how might their views be different? How can this kind of information be gathered and used?

4 What is important to you in the context of: your classroom? Learners? Teaching? Education as a whole? Society as a whole?

'A vivid image compels the whole body to follow.' *Aristotle*

Getting to grips with your vision

For some reason the concept of 'vision' seems to have been a neglected topic for many schools. While teachers can discuss at length intended learning outcomes, and school departments and managers wax lyrical about development plans, the wider concept of a vision is not well established within education. As a consequence this has resulted in some muddled thinking about what's important in our schools. It has also caused conflict between teachers and various government departments and agencies working with schools (especially the DfES), often because the two do not share the same vision about where we should be going – or indeed how we should get there. This chapter will allow you to focus on the critical area of vision, which underpins the whole of the Creative Teaching Framework.

What is a vision?

We begin by explaining what we mean by a vision, as well as explaining what stake-holders means in this context:

- A **vision** is a dream, a description of the future which shows what you would like to achieve in a particular aspect of your work or private life – this chapter puts the spotlight on your working life, but there's no reason to stop there once you begin the vision-building process. A vision can also be seen as a *preferred future* that is worth working to try to create. Vision also encompasses the *methods* that will be used to create that preferred future.

- A **stakeholder** is a person who has some personal stake in an issue and needs to be consulted to ensure their needs are accommodated – this chapter explores the need for congruence between the views of different stakeholders in order for you to be seen as fully effective as a teacher.

Multiple levels

At its broadest level a vision is a picture of the future which describes the kind of world in which you'd like to live and work. That world is usually a better and happier place than the one you currently inhabit. Your vision lets you imagine what needs to change in order for things to *improve* – and allows you to reflect on what *you* need to do to help make that future a reality.

In your role as a teacher, the most wide-ranging vision can best be summed up by what you see as *the aims of education*. More specifically, you can have a much narrower vision for what your students will achieve from carrying out a particular task within a lesson or unit of work – in other words the *intended outcomes* of a learning experience.

Between these two extremes there's a whole 'vision pyramid' which corresponds to the different levels at which decisions are made (Figure 2.1). At each stage the vision describes the intended outcomes or benefits you're looking for.

'When we set out on a journey we usually have a clear idea of where we're going and a mental picture of what our destination will look like. Why should our journey through life be any different?'

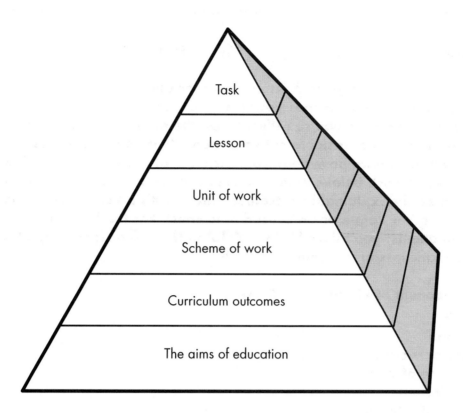

Figure 2.1: The Vision Pyramid

Component of vision	**Examples of decisions to be made**
Task	Specific learning outcomes
Lesson	General learning outcomes
Unit of work	What the unit of work should focus on
Scheme of work	What the scheme of work should cover
Curriculum	What the curriculum should engender
Aims of education	What education should achieve

'Vision without action is merely a dream. Action without vision just passes the time. Vision with action can change the world!' *Joel Barker*

Task 2.1: Clarifying your own vision

Study the Vision Pyramid. At one level or another you should be aware of the outcomes you're seeking at each level of the pyramid, whether you're reflecting on the aims of education or considering what tasks to set your students in tomorrow's lesson period 3. Explore how clear your vision is at each level by giving a score to each below, with 5 corresponding to a very clear vision (with easily explainable outcomes) and 0 with a very hazy vision (with rather vague or unfocused outcomes). For the first four components, you might find it helpful to think retrospectively about a specific lesson you taught recently:

Component of vision	Score
Task	
Lesson	
Unit or work	
Scheme of work	
Curriculum	
Aims of education	

Now consider the implications of these scores. What actions do they suggest? What might you do first to address the issues raised? How could this support you as you move forward with this thinking?

Why have a vision?

There are multiple reasons for building a vision at every stage in your working life (and outside it too!):

- It will make clear what you want to achieve.

- It will provide a guiding force that will enable you to make appropriate decisions.

- It will enable you to be faithful to your mission in the face of changes imposed from outside.

- It's an empowering exercise that can increase personal motivation and drive.

- It will help you focus in on the opportunities that exist to achieve your goals.

- It informs time management and resourcing.

- It links to your values and your mission and is a congruence check.

On the negative side, if you don't have a vision it's easy to be pulled in all sorts of directions by *other people's* visions, ideas or plans. A classic example is when a new government initiative is launched and teachers feel compelled to take it on board irrespective of whether

'A true leader is one who designs the cathedral and then shares the vision that inspires other to build it.' *Jan Carlzon*

it meets their own vision. 'Initiative overload' is now a familiar concept in many schools and is partly fuelled by not having a clear vision yourself of where you're heading.

But I don't have time to build a vision – my role is to teach!

This is a common belief, and it's vital not to let yourself fall into this trap. Remember you have real *choices* about what you can and can't do. Remember Henry Ford's quote, which warns against self-fulfilling prophecies?

'If you think you can do a thing, or think you can't do a thing, you're probably right.'

Henry Ford (1863–1947)

It's a tremendously positive step to take to spend time thinking about your vision – but you'll need to *make* time to do it. By reserving some time each week to focus on this key area of personal development, you'll soon begin to reap the rewards. Studies have also shown the many benefits to schools of building a vision (for example see case study 2.1).

Box 2.1: Vision-building tips

Five tips for creating more time to plan your vision:

- Carry a notepad with you around school to jot down ideas periodically when on duty or when waiting for people to attend meetings.

- Start the day with a five minute vision generator: e.g. 'If I could have anything for my class, what would it be?'

- Use a weekly planner and plan time in for 'visioning'.

- Write vision at the very top of your priority list – it's a high end activity that merits proper attention.

- Look for ways to delegate tasks to others (adults and youngsters) so that you have more time available to build your vision.

Case study 2.1: The value of having a whole-school vision

Summary

A research study has shown that schools who build a strong vision are more likely to be successful, and their staff less affected by stress, when facing government-imposed changes, than those who do not have a vision.

'It's a poor sort of memory that only works backwards.' *Lewis Carroll*

The study

Work was carried out in a range of schools at the onset of the national curriculum to determine how well they coped with the changes. Schools were selected which either had a strong vision, or did not have one.

Results

Overall schools that had a vision prospered despite the government-imposed changes, whereas those with no vision found these changes more challenging. Results also showed that staff in those schools with a strong vision suffered less from stress, disruption and inconvenience than schools with no vision. A vision appears to operate to provide a robust reference point for schools in the face of change, which helps them to navigate the changes while being true to what they believe in.

The study quotes the example of a school which had a unique vision built around its work in the environmental arena, having been spurred on by winning awards in this field. The school had gone public with its desire to become a leading centre nationally for environmental education. This helped it to focus on the elements of the new national curriculum which would allow it to move forward with its vision, rather than being swamped by all the new regulations. A year after the implementation of the new curriculum, staff at the school displayed impressive levels of motivation compared with those in other schools. The school continues to work towards its exciting vision, having embedded the national curriculum into its teaching and learning.

Conclusions

This case study helps to show the benefits of building a vision. Note that it's possible to scale things down from the whole school level to the faculty or departmental level, which are also subject to many changes imposed from above. Having a vision for your faculty, department or classroom can equally provide you with a clear reference point when trying to make sense of any changes.

Questions to consider:

1 Have any conflicts arisen at your school due to a lack of vision in certain areas of your work?

2 Which areas of your work are most subject to change?

3 How could a vision help you to work through changes?

4 How might a vision for your classroom be particularly beneficial?

5 What other factors, in addition to a having a vision, can be helpful when trying to manage change in your classroom or school?

'Make your plans as fantastic as you like because 25 years from now they will seem mediocre. Make your plans ten times as great as you first planned, and 25 years from now you will wonder why you did not make them 50 times as great.'
Henry Curtis

Building your vision

So far, this chapter has made the case for the need to build a vision for all aspects of your work. But what's the most effective way to actually build a vision? There's no doubt that building a vision is a specific *skill* which takes time to develop – so don't be too impatient if things seem slow to begin with!

Some of the key things to remember are:

- Give yourself *quality* time in which to work – don't try to do it at the end of a working day or week when you're tired and ready to put your feet up.

- Work in a comfortable environment – away from noise and other distractions and in a place where you'll not be easily disturbed.

- Use a range of approaches until you find the ones that work best for you – one particularly successful approach is described in Box 2.2.

- It helps to talk things through with a colleague or somebody from outside of education – this can help clarify your views.

- Focus on the *positive* aspects of the vision – don't be tempted to think about how things might change for the *worse*!

- Use visualization as a tool to go out into the future to a time when you have realized this vision. Explore what you see, hear and feel when you have accomplished this vision (see page 53 for practical guidance on 'visioning').

- Tell people about your vision, so that they too are clued into the opportunities you seek. But don't feel a failure if you don't manage to reach your vision in the timeframe you expected and remember that it's OK for your vision evolve.

Box 2.2: LogoVisual Thinking in action

LogoVisual Thinking (LVT) is a highly effective method of thinking through your ideas and bringing them into a coherent whole. It's an ideal method for building your vision. It takes advantage of a simple visual toolkit which includes objects (e.g. card/paper or Post-it notes) which can be written on and a display surface (e.g. flipchart paper) which can also be written upon and around which the objects can be moved. The approach enables many, often complex, ideas to be held together in one space at the same time, and repositioned to make clusters and new meanings to synthesize key ideas.

The LVT approach also works effectively when small groups of people are collaborating and discussing their ideas to build a shared vision. Additionally, it can be used to assimilate the views of people gathered through a variety of other methods of data collection, which do not rely on face to face interaction. LVT

'Your vision will become clear only when you look into your heart ... who looks outside, dreams. Who looks inside, awakens.' *Carl Gustav Jung*

follows a series of stages which help to break down the vision-building process, which correspond to:

1 **Focus** – stimulus question or questions are posed to provoke the creation of the vision.

2 **Gather** – ideas are written down by those who are participating in the exercise. These are recorded on separate sheets of card/paper or sticky notes. In this example these are direct responses to the stimulus question(s) by the participants.

3 **Organize** – the ideas are formed into clusters of related items, which are given short but meaningful titles. This is the stage of synthesis.

4 **Understand** – the ideas are assembled into a more holistic pattern or diagram which expresses their totality in a concise and meaningful way.

5 **Apply** – this takes the exercise one step further by using the results to respond to the task in hand at a more sophisticated level, i.e. the ideas are turned into a mission statement for your work as a teacher.

An example of a vision for a teacher's work created using LVT is shown in Box 2.3.

The LVT approach described here is also becoming increasingly recognized as a powerful teaching and learning tool, as well as a superb way to carry out a range of school management tasks. For more information, including 18 exemplars from schools showing practical classroom and management applications, see Best *et al.* (2005).

In addition to the methods described in Box 2.2 you could consider building your vision in the following ways:

- Brainstorming the possibilities.

- Drawing a mind map.

- Considering the pros and cons of various options.

- Listing the things you want to change and then listing how they'll be better in a brighter future.

- Imagining how someone else might deal with the situation.

- Preparing a collage to show what the future looks like – for example using cuttings from magazines.

- Writing an imaginary diary entry of a typical day five years in the future.

'Capital isn't scarce. Vision is.' *Michael Milken*

- Imagining what press coverage on your school would be like in the future and inventing some positive headlines.

- Making a presentation to an audience that crystallizes your views.

- You could be really creative by making up a song, poem or slogan which sums up your view of the future. Although this might sound a bit 'cheesy', remember we ask our students to do these kinds of creative things all the time – and they usually rise to the challenge!

Experiment with these methods, but remember not to hide within the comfort zone of your learning preferences. Remember that creativity, the key theme underpinning the whole of this book, is about experimenting to find new ways of doing things which bring powerful results.

Task 2.2: Which techniques top your table?

Consider the various techniques that you use to build your vision, at whatever level you're working. Draw up a 'league table' which shows how frequently you use, or how comfortable you feel about, each of the possible techniques mentioned in this chapter (including others you use that are not mentioned here). At the top of the league table place your favourite technique. Now consider what benefits could be gained from using the techniques in the bottom half of your league table. How can you ensure that in a year's time those currently unfavoured are pushing up towards the top of the league?

Ask colleagues about their own favoured techniques. This could begin a fascinating series of conversations, the like of which you may not have had before. It could also help you gain an insight into colleague's inner worlds. Perhaps some of your colleagues simply rely on instinct? Why not find out? If you're finding all this talk of visionary thinking a bit 'pie in the sky' remember that in the end it's simply about the *outcomes* that you're after in your work – and everybody surely has outcomes in mind?

Box 2.3: A teacher's personal vision

This model has been built using the LogoVisual Thinking approach described above, and outputted using a computer program called Visual Concept.

'Vision is the blazing campfire around which people will gather. It provides light, energy, warmth and unity.' *Bill Newman*

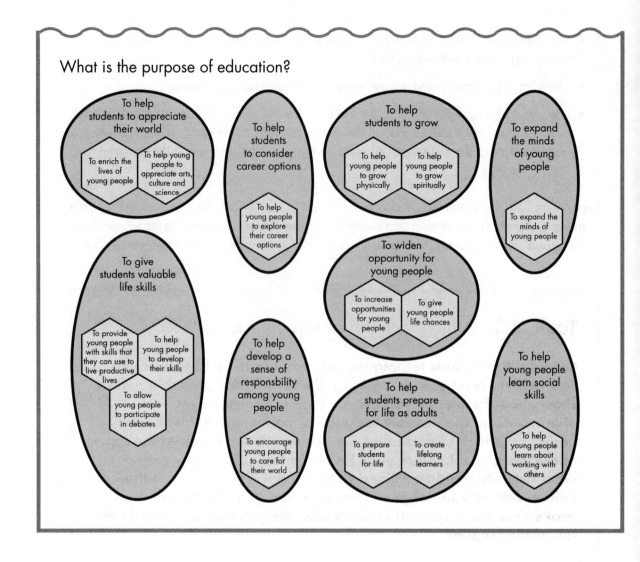

What is the purpose of education?

Integrating your vision with that of others

Have you ever stopped to think about whether your vision for education, an individual lesson or the teaching approaches you're using, is shared by your students? What about their parents and the wider community? And your teaching colleagues and senior management team? In common with many other teachers you'll probably find that this is something that you've not seriously considered before. It's because within education we're not in the habit of sharing our visions with other people and reflecting on the differences and areas of overlap.

However, if you think about it, it's really important to be clear about what others think, as you can only be seen as completely effective if you're meeting the vision of your students and other key stakeholders as well as your *own* vision. In an ideal world, all the key stakeholders would have a shared vision for education and how to achieve success. Remember,

'Whether carrying out a simple task or executing a grand plan, there's a vision, either conscious or subconscious, behind it.'

this could refer to the vision in terms of *outcomes*, together with the *actions* that are needed to get there. Figure 2.2 shows how the visions of different people can overlap to create a more powerful *collective* vision, but there's also the potential for divergence too.

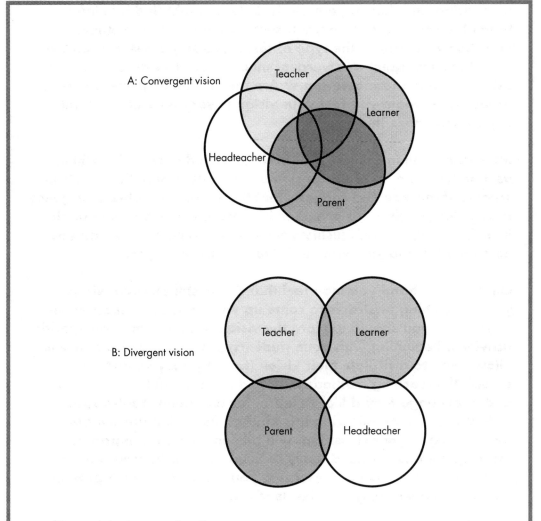

A: Convergent vision

Teacher

Learner

Headteacher

Parent

B: Divergent vision

Teacher

Learner

Parent

Headteacher

Figure 2.2: The power of collective vision

Where there's a *convergent* vision the views of the different stakeholders are broadly similar, resulting in a more harmonious working relationship. Each party is acting towards shared goals and this can result in a very powerful positive force for change. Within the classroom, the greater the degree of convergence, the greater the likelihood of teaching taking place which is judged as effective.

Where there's a *divergent* vision the views of the different stakeholders are broadly dissimilar, creating tensions in the working relationship. Each party is acting towards different goals, which can be a force which divides individuals and makes positive change difficult to achieve. Within the classroom, conflict is inevitable where there's divergence of this kind.

'Vision is the key to understanding leadership, and real leaders have never lost the childlike ability to dream dreams.' *Bill Newman*

Task 2.3: Who shares your vision?

Pause to consider the degree of day-to-day overlap between your own vision and that of your students (you might find it helpful to think about a specific aspect, such as the teaching methods you choose to use, or the type of tasks you set). Does it resemble most the convergent or divergent model? What evidence are you using to make these assertions? Are they reliable? Is there a key group from whom you feel your vision is very divergent? What implications does this have?

It's very helpful to explore this much neglected aspect of teaching, as it underpins a lot of the tension and dissatisfaction that exists in schools. If this exercise suggests that there's considerable divergence in key stakeholders' visions, then it's time to act. What can you do in order to explain and justify your vision to others? How can you persuade them to join with you? Are you always right?

On the other hand you may feel that this is still an area where you're clutching at straws to come up with sensible responses, in which case you should explore the vision of others through specific activities. Beginning with your students, plan an exercise that will allow them to articulate their vision (for why they should attend school, the teaching methods they find most helpful or the skills and knowledge they'd like to learn, for example). You're sure to find that just by allowing this kind of discussion the climate for learning in your classroom will be enhanced. An important message here is the need to try to keep clear of 'teacher knows best' approaches, while preserving your professional integrity as an expert on learning and the 'lead learner'.

Being clear about the vision of different stakeholders can be a powerful exercise. Sometimes, it can reveal that although there's a shared vision of the future and what should be achieved, there's disagreement about the *methods* that should be used to get there. This presents an opportunity to tackle the areas of disagreement to produce a more harmonious partnership – see Case Study 2.2 for a fascinating case study of this.

Case study 2.2: Exploring the vision of students and teachers

Summary

A recent project in Stoke-on-Trent has helped to cast light on the value of exploring the concept of 'vision' with teachers and students, and has shown that when given the opportunity students are able to articulate their vision effectively.

'Throughout the centuries there were men who took first steps down new roads armed with nothing but their own vision.'
Ayn Rand

The project

The aim of the project was to improve lesson design for more able students within four schools by exploring students' and teachers' views of effective lessons. It was initiated by a cluster co-ordinator who was keen to explore the extent to which more able students in Stoke-on-Trent could be engaged in an exercise which provided a high level of challenge, as well as providing meaningful information on the students' vision of an effective lesson.

Students' views

Working with external facilitators, the students were first asked to identify who the main **stakeholders** in their education are and what these people care about (the latter equated to their vision). The students' responses were as follows:

- *Main stakeholders* – students, parents/carers, teachers, LEA staff, government, employers.

- *What they care about* (*vision*) – students should be successful, pass exams, be happy, have appropriate skills.

A whole group discussion then took place, during which the following observations were made by the students:

- All the stakeholders agree that educational progress of one sort or another is what is really important: this is the vision.

- The stakeholders agree **what** is important, but they sometimes disagree about **how** to achieve the common goals: this leads to conflict.

This latter observation is especially insightful as it helps to explain the kind of conflicts that go on in classrooms and students' homes on a day-to-day basis.

Moving on from this broad exploration of vision, students were then asked to comment specifically on how lessons could be improved to challenge, inspire and motivate more able students. Working in small groups, the students carried out an exercise similar to that described in Box 2.2, with the following group vision being produced.

The participating students were highly engaged in this exercise, gave thoughtful answers and made it clear that they believed *passionately* in what they were saying.

'Every man takes the limits of his field of vision for the limits of the world.' *Arthur Schopenhauer*

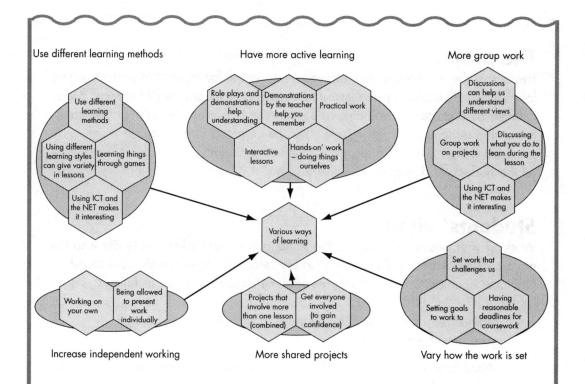

Use different learning methods

Have more active learning

More group work

Use different learning methods

Using different learning styles can give variety in lessons

Learning things through games

Using ICT and the NET makes it interesting

Role plays and demonstrations help understanding

Demonstrations by the teacher help you remember

Practical work

Interactive lessons

'Hands-on' work – doing things ourselves

Discussions can help us understand different views

Group work on projects

Discussing what you do to learn during the lesson

Using ICT and the NET makes it interesting

Various ways of learning

Working on your own

Being allowed to present work individually

Projects that involve more than one lesson (combined)

Get everyone involved (to gain confidence)

Set work that challenges us

Setting goals to work to

Having reasonable deadlines for coursework

Increase independent working

More shared projects

Vary how the work is set

Teachers' views

Next came the turn of a group of teachers from the students' schools, who had responded to an open invitation to all staff. The teachers were also asked how lessons for more able students could be improved, and worked in a similar way to the students in small groups. They produced their own vision for how lessons could be improved which was displayed on boards for the whole group to see. The teachers then compared what they had come up with against the students' ideas, and a lively discussion resulted.

Results

There was close congruence between the views of the teachers and those of the students as outlined in the diagram, especially concerning active learning, everyone pushing the boundaries and teachers planning effectively. The principal difference was that the students stressed the value of interaction and groupwork in learning, something which was not picked up by the teachers.

The results of the work led the teachers to discuss ways of profiting from the views of the students and staff, which involved work at the student, staff and parent level. A particularly exciting development was the proposal to ask the students themselves to get more actively involved in training staff, including senior managers, to improve provision. Specific teaching innovations were also devised by the teachers, in response to the students' views. It should be noted that many of the responses given by the more able students were judged by the teachers to be equally beneficial for other students.

'A man to carry on a successful business must have imagination. He must see things in a vision, a dream of the whole thing.' *Charles M. Schwab*

Conclusions

While teachers wouldn't want to use students' views as the *only* source of data on which to reflect and improve their lessons, the results obtained in this project have underlined the value of giving students the opportunity to have a voice and outline their vision.

The work also served to highlight the fact that student consultation can be used as a stimulus for high quality dialogue about teaching and learning, that can result in positive changes.

It's interesting to note that when challenged to consider the changes needed to engage more able students in lessons, teachers came up with a range of appropriate responses. However, they missed out on some of the students' suggestions, and clearly most of the teachers' ideas were not already being implemented by the majority of staff in their schools.

Questions to consider

1   Have you ever asked students for their views on lessons in this kind of way?

2   In this example the students identified considerable congruence between the visions of the different stakeholders, including their own (a fascinating and reassuring finding in itself), as to what they care about. But what would you do if there were marked differences in the visions of the different stakeholders? Reflect on whether this is an issue which you are facing in your school and what could be done to tackle these opposing views.

3   How can teachers' concerns about using students' views be addressed, so they're more willing to take such views seriously?

Further information

The work is described in more detail in the December 2004 issue of *Gifted & Talented Update* (www.optimuspub.co.uk).

'It's not what the vision is, it's what the vision does.' *Peter Senge*

The importance of values

An individual's vision does not just materialize out of thin air. Their vision is born from their *values*. We often glibly talk about values in relation to vision. But what are values, exactly? How do we create them and store them? What's the impact on us of the value sets that we've developed? How are values stored collectively in an organization? What happens when there's conflict between sets of values? How can we resolve these conflicts? These are just some of the questions we'll explore as we connect the process of vision-making to that of values. You'll see that as well as being a fascinating topic in its own right, by understanding our own values and those of others, we're much better equipped to deal with challenging or unhelpful behaviours – from our students as well as our colleagues.

What are values?

Values are the things that are important to you. They are 'what we desire and want' (Dilts 1999) and can be called 'drivers'. Values act as inner motivators or drivers of behaviour and influence what we think, say and do. So what are values exactly? Values are nominalizations; they are deeply held entities which when expressed verbally often come out as labelled single words. These words might include 'fairness', 'honour', 'success', 'happiness', 'love', 'equality' and so on. Such nominalizations are highly generalized, and this is typical of a value. Values can be applied to any context, and together they form our personal values set. This can be different according to the context in which it's expressed – our 'work' values set might be different to that for 'family life'. We can use our values set to explore any conflicts in our thinking, as Box 2.4 shows.

Box 2.4: Exploring an individual's value set

Jane desperately wants to allow her students more creative freedom. She knows at some level that it's essential for them to develop as effective learners. She is, however, frustrated by the limitations of the curriculum and her perceived need for good order in her classroom, and what that means. Jane's values are elicited and come out as:

- Truth
- Learning
- Fun
- Status
- Community

'Vision is the art of seeing the invisible.' *Jonathan Swift*

- Organization
- Rules
- Inspiration
- Creativity
- Success

Jane is asked to put these values in order by asking of each value, 'If you could have value X, but not value Y would that be OK?'.

The result is a list that looks like this:

Rules
Creativity
Success
Learning
Truth
Fun
Community
Organization
Status
Inspiration

Jane is having real challenges with getting her classes to be creative, because she has 'rules' at the top of her list of values. There's a *values conflict* emerging where she requires hard and fast rules in her classroom, yet she cherishes the idea of thinking creatively beyond the boundaries.

Interestingly, another person might have the same values set, but not be in conflict. Here we need to introduce another concept, that of 'criteria'. Criteria are the evidence for judging whether a value has been met. Jane feels uncomfortable because she's driven by the need for order and rules and yet is almost as strongly driven by the need for creativity, which she interprets as operating without rules, e.g. 'thinking outside the box'. Another person may believe that in order to have creativity happen, one must be aware of the current rules and parameters, after all, how can one think outside of the rules in creative ways, unless one knows what those rules are! Similarly they believe that there are in fact rules to being creative. There is a process that works for them, in other words there are steps and conditions which they must put in place so that they can be creative.

This kind of values conflict is common. And it grows from the interpretation that is placed by an individual as to what is important and what the criteria are for judging that importance. What you can see from this example is that the resolution of conflict is in the interpretation of these values, not the values themselves.

'The eye sees only what the mind is prepared to comprehend.' *Henri Bergson*

Are values, which are defined by our whole lifetime's experiences, fixed and unchangeable? Values might seem unchangeable because they provoke such strong reactions when they're violated. Both authors meet individuals from time to time, in their training courses, whose values are sometimes challenged by the concepts in the training. Strong emotional responses can emerge and these signal the crossing of values boundaries. In fact, our values are far more malleable than we think. The secret to shifting values is uncovered when we look at the way in which they're constructed.

Task 2.4: What are your own values?

Try this activity to elicit your own values and consider the reflective questions at the end of the activity.

Making a pen and paper available, ask yourself the question: What's important to me in relation to my classroom? Listen to what your mind conjures up in response to this question. Avoid thinking hard about this, simply take what flows into your mind. Once you've listed the words that flow, ask yourself: What else is important to me in relation to my classroom? Allow a further flow of words to come through and write them down.

Once you've exhausted the flow of words that represent what's important to you, consider these questions which will help to generate any further values that have not yet come through. If you had all of the values in place in your classroom, what would still cause you to want to leave? Write down any response. If you did not have any of the above values operating in your classroom, what would cause you still to want to stay? Write down this response.

What you will have now are a series of values. From your list pick the first ten most important values for you. Place them in order of importance, from 1 which is most important to 10 which is the least important on that list. This list is now your top ten values in relation to your classroom.

Operating within your classroom in a way which is line with your values will bring you fulfilment and a sense of being on track. If any of these values are missing, there may be conflict. Understanding more clearly where the conflict is enables you to address it more readily. It can also help you to consider conflicts between your values and those of your students.

Consider the following questions:
- **What conflicts exist between your values and those of your students?**
- **What are the conflicts between your values and the school's?**
- **How are your values and your students' values in line?**
- **How are your values and the school's values in line?**

'The secret of success in life is for a man to be ready for his opportunity when it comes.' *Benjamin Disraeli*

How values are constructed

Values are constructed from our *belief systems*. Belief systems are constructed from collections of beliefs. A belief is an idea we no longer question and is developed from a generalized decision we have made in response to a life experience, or something we have been told and take to be true (e.g. autumn begins in October; train travel is more environmentally friendly than car travel etc.).

It is thought that collections of beliefs are clustered together to form our values. What is common to our beliefs forms the highly generalized nominalizations we call values.

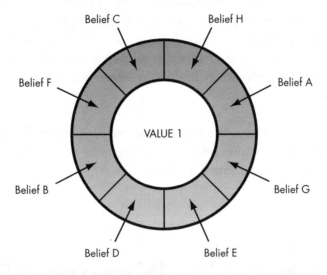

Values and beliefs

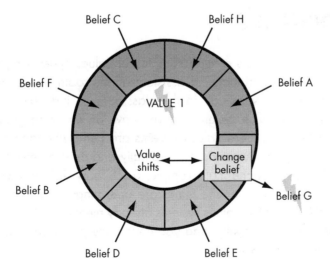

Values–beliefs relationships

Figure 2.3: Values and beliefs

'Chance favours only the prepared mind.' *Louis Pasteur*

For example, a set of beliefs such as 'lying hurts people', 'trust is built through honesty', 'being open creates useful dialogue' and 'let me down more than once and it's time to end our friendship', might cluster together to form the important common denominator which is 'honesty', which in turn creates that value in an individual. Now if this doesn't make absolute sense to you as an example, be aware that this may be because you're using your own experiences and values to filter the example! These ideas can get very complex! So let's make it simple.

It's a helpful analogy to think of the relationship between beliefs and values as being like a mint with a hole in it. The fabric of the mint is made up of a series of linked beliefs and the hole represents the value (Figure 2.3).

All the while that this set of beliefs hold (that is, they continue to be believed as true), the mint is intact and the value exists. The minute that one of the beliefs is challenged successfully, the mint is no longer complete, and the hole is no longer intact. The outcome is that the value changes. Consider then that this value is not in isolation but part of a complex of values – a kind of 3D matrix of mints, many sharing common beliefs to form their value. You then have some idea of the complexity of value systems. You also have an understanding of the fragility of values.

Change one belief and you affect one or sometimes many values at the same time. As we'll explore later in this book, changing beliefs is actually quite easy and it's something we do every day for ourselves and facilitate it in others.

What is the significance of this theoretical model to classrooms?

Inevitably, in a classroom there's a huge complex of values systems represented in every student and in the teachers and teaching assistants in the room. These value systems interrelate at every moment of every day in the classroom as individuals interact. Overlay on this the organizational value system and you have an amazing group of interrelating values sets. Add to this, that these values systems are being changed daily, and that the organizational value systems may exist conceptually and exist differently in reality, and it all gets to be a bit of a headache! For example, a school is likely to have the values of its headteacher, the values that he or she thinks are operating, the actual values operating, which are mediated by all of the values systems already mentioned (students and staff), plus those of government and community, and you have enough variables to blow your mind. Once again let's try to make it simple.

'If one is the master of one thing and understands one thing well, one has at the same time, insight into and understanding of many things.' *Vincent van Gogh*

Working with multiple values sets

When we're working with groups of teachers or students we're setting together multiples of different values sets. It becomes overwhelming to try to consider each individual value set and a more manageable model is called for. The *Values Clusters Model* presents six key groups of values. These might represent the values sets of an individual, a group or subgroup (e.g. a class, or friendship group within it, or an organization). It's possible to try and oversimplify this, and so as we explain the drivers and operating approaches of each values cluster, we would ask you to be aware of the blurred edges to the boundaries between the clusters. One can operate in more than one cluster group at any one time and over time this can change. We would also point out that each cluster has its strengths and weaknesses for both for teachers, learners and organizations, and so it would be helpful to you in considering this model initially to accept the presupposition that there's no right or wrong value set, they just represent a spectrum of human drivers.

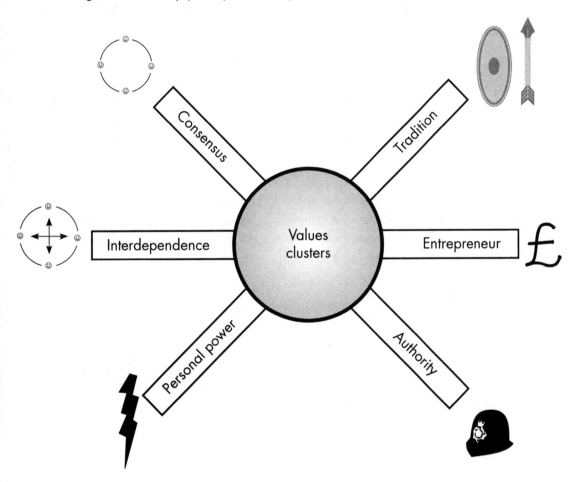

Figure 2.4: Values Clusters Model

The following table outlines the six values clusters and expands on the characteristics of each cluster.

Values cluster	Description	Key motivators	Plus points	Minus points
Consensus	The cluster of 'self sacrifice for the good of all of us'. Characterized by exploration of feelings of the group and seeking absolute agreement at every stage of decision making.	Connection, emotion, rights, participation, equality, celebration of diversity.	An inclusive, trust-building value set, which allows individuals to feel part of a supportive climate for development. Has potential to develop solutions which are focused on collective rather than individual power. Explores feelings and works towards social improvement.	Working with this values cluster is time-consuming and it can be very difficult to reach consensus. Outcomes may be difficult to agree and once agreed, the thoughts and feelings of individuals may derail progress. These feelings need to be explored before the outcomes can be worked upon further.
Tradition	There are ways we have done things for many years, why change? The history is already written and we follow it loyally.	Custom, tradition, mystique, rituals, belonging.	There's a ready, available set of guide-lines, rules, and practices which have been proven over time to work. Often time efficient, with elements of mystique surrounding some practices, people and objects.	It may be exces-sively ritualistic or intimidating. There may be a lack of creativity, individuality and freedom of expression. This can be demotivating for teachers or learners.

'Initiative is key. Anybody who wants to be somebody is going to work as hard as they can to fulfil that dream.' *Anonymous*

Values cluster	Description	Key motivators	Plus points	Minus points
Entrepreneur £	A competitive and goal-centred cluster, likely to be possibilities-oriented. Individuals are drawn to rapid change and the blazing of new trails.	Success, riches, competition, personal gain, wealth generation, exploitation, opportunity, drive.	Entrepreneurs exploit opportunities and can have gains on multiple levels. In the classroom the entrepreneurial teacher can market the learning in varied and interesting ways, allowing learners to develop their own goals. This creates highly motivating lessons.	This can be in conflict with a more traditional curriculum. Learners who do not have a learning pathway provided which gives an outlet for their entrepreneurial values, will find other outlets for this and exploit other ways of working which may not support learning more widely in class.
Authority	There is a right way to do things, and come what may we stick to it. Erring leads to punitive action.	Responsibility, law, conformism, discipline, procedure, establishment.	Rigid rules and regulations provide safe and comfortable working conditions for the majority. Providing clear rails for learners and teachers to operate on cuts down on the stress created by too many choices. Individuals in an organization know what's expected.	An over-authoritarian value cluster can stifle creativity. Limiting or cutting out choice for many learners and teachers can be demotivating. It can also trigger subversive behaviour in some people. When circumstances change, the authoritarian culture can be slow to adjust its boundaries and chaos can develop as old structures fail.

'The major reason for setting a goal is for what it makes of you to accomplish it. What it makes of you will always be the far greater value than what you get.' *Jim Rohn*

Values cluster	Description	Key motivators	Plus points	Minus points
Personal power	The cluster of immediate self gratification. 'I can have what I want and I want it now'. Driven by status.	Go for it!, impulse, self, fun, excitement, today, instant gratification, respect through non-conformity.	It empowers individuals to be, do, and have what they want. It's the typical value set of the so-called 'selfish teenager'. It may be a necessary transitional values cluster from childhood to adulthood. It's characterized by flouting rules, and seeking immediate gratification.	It's immediately fulfilling and can get the individual what they want at the expense of others. This cluster can be highly disruptive to group dynamics and challenges the striving for collective good.
Interdependence	Embraces change as a normal part of life. It recognizes that interactions are two-way processes and bring benefits to both; there is a long-term plan. Working with others generates more than could be achieved individually. Working 'on the edge of chaos' generates creative solutions.	Metathinking, complexity, valuing others, accumulation, change, synergy, creativity, out-of-the-box, flexibility, fluidity.	A heightened state of working. This recognizes the needs of individuals and the strengths they bring to a team, as well as the goals of the organization. When interdependence is operating, everyone is offering their skills and knowledge and the whole is more than the sum of its parts. It generates new, creative solutions to problems. It is exciting, inclusive and effective.	It requires the establishment and re-examination of the purpose and operating agreement of a group. This needs to happen periodically and when problems arise. Interdependence can involve rejecting past approaches and even current plans; it may be working 'at the edge of chaos'. For some people this is too dangerous and can trigger defensive behaviours.

'I have often wondered how it is that every man sets less value on his own opinions of himself than on the opinions of others.' *Marcus Aurelius*

Working with values clusters in the classroom

The Values Clusters Model is just a model. If we attempt to box ourselves, our classes, or our organization into one cluster, we're oversimplifying the picture. In all likelihood, there are elements of a number of clusters working in any one individual or group of individuals. We have listed some of the positives and negatives of each cluster, so that you can begin to notice the ways in which there are benefits to each and every one, just as there are negative aspects.

There are a number of ways or steps we can take to work with values, using this model. Many of these have key relevance for behaviour management in schools:

1 **Appreciate**: we can use the model to broadly group an individual or group behaviour set. By considering where they're currently operating from we can more fully understand their needs and their motivators. This in its own right helps us to de-emotionalize our relationship with others. This can happen by accepting the presupposition that we should respect other peoples' model of the world and we can appreciate that others are different from ourselves. We can also understand what they're getting from operating from their values clusters. We don't have to agree with their values, but it gives us a non-emotive starting point to understand where they're coming from.

2 **Analyse conflict**: we can honestly align ourselves with others by identifying the values cluster(s) we most strongly affiliate to and reflect on the motivators we have and the motivators of the individuals or groups we're operating with. This allows us to rationally analyse where differences and similarities lie.

3 **Build bridges**: using the analysis of differences and similarities we can create motivational bridges between ourselves and others. For example, if a teacher operates from a *tradition* cluster and learners from a *personal power* cluster, recognizing what learners need can help the teacher plan for their needs. This might mean the teacher tapping into areas of mystique (of tradition) and excitement and status (of personal power) about the traditions of the institution or group. For example, telling stories of legendary past students or teachers who demonstrate the duality of conformism and non-conformism, like a cricket captain who had an unusual ritual before running up to the crease and devastating the opposing batsman. Looking for examples of ambiguity between values clusters is helpful. This builds rapport and enables the next stage to take place. It also values the strengths and contributions of those you seek to connect with.

4 **Lead to new ground**: here, with strong rapport with others, we can introduce more of our preferred values clusters and influence others. This is a critical task for a teacher, who may be confronted with students' values (and resulting behaviours) which are not conducive to effective classroom learning.

Of course, you could argue that there is a values system behind this approach. You're probably right. If we were to strongly advocate one values cluster it would be *interdependence*. Stephen Covey in his book *The Seven Habits of Highly Effective People* (1989)

'Things only have the value that we give them.' *Moliere*

champions the interdependence values set. He connects three key elements to making this work:

- **Thinking win/win** – ensure that both parties in an interaction benefit.

- **Seeking first to understand, then to be understood** – find out the circumstances before acting.

- **Synergy** – utilize the strengths of others to create a whole which is more than the sum of its parts.

Utilizing the four approaches above, as steps, can help you to both connect with people and move them towards your vision.

We would suggest that all meaningful change occurs when individuals buy into the benefits of the change – and this can take some time. The more investment they have, the smoother and more effective the change is. Therefore, if you're committed to developing the best opportunities for your learners, we advocate an approach which champions creativity as part of an interdependence values set. Whilst advocating creativity and interdependence, let's not forget that every values cluster has its strengths as well as its weaknesses, and respect other peoples' models of the world.

Linking vision and values in school

In the early part of this chapter, we outlined the importance of vision as 'a description of the future which shows what you would like to achieve in a particular aspect of your work or private life'. Values being your underlying drivers or motivators for life and work, it would be difficult for them to be anything but intrinsically involved in the development of your classroom vision. As you move forward in developing your vision you might wish to use the analysis of values clusters as a tool to identify what you would like to see in your classroom. This may be in terms of resources and exam results, but also in terms of relationships, interactions and motivators amongst your learners.

A vast body of research in the field of Neuro-Linguistic Programming (NLP) shows that a clear focus on exactly what you want to achieve propels you towards it. An unclear internal representation of the outcomes you wish for, or one which harbours conflict about what you want, will leach energy and derail your endeavours. We cannot advocate enough the importance of building a vision, and what's more, growing a vision which embraces your motivators and looks for bridges with the youngsters and the organization. You may even need to challenge your current values set and will almost certainly have to challenge the values set of others. Go on, we dare you!

'It is never easy to keep reaching for dreams. Strength and courage can sometimes be lonely friends, but those who reach, walk in stardust.' *Flavia Weedon*

Relating your values and vision to the Creative Teaching Framework

We draw this chapter to a close by considering how the concept of values and vision relates to the Creative Teaching Framework which is the foundation of this book.

While all of the components of the framework are important, it's difficult to overemphasize the importance of vision, which inevitably stems from our own sense of what's important (our values). Without a vision underpinned with the motivational drivers – at whatever level you're operating – it's very hard to know what specific actions you should be carrying out on a day-to-day basis to ensure that you're true to what you believe in. The danger is that you'll be easily pushed and pulled in all sorts of directions, probably against your will, because you have no alternative vision to work towards which you own.

The Creative Teaching Framework allows you to focus on a variety of levels which are appropriate to your work – the task, lesson, scheme of work, curriculum chosen, etc. But it also suggests that an essential guiding force for all this work at a more specific level is your vision for what education is really about. In many ways, therefore, building a vision can be seen as the *starting point* for becoming a more effective teacher.

We firmly believe that a considerable amount of teacher dissatisfaction and stress is caused by individuals not having a clear vision of where they're heading. So why wait? If you've not yet protected some quality time to begin building your own vision then now is the time to start.

We encourage you to fish beneath the surface in the realms of your beliefs and values. We urge you to analyse your motivations and those of your learners and construct and work towards your vision. Seek to bridge the gap between where learners are and where you want them to be. We'd go further than that, in that we'd encourage you to encourage your learners to be part of that vision in both its building and its execution. If you want change, then sell the benefits of change and make those affected by it part of its process.

'The most important thing about having goals is having one.' *Albert F Geoffrey*

- -

⟳ Review

This chapter has sought to emphasize the following key points:

- Vision is fundamental to becoming a more effective teacher.

- It's vital to be clear about your own vision at many levels – from the aims of education to the purpose of a specific task within a lesson.

- A variety of tools and approaches exist which can help you to build your vision – which is a discrete skill in itself.

- The most effective teachers will take account of the views of students and other stakeholders to build a powerful collective vision.

- Gaining insights into students' and other stakeholders' visions requires you to open up, actively listen and value others' views.

- Values underpin vision and are in turn affected by our beliefs.

- Values are intrinsic motivators of learners, teachers and leaders, but they're not fixed and are subject to regular reorganization.

- Values can be conceptualized as six clusters and this can be used as a basis for understanding and planning for learning.

⇨ Action points

Consider the following actions in the light of this chapter and using the self-evaluation tool select those which are most appropriate to your particular needs:

- Build a vision for what you believe to be the aims of education – consider the implications of this for your department, lessons and the tasks you set. Make sure you write this down.

- Explore your students' vision for what they want to get out of school.

- Explore with other stakeholders what their vision for education is.

- Use the Values Cluster Instrument to analyse your own profile of values and consider using it to support your understanding of the values sets of others in your school.

- Use the Values Cluster Model to analyse, informally, the motivators of your students and colleagues and experiment using the motivators to influence them.

- Use your vision to think about the Creative Teaching Framework and what actions you need to carry out to make your vision a reality.

'Aim for success, not perfection. Never give up your right to be wrong, because then you will lose the ability to learn new things and move forward with your life'. *Anonymous*

👁 **Further reading**

The topic of vision is not covered extensively by other educational literature. The following will help take your exploration of vision further.

Best, B, Blake, A & Varney, J (2005) *Making Meaning: learning through logovisual thinking.* Cambridge: Chris Kington Publishing.

- Explains the background to the LVT approach which can be a powerful means of building vision, and includes 18 examples of teachers' and school managers' use of the approach.

Covey, S R (1989) *The Seven Habits of Highly Effective People.* London: Simon & Schuster.

- Covey's second habit focuses on vision which he sees as vital to personal and professional life.

Dilts, R (1999) *Sleight of Mouth: the magic of conversational belief change.* Capitola: Meta Publications.

- Provides an in-depth discussion of the nature of beliefs and values and the criteria which individuals attach to values to determine when they have been fulfilled.

McDermott, I & Jago, W (2003) *The NLP Coach.* London: Piatkus.

- A comprehensive, yet accessible examination of how rapport is built and how beliefs and values can be challenged and changed.

Straessens, K & Vandenberghe, R (1994) Vision as a core component in school culture. *Curriculum Studies* 26:187–200.

- This journal article provides a helpful discussion of how vision relates to practice within school.

Wallace, R (1996) *Vision for Practice.* London: SAGE.

- Provides guidance on how to establish a vision through a preliminary needs assessment.

'The aim of education is the knowledge, not of facts, but of values.' *William S Burroughs*

> **End of chapter metaphor:** Read the story and use the questions that
> follow to consider further aspects of the chapter content.

The tree and the robin

As a plump robin landed in the canopy of the top of a small oak, it flexed its branches. "Morning robin," said the oak.

"Hello," replied the bird.

"Do you know, robin, I'm tired of being a little tree, I want to grow big and tall like all the other trees. I am fed up being down here in the dark and missing out on all of that light that the others get." The robin hopped onto the uppermost branch of the little tree.

"Such sad words," said the robin. The little oak sounded so down.

"I seem doomed to be small all of my life," said the tree.

The robin drew breath and asked the tree a question. "Hey tree, what do you *really* want?"

"I want to grow tall and feel the warmth of the sunshine on my leaves."

"So why don't you?" said the robin.

"I can't because the other trees crowd me out."

"What have you tried?"

"Nothing, there's just no hope!"

"If there was hope, what would you try then?"

The little tree paused for several long seconds. "Well," said the little tree, excited now, "I'd put a little energy into lifting my leaves up to the sun and catch what light I could to grow taller."

"What else?" asked the robin.

"Why I'd stretch my roots to get a little more water and minerals from the soil!"

"What would that get you?"

'Leadership is the capacity to translate vision into reality.' *Warren G Bennis*

"I'd be able to grow a few feet this summer and I'd be closer to the other trees and closer to the light."

"And what would that achieve?"

"Well, next summer I would be able to grow even quicker, because I'd have more light still."

"That would be great, wouldn't it?" said the robin.

"It would be amazing – and what's more next year some of the bigger trees will be cut down and taken away, and that will give me even more light – within two years I could be a really tall tree!"

"So what will you do?" asked the robin.

"Well, I'm going to start stretching right now."

"Well, I will visit you every day to see how you're getting on."

And so he did. The little tree grew bigger and, in the second year, he was as tall as all the other trees; he was right up there in the light.

<hr>

You might wish to consider

1 What thoughts about your classroom does this story throw up?

2 Are there any negative thoughts that you need to work to eradicate?

3 How is this story adaptable for use with your students?

<hr>

'There is only one certain thing you will need for success ... that is the belief you can, and where that does not exist, you must surely still believe that you might.'

Chapter 3

Climate for learning

CLIMATE

'Unless students learn within a physical and emotional climate that supports their learning, no teaching method can be truly effective. It's like trying to set off on a car journey when there's only a dribble of petrol left in the tank.'

Jarvis Hayes

Message to the reader

In recent years, climate for learning has gained in popularity and it's likely that you're already addressing this issue on a variety of fronts. This chapter contains a comprehensive range of ways in which you can enhance still further the climate for learning in your classroom, as well as an explanation of how climate for learning influences three inter-related factors that allow students to enter their Effective Learning Zone. The chapter should help to reinforce just how important climate for learning is – but it is just one component of The Creative Teaching Framework which is explored fully in the other chapters of The Creative Teaching and Learning Toolkit.

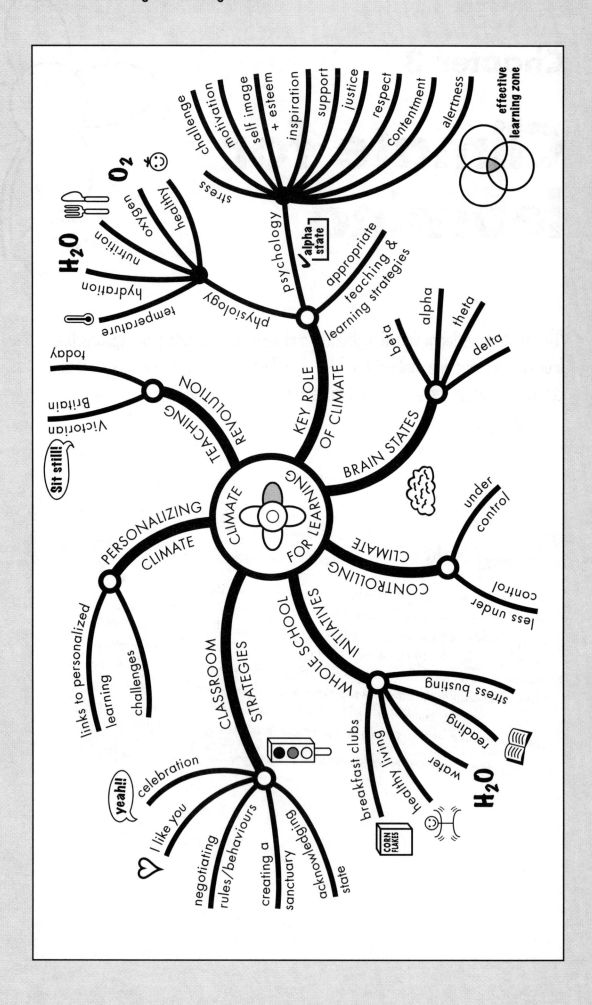

'When people are least sure, they are often most dogmatic.' *John Kenneth Galbraith*

Preview

This chapter explores the vital role of climate in effective teaching and learning, a domain which has so far tended to be neglected in many texts on teaching.

Key learning points:

▶ Why climate is essential to effective teaching.

▶ The two components of climate for learning: physiology and psychology.

▶ How to create a highly effective classroom climate for learning.

▶ What can happen if you do not consider climate for learning.

Questions to ask yourself before beginning this chapter:

1 In what ways do you currently try to create a positive physical climate for learning in your classroom?

2 In what ways do you currently try to cultivate a supportive emotional climate for learning?

3 Consider a classroom you have been in which did *not* have a positive climate for learning – what were its features?

4 Reflect on *your own* ideal climate for learning as a student – what would this be like? Have you ever studied in such a place? What was it like to study there?

'An essential aspect of creativity is not being afraid to fail.' *Edwin Land*

The teaching revolution

The classrooms of Victorian Britain were very different to those of today. Teachers were usually seen as all knowing, authoritarian figures, who did not tolerate ill-discipline and the quirks of children. The schools they taught in must have been very scary places for young people.

Thankfully, students are no longer encouraged to 'sit still, listen, repeat and learn', and are not routinely beaten if they step out of line. No longer are students who struggle forced to sit in corners wearing humiliating dunces' hats, or punished simply because they did not understand something.

When we reflect on the dramatic changes that have occurred in how we teach young people in our schools, it's clear that teaching methods have undergone something of a *revolution* – but one that lagged some way behind the industrial revolution of the golden era of British history. And we would argue that this teaching revolution is still underway.

The raft of new approaches to teaching has provided a major impetus for practitioners to think again about the *aims* of their teaching and the *methods* they'll use to achieve these. One of the most profound changes occurring centres on the *climate* teachers create for learning. This encompasses the *physical* and *psychological* factors that provide an environment that allows learners to flourish.

In the last decade there's been a realization by many teachers that unless learners are in an appropriate state to learn, any teaching approach is likely to be compromised. This has been slow to be picked up in many handbooks for teachers, though the accelerated learning movement has embraced the dimension of climate more warmly than most.

The key role of climate

We believe that an individual's most effective learning takes place in the zone of *overlap* between the three areas of physiology, psychology, and teaching and learning strategies (Figure 3.1, page 86). We call this area of confluence *'The Effective Learning Zone'*. It recognizes that learning will be maximized if due consideration is given to the following three factors:

* **Physiology** – learners need to feel comfortable with their physical environment and their brains should be in an appropriate physical condition to learn. This includes:
    - *A comfortable temperature*: not too hot or too cold, as either can affect brain function and motivation.
    - *Hydration*: the brain is about 75 per cent water and dehydration causes lethargy and hinders learning.
    - *Nutrition*: the brain relies on nutrients in order to work properly, and hunger can prevent learning, or slow it down.

'Creativity flourishes when we have a sense of safety and self-acceptance.' *Julie Cameron*

- *Good oxygen levels*: learners need a good supply of oxygen in order for their brains to be in tip-top condition.
- *Free of illness*: illness suppresses the immune system and causes the brain to direct the body's resources to recovery, thereby making new learning less easy.

- **Psychology** – learners need to be in an appropriate emotional state to learn, which can be characterized as being 'intellectually challenged and motivated, without being negatively stressed'. This will help them to enter what's called the 'alpha state' of relaxed alertness, which is most conducive to effective learning (see Box 3.1). The following factors should be considered – all are concerned with learners' feelings:
  - *Stress*: high levels of stress can prevent learning.
  - *Challenge*: high challenge or expectations are important, but if challenge is too high it can cause negative stress.
  - *Motivation*: highly motivated learners are those who are engaged with their learning and see its personal benefits.
  - *Self-image and esteem*: learners who have a positive self-image are more likely to have high self-esteem, which will help them to engage in effective learning.
  - *Inspiration*: learners can be inspired by teachers, stimulus materials and teaching and learning methods.
  - *Support*: learners who feel supported as they learn (by the teachers, teaching assistants and other learners) are more likely to take risks and achieve their potential.
  - *Justice*: learning is most effective in an environment which is seen as fair and just.
  - *Respect*: it's important for learners to feel respected as they learn, which helps them to feel valued.
  - *Contentment*: learners who are feeling happy and fulfilled are more likely be successful learners; they're likely to feel happier if they achieve success.
  - *Alertness/attention span*: learners need to be fully alert to learn, and lack of sleep or too much day-dreaming can interfere with the learning process, meaning they can concentrate for shorter periods of time.

- **Appropriate teaching and learning strategies** – physical and psychological climate are important, but effective learning clearly only takes place if learners also experience teaching and learning approaches which are successful in achieving the intended outcomes. This theme is explored in much more detail in Chapter 4.

'We need to make the world safe for creativity and intuition, for it is creativity and intuition that will make the world safe for us.' *Edgar Mitchell*

Box 3.1: Brain states

Our brains continually generate minute electrical impulses. Scientists who have attached sensitive electrodes to people's heads have discovered that our brains emit four quite different types of electrical signals, or 'brain waves':

Alpha: characterizes relaxation and meditation and facilitates inspiration, fast assimilation of facts and heightened memory.

Beta: characterizing the conscious mind: you are wide awake and figuring out complex problems.

Theta: characterizing deep relaxation, where flashes of inspiration can occur.

Delta: characterizing deep, dreamless sleep.

While the first three states are all important to one degree or another in learning, the alpha state is the ideal state for classroom learning and teachers should strive to allow learners to enter this state and keep them there.

Note that physiology, psychology and teaching and learning strategies are clearly *inter-related*. If students experience engaging teaching and learning strategies in one of your lessons, they're more likely to feel motivated and content in the next. Equally, many of the factors listed under 'physiology' have direct effects on students' psychology. In reality these factors serve as a tapestry of interconnected influences which, when they come together, create a rich environment allowing effective learning.

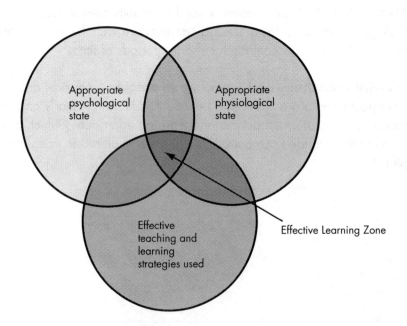

Figure 3.1: The Effective Learning Zone

'Never tell people how to do things. Tell them what to do and they will surprise you with their ingenuity.' *George S. Patton*

Task 3.1: Exploring the Effective Learning Zone

Redraw the Venn diagram in Figure 3.1 to express your own views on how to help students enter their Effective Learning Zone. Make the size of the circles proportional to how important you feel they are, and position the circles according to how the three variables interrelate.

This is a very interesting exercise to carry out with a colleague, or as part of a departmental meeting, as it encourages you to explore in detail the various elements of effective teaching and learning. It will help you to begin a critical dialogue around what is effective in your classroom, which should enable more of your students to occupy their Effective Learning Zone. As you redraw the diagram, you could adapt it by adding any additional elements that you think are missing or adding annotations that explain your thinking. In this way you'll be able to create something which has much more personal meaning.

Complete this exercise by reflecting on the degree to which your students occupy their Effective Learning Zone in your classroom, in your department and across your school. What are the implication of this?

Figure 3.1 helps to illustrate that creating an appropriate climate for learning should be an essential endeavour of any teacher. Though we recognize that selecting the appropriate teaching and learning strategies is critically important too, we feel that the importance of climate for learning has been underestimated in the past. Our Creative Teaching Framework (page 43), therefore, includes 'Climate' as one of its five key components.

The central mission of a teacher is surely to ensure that his or her students occupy their Effective Learning Zone for as long as possible. If this is to take place then learners' physiology and psychology must be carefully considered, and appropriate actions carried out.

Having explained why we feel that climate is so important for learning, the remainder of this chapter will address the question of how teachers can actually *create* an appropriate climate for learning in their own classrooms. The good news is that there's a whole host of simple steps and practical measures you can take as a teacher to address this vital area.

'We're in the age of the idea. The organizations that can develop a culture of creativity and idea generation will be the winners.' *Kevin Roberts*

Assessing which aspects of climate you can control most easily

At this point it's useful to pause and reflect on whether some of the elements which combine to create an appropriate climate for learning are under more direct control of teachers than others. Indeed, we should ask the question, 'Are some of the factors actually *beyond* the influence of teachers?'

Task 3.2: Which aspects of climate for learning are under your control?

Study the section on pages 84–5 which details the aspects of students' physiology and psychology which need to be considered in creating a positive climate for learning. On the continuum below, mark where you feel each of the aspects mentioned lies, showing how much direct influence you can have over it as a teacher.

←--→

No influence   **Considerable influence**

As you carry out this exercise it should quickly become apparent that some aspects stand out in terms of your ability to influence them, whereas others are more elusive. What are the implications of this for your teaching? What action points does it suggest? Note that the third component of Figure 3.1 (teaching and learning strategies) should be something which you feel you have *very considerable* control over – if not then you clearly have some major issues to wrestle with!

Task 3.2 reminds us that teachers are clearly not able to control *every* aspect of their students' climate for learning. We'll all recognize times when our students have shown up to lessons bringing emotional or psychological baggage from previous subjects, or from their lives outside school. Sometimes this baggage can be so heavy it weighs students down to the point where no new learning is possible, however well it is presented. Every student is then entitled to time out to recover their resources and energy levels. Unfortunately, our pressured education system does not always make this easy.

We do believe, however, that teachers have more far-reaching influence over the climate for learning in their classrooms than is often recognized. It's vital that we do not bury

'Keep away from people who try to belittle your ambitions. Small people always do that, but the really great make you feel that you, too, can become great.' *Mark Twain*

our heads in the sand and blame factors outside our control for the lack of learning of some students in our classroom. Indeed, we have taught or observed many lessons where students have arrived feeling de-motivated and stressed, but left feeling engaged and empowered.

With a determined approach it *is* possible to create a kind of 'learning oasis' in your classroom where students are buffered from many of the stresses and pressures of their young lives. We know this because we have worked with young people who have told us that their teachers have successfully created just this kind of oasis. So how do teachers achieve this kind of transformation, allowing their students to enter their Effective Learning Zone despite the odds being stacked against this?

Creating an appropriate climate for learning

Some teachers seem instinctively to know what to do in order to create a better climate for learning; others are able to put some of the foundations in place, but are not sure how to complete the picture; and still others understand what needs to be done, but do not have the confidence to carry these actions though. And some teachers seem to feel unable to let go of their traditional view of what a teacher should and shouldn't do.

Box 3.2 provides some practical ways in which you can help to develop a better climate for learning in your classroom. It's important to acknowledge that progress may need to be made on *many fronts* in order to ensure that your students are able to work consistently within their Effective Learning Zone. Simply adjusting the room temperature, playing music or doing 'brain gymnastics' will not by themselves result in an ideal climate for learning.

Box 3.2: How to develop a better climate for learning

The table overleaf outlines a range of ways in which the different factors that help to create a better climate for learning can be addressed. Note that the key aim of all these actions is that students' brains can be enabled to enter the 'alpha state' of relaxed alertness, which is the most effective state for learning.

'Trust your hunches. They are usually based on facts filed away just below the conscious level.' *Joyce Brothers*

Factor	Suggested actions
Physiology	
Temperature	– Adjust room thermostat/radiators. – Open windows/doors. – Use fans in summer. – Turn computers off when not in use.
Nutrition	– Encourage healthy eating. – Have snack breaks for fruit.
Hydration	– Encourage students to drink water as they learn. – Encourage students to drink regularly outside lessons (avoiding sugary drinks which can make students 'high').
Oxygen levels	– Open windows/doors. – Ensure good ventilation (e.g. extractor fans in science labs or technology rooms). – Have plants in the room.
Illness-free	– Encourage students to live healthy lifestyles, exercising regularly.
Psychology	
Stress	– Relaxation exercises/meditation. – Acknowledge students' levels of stress/state of mind in your lessons (e.g. traffic light system, see Case Study 3.3). – Have agreed rules/behaviours for students (see Case Study 3.1). – Play relaxing music. – Develop a 'sanctuary area' in your classroom (see Case Study 3.2). – Have a time-out for circle time.
Challenge	– Ensure expectations of all students are high. – Make activities challenging for all students. – Include thinking skills activities.
Motivation	– Set tasks which appeal to different learning styles. – Give students choices. – Give students ownership of learning.

'A hunch is creativity trying to tell you something.' *Frank Capra*

Factor	Suggested actions
Self-image & esteem	– Praise frequently, criticize constructively. – Carry out specific tasks that help build self-esteem (e.g. I like you because..., Box 3.4). – Display students' work on walls. – Publicize student successes.
Inspiration	– Use positive role models. – Be prepared to go outside the usual curriculum from time to time to inspire students about the wider world. – Carry out real life learning projects.
Support	– Try to develop close and supportive working relationships with all students. – Get to know students as individuals, including their lives outside school. – Form a partnership with parents to provide 24/7 support for students.
Justice	– Ensure that you're scrupulously fair with all students, especially regarding rewards and sanctions. – Be prepared to admit you were wrong to your students.
Respect	– Treat all students with respect. – Value the individual. – Engage in positive behaviour management (e.g. criticize the behaviour not the person).
Contentment	– Praise students frequently. – Make learning fun! – Make time for celebrations. – Show you care about the progress of your students. – Develop a 'sanctuary area' in your classroom (see Case Study 3.2).
Alertness/ attention span	– Do 'brain gymnastics' at the start of the lesson or during 'brain breaks'. – Encourage students to drink water as they learn. – Encourage healthy eating (e.g. as part of 'eating for learning' initiatives).

'I call intuition cosmic fishing. You feel a nibble, then you've got to hook the fish.' *Richard Buckminster Fuller*

91

As you study Box 3.2 it should be apparent that quite of few of the suggested actions are things which need to be tackled at the *whole school* level, as well as in your own classroom. There are some outstanding examples of schools that have tackled issues, often as part of citizenship or PSHE lessons, which have resulted in students arriving at lessons in a more positive state in which to learn (see Box 3.3). In these schools, large numbers of students are working consistently in their Effective Learning Zone. It would be surprising if you did not recognize that you are *already* working on many of areas highlighted in the table – this is to be celebrated. The next step is to identify which additional areas can be targeted, or to develop a wider repertoire of approaches to target those aspects of classroom climate that you feel especially strongly about.

Box 3.3: Whole school initiatives to promote a better climate for learning

Breakfast clubs

Many schools believe that setting up breakfast clubs has improved the morale, behaviour and concentration levels of students. A worrying proportion of young people do not eat a nourishing breakfast before they leave home in the morning; others scoff a packet of crisps and slurp a can of coke on their way to school. By providing breakfast cereals, fresh fruit, juice and yoghurt, schools are encouraging their students to eat a better diet for learning. Breakfast clubs are often also used to provide additional support for students with homework or other school-related issues, or allow students to play fun but educational board games with adult helpers and friends.

Healthy living projects

In the last few years there's been a big upsurge in interest in schoolwide projects that encourage students and their families to live healthier lifestyles. The most effective projects are those which are launched with parents at high-profile events, supported by suitably-skilled health professionals. The aim is to encourage families to enjoy a better balance of exercise and healthy eating, which many schools believe is having a profound effect on students' climate for learning in school. Schools have been successful in gaining grants for these kinds of projects from organizations such as Awards for All (www.awardsforall.org.uk). They help to develop the community responsibility of schools which will become increasingly important as the extended schools agenda gathers pace.

Water for learning initiatives

The role of water in promoting a better climate for learning has been overlooked in the past. The problem seems to be that young people are routinely dehydrated at school, or are consuming sugary or caffeine-rich drinks with additives that are not good for their teeth or their behaviour. Large numbers of schools are installing water coolers and encouraging students to drink water regularly during the school

'If I have seen further it is by standing on the shoulders of giants.' *Isaac Newton*

day. Many teachers are also allowing students to bring in their own water bottles so they can drink as they learn. Despite concerns from some teachers about the interruptions or distractions that this might cause, schools have found that water bottles quickly become part of the classroom furniture, along with pencil cases and other equipment. Extra care is clearly needed in situations where water might be especially hazardous (e.g. in computer suites or science labs). Students really appreciate being given the opportunity to drink during their lessons, perhaps because they feel they're able to gain more control over their climate for learning by doing so. This brings additional benefits in terms of motivation.

Reading period

The start to a school day can be very rushed, with assemblies, registers, and the giving out of notices and information. A more relaxed start can provide a pleasant change and lower stress levels. A number of schools operate a system whereby on one or more mornings a week the whole school falls silent and everyone reads – in some schools this even includes the school office and phones are taken off the hook! Reading material is available for anyone who forgets and comics, newspapers and books of all kinds can be read. The usual announcements are pinned up or displayed on screens instead of read out. These initiatives have helped to develop a sense of calm during what can be a very hectic start to the day, and have enabled students to enter a more appropriate state for learning.

Stress busting

As an alternative to sporting activity, part of the lunch break in some schools is given over to a relaxation session. This is open to staff and students and can take the form of meditation, Tai Chi or visualization. Where schools are fortunate enough to have any staff trained in therapies such as reflexology or head massage they could be persuaded to demonstrate these skills or even make them available to others. General relaxation techniques can also be taught, such as deep breathing. The key is to provide a quiet environment during what can be another busy period of the day. This can be a particularly valuable activity during times of intense activity in school such as during the exam period, or report writing times. The busier the schedule the more need there is for a chance to switch off and recharge.

An important point about the above five initiatives is that they can help both students and staff to become more relaxed and help prepare them for teaching and learning activities. Although the thrust of this chapter concerns students' climate for learning, the important area of teachers' readiness to teach shouldn't be forgotten. This is dealt with in much more detail in Chapter 6.

Box 3.4: I like you because...

This exercise can be carried out with any class in order to help boost self-esteem. The aim of the task is to write **positive** comments about a person on a sheet of paper which has their name written at the top. The pieces of paper are left on the desks and students circulate the room, writing positive comments on *every other* student's sheet. It's vital that students understand that only positive comments are allowed. The result of the exercise is that every student leaves the lesson with a list of reasons why others value them, which can be a significant boost to their self-esteem. Because we do not routinely ask students to praise others in this way, many students are genuinely surprised by the positive comments which are made about them. This is an ideal exercise to carry out at the end of term, or when reviewing work done on a topic. The exercise can also be tailored to a particular aspect of a subject, or could refer to students' work which is displayed next to the comments sheet. Form tutors can also make use of this activity to help develop a cohesive team spirit. You may also wish to open things up by having students write comments about you as the teacher! See also Case Study 3.1 and page 101 for more information on using students' comments to improve your teaching.

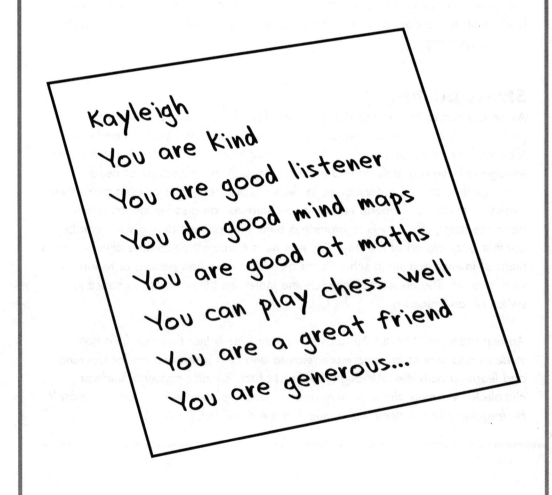

Kayleigh
You are kind
You are good listener
You do good mind maps
You are good at maths
You can play chess well
You are a great friend
You are generous...

'There are two ways of spreading light: to be the candle or the mirror that reflects it.'

Case study 3.1: Negotiating classroom rules and behaviours

A geography department at a 13–19 school in the north of England achieved impressive results in creating a better climate for learning by negotiating classroom rules and behaviours with students. The premise for the work was that if students are involved in setting the expectations for positive classroom behaviour, they're much more likely to keep to them. The work was carried out during the first three lessons that the teachers had with their classes at the start of the school year. The decision was made that students should also be asked for their views on what they expect of their teachers, which resulted in a much richer exercise than would have been possible if students had confined their comments to those about student expectations.

Lesson 1: Students were asked to state their views on what their teacher needs to do to help them to learn. These were written on sticky notes to be shared with the whole class as part of a discussion session. Any 'inappropriate' responses were then discussed. Typical responses included 'Help me when I am stuck', 'Treat me fairly', 'Realize that I have a life outside your subject', 'Do not shout at me if I get something wrong', 'Do not pick on me or humiliate me'.

Lesson 2: The teacher shared with the group a list of class expectations of the teacher which came from lesson 1, and agreed to try their best to keep to these. The students then repeated the exercise but referring to what *other students* can do to help them to learn. These views were fed back to the class and formed into a set of class rules, once again with any 'inappropriate' responses being discussed.

'It is always with excitement that I wake up in the morning wondering what my intuition will toss up to me, like gifts from the sea. I work with it and rely on it. It is my partner.' *Jonas Salk*

95

Lesson 3: The teacher shared with the class a written summary of the agreed class rules, simplified into five easy to remember principles and phrased in positive language (e.g. We'll try our best in this subject; We'll cooperate with each other; We'll put our hands up if we want to speak to the class; We'll ask for help when we need it; We'll respect others and their property). These were printed out and stuck into the students' exercise books/files, as well as being printed out on poster-sized sheets and placed on the wall, entitled 'Our agreed classroom rules'.

This work helped to foster a sense of a learning community where students and teachers have responsibilities as well as rights. When students' behaviour was not helping others to learn, the teacher was able to point to the agreed rules that other students had been involved in setting. This in itself often resulted in the behaviour being corrected, as otherwise students risked the disapproval of their peers, which tends to be more important to them than the disapproval of their teachers!

By asking students for their views on what makes an effective teacher, students felt empowered. Teachers gained respect from this exercise because they showed respect for students' views. By opening up to students in this way, an atmosphere was created where everyone is seen as learning. It made it easier for students' work to be constructively criticized, and the most effective teachers encouraged students to give their feedback on the effectiveness of teaching at regular intervals during the year.

The teachers found – and this is supported by many other projects of this type – that when given this opportunity to state their views, students gave uniformly helpful, thoughtful and highly practical suggestions for what other students and their teachers needed to do to help to create a better climate for learning. There were very few, if any, suggestions that were not appropriate, and any that were offered were quickly retracted when students were asked to justify them. The work reinforces that fact that students share a common view of what is effective in helping to maintain a positive climate for learning, and are happy to work together to achieve it. It provided the teachers in the school with a very optimistic view of the attitudes of their students, with contributed to an environment where learners flourished.

'If you train yourself to listen to your intuition and to follow its bidding, you will greatly increase your percentage of success in life.' *Harold Sherman*

Case study 3.2: Creating a sanctuary area in your classroom

A teacher in a rural comprehensive school in North Yorkshire, established a 'sanctuary area' in her classroom which allowed students time out from the hustle and bustle of the curriculum.

'Many primary classrooms operate the idea of a "quiet corner" and I decided to adapt this for my classroom with secondary-age students. By rearranging two low level book cases I was able to semi-screen an area in the corner of the room. I fitted this out with a remnant of carpet, some cushions and a floor cushion and added a large teddy bear.

Originally I had thought that this would be just used by my form group – who spent most of their time in the room and spent several of their lessons with me. I explained that it was an area which could be used for "time out" and uninterrupted quiet reading or study, but not for small group discussion work. My intention was to provide a quiet place where individuals could take time to calm down if need be or to seek refuge – in a comfort zone or sanctuary. I was inspired to do this because in a previous school a group of subject teachers with inter-connecting classrooms had used the link-way between them – nominally a book storage area – for a similar purpose.

Anyone could move themselves to the area whenever they wished and wouldn't be disturbed. I had to take a few risks to establish the sanctuary. Perhaps inevitably it was first seen as a novelty and was used to "escape" tasks, but it was simple to monitor and soon began to be used for its genuine purpose. It also became easy to spot which students used it on a regular basis and who might be using it as a way of getting one-to-one help or alerting me to other problems. I also began to use it myself when I needed time or space to get my thoughts together or finish a task uninterrupted – a situation which my own form soon began to appreciate, happily granting me the time I needed. Over the course of a term a number of unexpected developments took place. Students other than my own form began to use it and soon it became a feature of my room which students in all my lessons began to appreciate and use positively. Students also began to personalize the area, adding extra cushions and soft toys.

The idea of the sanctuary obviously appealed to all ages and both sexes; it was not uncommon to find boys from older forms sitting reading in the corner cuddling a teddy bear! Frequently at the start of a session it would be used as a way of calming down if the student had experienced frustrations in their previous lesson. It was also very popular first thing after lunchtime.

The sanctuary also became an area which students used at breaks and lunch-times, and while occasionally books went missing they were generally returned (anonymously) when I held an amnesty at the end of a term. There were

'Risk-taking is at the root of innovation, but it must sit on a foundation of some certainty.'

never any instances of vandalism in the area and when, during a process of reorganization I removed the area, students who had grown used to it being there lobbied to have it re-instated.

One of the key points was the fact that no-one was ever "sent" there – it was a totally voluntary move. Nor was it ultimately seen as a way of "opting out". Students who used the facility still completed the work covered in the session but could do it either in the sanctuary or afterwards. It also was not totally removed from the room, so that I could see who was there and what was going on – but choose not to intervene, unless circumstances obliged me to do so.

Introducing the idea was viewed with scepticism by other members of my department, and initially it was designed simply to be used with my form. However, the idea spread by osmosis through other classes taught in the room that then began to use it. It clearly relies on trust and therefore is open to abuse in the early stages. However it can be a valuable tool and a helpful way of catering for situations when students are not ready to learn for external reasons.'

Personalizing the climate for learning

Effective teaching and learning takes place when teachers strive to make learning *personally* accessible and relevant to all learners. The new government emphasis on personalizing learning is simply adding weight to teachers' long-held belief that personalization is central to the most effective teaching. And an important principle embodied in this book is the notion that the most effective learning takes place when an *individual's learning preferences* are respected.

However, the quest to personalize education presents teachers with a number of challenges when it comes to creating an appropriate climate for learning. In any class it's likely that different students will have particular preferences for their ideal climate for learning, much as they have their own unique learning style profile. For example, some students may appreciate more attention being paid to activities that help to bolster their self image, as they may be especially fragile in this area. Others may simply prefer the room temperature to be higher than the majority, or better ventilated.

While it's vital to respect these differences, it's equally important not to think that they're so challenging that work in this area is simply too taxing to carry out. There is, after all, much common ground in terms the classroom climate that most students prefer (it's worth sharing students' diverse preferences with your classes, as they find it quite enlightening to realize that others have quite different views to their own). And just because we recognize that our students have unique preferences for their ideal climate for learning, it does not mean

'One of the reasons mature people stop learning is that they become less and less willing to risk failure.' *John W. Gardner*

that we have to create 30 'micro-climates' for every student in a class! This chapter has hopefully emphasized the importance of the climate for learning, as well as providing you with a range of ways in which you can create a better learning climate for your students.

Case study 3.3: Acknowledging students' psychological state

A 'traffic light' method has been successfully used by several schools that wanted their teachers to gain a greater insight into the psychological state of students at different stages during the day. The hope was that by gaining this – usually hidden – information, teachers would be able to modify their practice in order to help students to enjoy a better climate for learning and thereby enter their Effective Learning Zone.

The system works by every teacher being issued with green, amber and red traffic light symbols for student use. When prompted, students hold up the traffic light that best sums up how ready they feel to learn. This gives them an immediate and confidential way to give feedback to the teacher about their readiness for learning.

The table illustrates this by explaining the traffic light system and including some possible reasons for the responses – note that there can be quite varied reasons behind the student responses. The initiative is best launched in assemblies so that all students know why the school was carrying it out, and how it will work.

Traffic light colour	Meaning	Possible reasons for response
Green	I am ready to learn	– I'm feeling lively – I enjoyed the lesson I just had – I liked the previous lesson in your subject – I like the topic we're studying at the moment – I'm looking forward to my holiday to France – I think you're a great teacher!

continued overleaf . . .

'We fear things in proportion to our ignorance of them.' *Titus Livius*

Traffic light colour	Meaning	Possible reasons for response
Amber	I am not totally ready to learn	– I'm feeling a bit tired – Somebody annoyed me earlier in the day, but I'm getting over it now – I'm thinking ahead to my dental appointment tonight – I think I've got a headache coming on – I'm not that into the topic we did last lesson – I'm thirsty!
Red	I am not ready to learn	– Something bad happened last night that I'm still thinking about – I've got tummy ache and I want to go home – My boyfriend just dumped me – The work you set me is always too hard/easy and I am not feeling motivated – I'm being bullied and the girl who is calling me names is in this lesson – I don't like your subject!

Teachers ask students to hold up their traffic light at different points in the lesson to gain vital insights into students' readiness to learn. The examples below show how the teacher can use the information gained, where it indicates that some students are not in a positive state to learn.

'If you think there are no new frontiers, watch a boy ring the front doorbell on his first date.' *Olin Miller*

Example	Suggested actions by teacher
1 Many students hold up amber or red traffic lights	– Carry out relaxation exercises or 'brain gymnastics' – Discuss with the group what is hindering their learning today (perhaps their team lost in the lunchtime interform hockey match, or the headteacher has made an unpopular rule). It may be that the issue simply needs talking through – Ask if there's anything you can do to help students feel more positive about learning – Find time to talk later with the students who held up red lights
2 One or two students hold up red traffic lights	– Wait for a quiet moment and speak to these individuals privately, so that an appropriate solution can be found (e.g. send them to the school nurse, have time out in the 'sanctuary area') – Be prepared to set different work, or have different expectations of these students in the lesson, now you know how they're feeling – General relaxation or 'brain gymnastics' may help these students

Some teachers may feel that allowing students to bring in feelings or issues from outside the lesson is not conducive to effective learning. Perhaps they feel that this is not the role of the classroom teacher, who has a substantial curriculum to get through? While it's clearly true that a classroom teacher cannot allow large proportions of their lessons to be taken up with dealing with these issues, which may traditionally be seen as the preserve of pastoral staff or form tutors, to ignore students' feelings and emotions is to assume that our students are always in a ready state to learn. We all know that this is not the case, and young people cannot simply turn off their emotions or forget about the other issues in their lives simply because they a have science, maths or RE lesson. By acknowledging the personal climate of students, and carrying out actions that help them to enter their Effective Learning Zone, we're taking powerful steps towards creating a classroom climate where highly effective learning for all can take place. If you ignore the psychological state of your learners you're sure to be heading for frustration and disappointment no matter how effective you think your teaching methods are.

'When I'm trusting and being myself as fully as possible, everything in my life reflects this by falling into place easily, often miraculously.' *Anonymous*

Case study 3.4: The value of celebration

Teachers can help to create a better climate for learning by ensuring that there are regular *celebrations* of students' learning. Celebrations help to create a feeling of group identity, as well as marking publicly the progress that students have made. Last but not least, they help to inject fun into the classroom.

Case study

One of the authors (BB) developed a particular interest in the value of such celebrations during his career as a teacher and head of department at Settle High School in North Yorkshire. Faced with students with impressive levels of engagement and effort in their learning, he felt the need to respond with a targeted programme of 'celebrations' – in the widest sense. The hope was that this would also contribute to the emotional wellbeing of students.

The celebrations took many forms, and ranged from quite small measures to more elaborate events and activities, including:

- Keeping a portfolio of high quality work in each year group, to provide inspiration to others.

- Attractive displays of students' work around school and in the community (e.g. public library, foyer of local supermarket, tourist information centre).

- Reports on students' projects and examples of especially effective work included in the school newsletter/magazine.

- Articles about successes sent to the local paper, with an archive of published cuttings kept.

- End of term celebrations with subject-relevant games, food and dancing.

Results

The response by the students to the celebrations was excellent. Brin felt that their levels of enthusiasm improved still further and that a better, more cohesive, class climate was cultivated. Students' impressions and expectations of their teacher were altered significantly through the celebrations, especially those that required their teacher to lead subject-themed games or teach salsa dancing lessons!

As well as proving popular with students, these celebrations helped to raise the profile of the department and led to many positive comments from staff, parents and the community. The measures formed part of a range of initiatives to encourage excellence and high expectations in the department.

'The only way of finding the limits of the possible is by going beyond them into the impossible.' *Arthur C. Clarke*

Memorable events

The scale of celebrations gradually increased as Brin realized the positive effects they were having on the students – and they culminated in some truly memorable occasions. Some of these were highly creative, and indeed rather unusual for a geography classroom.

One of the major highlights involved an end of term celebration with a Year 10 class who had worked extremely hard during the year, despite not being the most academically able group. The event included a geographically-themed 'pass the parcel', a multicultural buffet prepared by the students and culminated in a Cajun dancing lesson led by the teacher (links were made to the geography of the Louisiana swamps and the management of floods which had been studied earlier in the term).

The sight of a group of self-conscious fifteen-year-old boys and girls losing their inhibitions to dance with partners in Cajun style for fifteen minutes had to be seen to be believed! It demonstrated much about the strength of relationships in the group. Ten years on from such celebrations, some students who took part – now adults with their own children – still talk about these memorable events...and a few are still enjoying their dancing.

But is this really teaching?

Anybody observing some of more elaborate celebrations could be forgiven for wondering what lesson they were watching. Games, food, music, acting...all in a geography lesson? Others, including Ofsted inspectors, might question what the learning outcomes of these 'lessons' were. Perhaps parents might be reluctant to send their children to school for such lessons, often held on the last few days of term, because they failed to see their relevance for learning? (and Christmas shopping or missing the holiday rush on the roads seemed more important).

Such celebrations are important because they demonstrate that learning takes place in the context of a working *relationship* between a teacher and his or her students. The relationships between members of the group – which can be cemented through such celebrations – are vital to creating a positive climate for learning.

Successful results

Despite attracting some controversy from Brin's fellow teachers – and one or two senior managers – the innovative approach to celebrations, in conjunction with a range of other measures, helped to bring his department's results to among the top three in North Yorkshire out of 50 secondary schools. They eventually attracted positive comment from LEA advisers, and strong student–teacher relationships were the one of the key highlights of the Ofsted inspection carried out at the time.

'The power of imagination makes us infinite.' *John Muir*

A note of caution

There has been a fair amount written about the role of *rewards* in learning, including some critical research and articles, which have suggested that *routine* rewards are not helpful to learners. Such rewards are those which learners come to expect, irrespective of the effort that has been put in. It has been suggested that routine rewards can be counter-productive because the students come to value the reward over and above the learning. The key message is that while celebrations – organized in response to genuine effort – are an important part of a teacher's repertoire, routine rewards, especially for low level effort, are best avoided.

Conclusion

We believe that every teacher must embrace the principle of celebration in their own classroom. Celebration has a vital role to play in creating an appropriate climate for learning, that can underpin effective teaching strategies on a day to day basis. We feel that it is certainly worth devoting at least one lesson per term to a focused celebration of learning – and we believe passionately that this is *not* a waste of a lesson, despite the fact that the learning objectives may not be focused on the national curriculum. Celebration can be a highly creative tool to help learners to reach their potential. It also has an important role in developing students' emotional intelligence.

Further reading

The topic of celebrating learning is not well covered by the educational literature – it seems to be another area which has tended to be lost among the sea of recent educational initiatives. The following book, though pitched mainly at whole school efforts, contains useful information about how you can celebrate learning in the classroom:

Best, B, Grebot, M and Donnelly, I (2006) *Promoting Your School*. Alresford: Teachers' Pocketbooks.

'Go confidently in the direction of your dreams. Live the life you have imagined.' *Henry David Thoreau*

Task 3.3: Exploring climate for learning in your school and local authority

This chapter has highlighted a range of ways in which you can improve the climate for learning in your classroom. Take the chance to review the techniques which have been *already* tried in your own classroom, school and other schools locally that you know about.

Draw a table as shown below. In the left-hand column record the approaches that have been tried and tick the appropriate column according to whether these have been tried in your own classroom, school or another local school (to your knowledge). You may need to do a little research to find out what's been done in your school and further afield, but don't go overboard with this.

Technique	Your classroom	Your school	Local school

Which techniques, that have been attempted in your school or locally but not in your classroom, would you like to introduce? Who could you ask to find out more about these methods, and how can they support you as you try to implement them? Remember that visiting neighbouring schools can be very rewarding, as you get the chance to enter a different culture, where things that do not seem possible in your own school simply happen!

 Review

This chapter has sought to emphasize the following key points:

- The *climate for learning* is an important factor to consider when designing effective learning experiences.

- Climate for learning includes two distinct elements: the *physiology* and the *psychology* of learners.

- Appropriate physiology and psychology combine with appropriate teaching and learning strategies to create an *Effective Learning Zone* where the most powerful learning experiences take place.

- Teachers have much control over students' climate for learning, but there are some aspects which are harder for teachers to influence than others.

- Specific measures can be taken by teachers to develop a better climate for learning.

- Work to develop a better climate for learning is most effective when it's part of a schoolwide effort, supported by a range of curricular and extra-curricular approaches, and championed by school leaders.

⇨ Action points

Consider the following actions in the light of this chapter and using the self-evaluation tool select those that are most appropriate to your needs:

- Consider the climate for learning you try to create for students in your classroom. Describe it from the point of view of the student – how might a student who is in the 'green', 'amber' or 'red' state react to the day-to-day climate you create?

- Consider which aspects of the climate for learning you create you're happy with? Why? What about those aspects that you are not so happy with? What would you like to do first to improve things further? Write a mini action plan that sets out a timeline for addressing this key aspect of your practice.

- Who else can support you as you strive to create a better climate for learning? How can they help? What support could you find outside your school? Devise a *Continuing Professional Development route map* that will help you to create a better climate for learning.

- What concerns do you have about addressing the climate for learning in your classroom? Make a note of these and discuss them with a senior colleague who is sympathetic to this type of work.

👁 Further reading

Some of the major texts on accelerated learning are strong on classroom climate, as this movement has sought to place considerable emphasis on this particular aspect of teaching and learning. The following texts are particularly illuminating on this subject:

Best, B (2003) *The Accelerated Learning Pocketbook*. Alresford: Teachers' Pocketbooks.

- A handy pocket-sized guide to the subject which is part of an award-winning series for teachers.

Corrie, C (2003) *The Emotionally Intelligent Child*. London: Network Educational Press.

- A particular focus on the emotional aspects of classroom climate.

Smith, A (2000) *Accelerated Learning in Practice*. London: Network Educational Press.

- Contains a thorough examination of all aspects of classroom climate.

Smith, A, Lovatt, M & Wise, D (2004) *Accelerated Learning: a user's guide*. London: Network Educational Press.

- The latest volume from Britain's most passionate advocates of accelerated learning.

'Risks must be taken, because the greatest hazard in life is to risk nothing.' *Leo F Buscaglia*

> **End of chapter metaphor:** Read the story and use the questions that follow to consider further aspects of the chapter content.

What, how and why

It was in September, week one swimming lessons, that I first realized that I didn't fit in. They pushed me up against the glass at the swimming pool and called me names. They said that I was weird because I wore glasses and then they hit me. In the swimming class itself, they carried on and tried to hold me under the water, but Miss caught them and told them off. Very soon I was terrified to go to swimming classes and I protested to my mum and said I didn't need to go; to no avail.

Eventually these boys left. They got really good at swimming, and I floundered in the shallow end constantly worried, too scared to try stuff. I was ready to fend off the jibes and taunts, but not to swim. New boys joined the group and once again the taunting began. A little while later I decided I had to take a stand. I'd had enough. I had to toughen up. So I joined a martial arts club. I was so scared. This time round any bigger boys at the club could legitimately beat me up; what was I doing? But I had to get some ways of fighting back.

What a surprise I had when I got there. I had such a good time on the very first night, and it's continued. Why was it so different? Because there were rules and there was respect, not just for the Sensei but for everyone. And not just **what** you're supposed to do, but **how** you're supposed to do it, and most important of all **why** you're supposed to do it. Sure I get battered and bruised, and yes it hurts, but this time it's my risk and I know where I stand, and I'm really learning.

Based on a true story.

> **You might wish to consider:**
>
> 1 How do the key themes of this story relate to your own experiences at school?
>
> 2 How do the key themes of this story relate to your current professional experiences?
>
> 3 What questions might you need to ask of your practice or that of others?

'Listen to your intuition. It will tell you everything you need to know.' *Anthony J D'Angelo*

107

Chapter 4

Teaching and learning strategies

TEACHING AND LEARNING STRATEGIES

'Most ideas about teaching are not new; but not everyone knows the old ideas.'

Euclid (c.325–c.265 BC)

Message to the reader

The teaching and learning chapter is the most substantial in *The Creative Teaching and Learning Toolkit* and we suspect it is the one you will refer to most. We have tried to provide you with hundreds of strategies and tools that you can select from, depending on the particular topic, students or learning outcomes you're working with. Do not forget, however, that effective teaching and learning takes place within the context of the Five Domains (page 40), of which teaching and learning strategies is only one component. The Creative Teaching Framework makes it clear that unless all components are addressed, learning will not be maximized. Make sure that you study the other chapters in the book and consider their implications, as well as immersing yourself in ideas for new teaching and learning strategies.

'The man who views the world at 50 the same as he did at 20 has wasted 30 years of his life.' *Muhammad Ali*

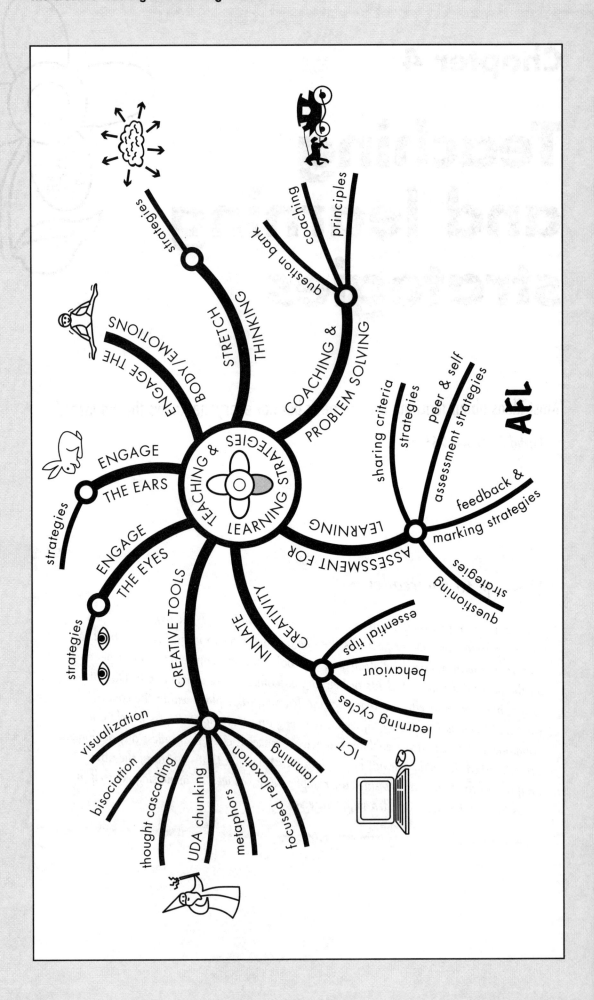

'It is what we think we know that keeps us from learning.' *Chester Barnard*

Preview

This chapter focuses the core domain of teaching and learning, especially the importance of motivating and engaging students to promote learning:

▶ It presents a collection of over 100 strategies for promoting creative thinking and for engaging learners across a spectrum of learning preferences.

▶ It provides approaches and examples of these strategies under the headings of:
  • Creative tools – strategies for developing creative thinking.
  • Strategies to engage the eyes – for appealing to the visual sense.
  • Strategies to engage the ears – for the auditory sense.
  • Strategies to engage the body – for the movement and emotional senses.
  • Strategies to stretch thinking – for stimulating the capacity to think at varying levels of sophistication.
  • Strategies for coaching and problem solving – for promoting resourceful thinking.
  • Strategies for assessment for learning – for promoting a formative assessment process.

▶ The key principle of the chapter is that teachers need to select from a wide repertoire of teaching and learning approaches in order the meet the needs of the learners they're working with on a particular unit of work, lesson or task.

Key questions to ask yourself before beginning this chapter:

1 How are you currently seeking to engage and motivate students?

2 What is currently working well and where are there challenges?

3 How would you describe the breadth and depth of activities currently being employed in your teaching?

4 To what extent do you use a learning cycle to design learning experiences for your students?

Centuries ago...

Centuries ago in China, what we now refer to as 'the martial arts' began when monks communicated. Shaolin monks were entrusted with the delivery of important documents and frequently came under attack from outlaws and those hired to intercept these scrolls. The monks developed techniques to defend themselves from these attacks. Over time the monks shared the approaches they used with other monks they met on their journeys. What evolved from this cross-fertilization of ideas was Shaolin Kung Fu. Underpinning this development and enshrined within the Buddhist culture was the concept of *enlightenment*. Attaining enlightenment demanded that the monks sought constant improvement or *bushido* (way of the warrior) as it became known in the East. This required a dedication and an openness to receiving new approaches and thinking. It required experimentation. Creativity existed within this pursuit of perfection.

Over time the westernization of martial arts practices has removed the thread of enlightenment. Some argue that the heart of these noble martial arts has been lost by the pursuit of a competitive practice and the need to attain the next graded belt. This grading system is very much a Western construct. To attain the belt is not necessarily to pursue *bushido*. One can achieve a belt without an underlying drive to perfect.

The classroom today

In this chapter we invite you to use your creativity to generate and plan for stimulating and well-crafted lessons. Whilst you're not protecting ancient scrolls from outlaws, you *are* involved in the evolution of teaching and learning, and we would encourage you to experiment, to be open to receiving and thinking about new approaches, and to refine that which is already good. Like those monks in China centuries ago, you're engaged in a vitally important vocation, which will have lasting effects on a generation.

A question frequently asked by teachers in training is, 'How can I motivate and engage my students?' In this chapter we seek to provide a wide range of strategies that will appeal to the intrinsic motivation of the young people that you work with. By intrinsic motivation we mean the innate interest that a student has in the tasks themselves, rather than relying on external rewards such as vouchers, letters to parents, points systems or praise.

The need for intrinsic motivation

A fascinating raft of research is building on the negative effects of external or extrinsic reward, and the positive effects of intrinsic reward.

'Personally, I am always ready to learn, although I do not always like being taught.' *Winston Churchill*

In the 1960s rats were trained to run to a location for a large reward. When compared with rats trained to run for a smaller reward, the rats that had first had the larger reward ran more slowly for the second smaller reward. In other words the smaller reward became comparatively less motivating, because it was smaller. The conclusion of the observers was that ever larger external rewards are required to maintain a similar motivational effect. This means that a bag of crisps today might need to be a burger and fries tomorrow and eventually an all expenses paid trip to Disneyland in due course!

Caution must clearly be exercised in the drawing of conclusions about children's learning from experiments with rats. More recent studies involving functional brain imaging techniques, coupled with behavioural research, has shed tantalizing insights into reward and states of creative flow. Oldfather *et al.* (1999) claimed to have discovered the so-called 'reward centre' in the human brain. It was found to be positioned just above our eyes in the pre-frontal cortex of the brain. They discovered that in the presence of a reward, this centre was activated. Tsigilis *et al.* (2003) report a study where one group of individuals were given rewards of money and sweets, as well as praise, to carry out stimulating tasks which involved creativity and game playing. Another group were not given the rewards, but just asked to do the tasks. The outcomes consistently showed that the reward stopped people from doing the tasks; in fact it demotivated them. Those not rewarded continued to enjoy the task for its own sake.

Further to these studies, evidence of the tendency for learners to abuse reward systems is growing. Davis and Weidenbeck in Persaud (2005) explain that any reward system will eventually be worked out so that 'the maximum reward can be obtained for minimum effort and so distracting them [workers or children] from the key engagement with the job in hand'.

Therefore, what we argue for in *The Creative Teaching and Learning Toolkit* are stimulating learning activities which have their own intrinsic draw. We encourage activities with their own built-in learning potential, to enable learners to find enjoyment and, in the words of Alistair Smith, to 'seek and secure connections' (Smith *et al.* 2004) rather than work for an external reward.

Mihály Csíkszentmihályi, a leading psychologist in the field of well-being, defined intrinsically motivated behaviour in terms of the emotional experience people have when they're engaged in an activity. This emotional state Csíkszentmihályi labelled 'flow' and it was characterized by, among other things:

- A feeling of being immersed in and being carried by an activity.
- Merging of action and awareness.
- Lack of self-consciousness. (Persaud 2005)

In 'flow' we would argue there's the potential to be at our most creative and at our most enquiring. If learning is about seeking and securing connections and about taking risks and problems, then surely this is a state we would want to facilitate in our students.

In this chapter we aim to set out a series of strategies which can provide a large variety of tasks that are likely to stimulate the high levels of engagement and result in flow. We divide these broadly into 'creative tools' and 'teaching and learning strategies', though the boundaries between the two are not as clear as that.

'The more I learn, the more I realize I don't know.' *Albert Einstein*

Task 4.1: Exploring motivation

Reflect on what you *think* motivates your students to learn in your lessons. Make a list of the factors you come up with. Then carry out an exercise where you actually *ask* what motivates them. An interesting way to do this would be to ask them what they look forward to about your lessons and what they dread (if anything!). You could then go on to ask them why they think it's important to work hard in your subject area, and whether there's anything that could change which would make them work harder, or enjoy their learning more. Having a dialogue with your students about this kind of thing can be very rewarding, and helps to suggest things that you might do differently to engage more students. To wrap up the exercise you could consider if there are any factors which you do *not* feel you can control which affect the motivation of your students, and the implications of this for your lessons.

'For teachers the time has come to move from being the sage on the stage to the guide on the side'

Creative tools

There's a vast range of creative techniques available to teachers. What we have attempted to do in this chapter is to distil the best and most practical for use in the classroom. Remember that this is far from a complete list; instead it's intended to provide a sample of the better techniques which are available. Your mission should be to allow your students to become immersed in a range of activities which *nourish* creativity.

While our initial focus in this chapter is on strategies to be creative, many of these techniques have key relevance for problem-solving and learning – both for teachers and learners. The section that follows deals with teaching and learning techniques more specifically.

The creative tools are broadly classified as:

- Visualization

- Bisociation and association

- Thought cascading

- UDA Chunking

- Metaphors

- Focused relaxation

- Jamming.

Visualization

Visualization is not what it seems; interestingly only about a third of us regularly visualize by creating pictures in our heads in our waking hours. Most of us do so in our sleep during the Rapid Eye Movement (Dream) Phase. We're all capable of creating representations of the world around us in the form of pictures, sounds, words and feelings. We may have some preferences for one or more of these. The visual, auditory and kinesthetic representations are our internal 'map of the world'.

Alfred Korzybski suggested that our senses pick up information about the world we inhabit, but that our brains filter and manipulate this information through our unconscious expectations (Talbert 1996). The effect he suggests is that what we think we see, hear and feel around us is potentially not the reality, but an illusion of the reality created internally. It explains why one person might believe that red cars are more prevalent than other colours, because their car is red and so they notice them more readily. The reality may be that black cars are more popular. We're constantly creating what we think we are aware of in our perceived reality.

Similarly, we have it within our gift to create future representations of reality that have not yet happened. In so doing we can generate new perceptions through tweaking our internal

'There is no learning without some difficulty and fumbling. If you want to keep on learning, you must keep on risking failure—all your life.' *John W. Gardner*

pictures, sounds and feelings. This provides us with the capability to create new representations of existing ideas or build new ideas internally from scratch. Visualization is a powerful tool for future goal setting in classrooms and for a range of other applications, including encouraging children to associate into particular states of mind or to put themselves into other people's shoes.

Box 4.1: Seven classroom applications of visualization

1 **History**: Close your eyes and pretend. Take yourself back on your timeline, to way before your birth and to a time when you were Anne Boleyn's servant. Knowing all that you know about living at that time, tell your story into a tape recorder. Imagine yourself all the way through – what are you seeing, hearing and feeling throughout?

2 **Science (physics)**: Close your eyes and imagine that you are a ray of light travelling from the sun towards the earth. What do you experience all the way until you land on the east coast of the USA? What gets in your way? How do you overcome this?

3 **Science (biology)**: Imagine life as a garden snail. You see yourself sliding around and leaving a trail. Feel the weight of your shell and then marvel at the world sensed through your retractable antennae. What are you aware of that is threatening your environment? How has the flavour and availability of what you eat changed over the years?

4 **Religious education**: Pretend you are in warm sunny place, it's a beautiful day and you have a long, cool drink beside you and a packet of your favourite nibbles. You are feeling really contented. What are you hearing, seeing and feeling? Now imagine being in a warm sunny place, it's a beautiful day and you have a stinking ditch full of dirty water to drink. You are sharing that water with bison and you fear there may be crocodiles lurking beneath the surface. You know it will make you sick but it's all you have to drink. You haven't eaten for two weeks, except for some seeds your father walked 10 miles to get from the back of an aid truck. As you look at the two pictures of you in the warm sunny places, what are you thinking? What are you feeling? What would you like to say to each other?

5 **Learning to Learn/PSHE and developing learning skills**: Take some deep breaths and relax. Imagine that it is Christmas Eve and you have hung up a stocking in the hope of gifts. You lie in bed and look at your stocking four metres away from your bed. You go to sleep and wake up at about 3am to see across the room in the dull light that presents are waiting for you. You are dying to open the gifts but you know that in the carpet at night are ghouls and gremlins hell-bent on stealing your toes, so you can't get out of the bed until it's properly light. How do you get to feel the presents? How are you resourceful to overcome the challenge?

'Education is the process of leading people from cocksure ignorance to thoughtful uncertainty.' *Dennis Hicky*

6 **Geography**: students need an Ordnance Survey (OS) map key in front of them for this activity. Close your eyes and imagine where you live. As you sit there, feeling your feet inside your shoes and listening to your breathing, pause. Decide to go on a journey of your area as if it were really an OS map. Stand outside your home and turn in any direction to walk away from it. As you walk around, picture the features of the area as an OS map, so instead of a church with a spire you see a black circle with a cross attached. Instead of a Tarmac main road you see a red line and instead of the post office you see two big black letters 'PO' standing where the post office is, swaying back and forth in the wind on a springy stand. Use your imagination and go around your neighbourhood to see everything as symbols on a map. If you need to check any symbol at any time, just open an eye and find it on the key. When you've practised it once, do it again and give a commentary out loud to another student.

7 **English**: Understanding characters. Think about the key character in the novel you're studying. As you close your eyes and focus on this character, what do you see? What does this person sound like when they speak? What gestures do they make when they speak and how do they move? What are they wearing and what are they carrying? Imagine this character right at the start of the book and fix the image in a frame on a wall in your mind. Now imagine them in the middle of the book and fix this picture in a frame and hang it on the wall next to the first picture. Now imagine a final picture of the character at the end of the book and fix this in a frame on the wall. As you stand back now in your mind and view the three pictures, what do you notice? How are the pictures different? How are they the same? Sit yourself down so you're really comfortable and in a 'Harry Potter-esque' style, allow the character to come to life in each of the pictures and move around, speak and go about their business. What else do you notice now, as you compare these movies of the character in each part of the book? How do the frames differ throughout the novel? What could this mean about the character?

Association and bisociation

Association is the act of connecting together two or more ideas, objects or thoughts. *Bisociation* is the bringing together of two or more ideas, thoughts or objects to make something new. The act of bringing together sometimes disparate and seemingly uncon-nected elements creates new wholes and can potentially solve problems. For example, when software meets time management, computerized diaries are created and new automatic personal organization processes are created. Or, when slippery soap meets a hole and a rope, soap on a rope is born, with no more hunting for the soap in the bath. Or, when microchips meet cats and you can mark ownership of your moggy without it needing to wear a collar.

'Anyone who stops learning is old, whether twenty or eighty. Anyone who keeps learning today is young. The greatest thing in life is to keep your mind young.' *Henry Ford*

Sometimes the connections between ideas, objects or thoughts are quite closely connected, while in other situations they're further apart. For example, application of lightweight foils used to cover space vehicles, which are then utilized by runners to retain heat after a race versus the use of classical music in shopping centres to ward off unwelcome youths.

Association and bisociation can be done through the natural associative processes of the brain. The brain is 'designed' to create connections between thoughts and ideas. There are also tools that can enhance this process. Three useful tools which lead young people to make associations are:

- The bisociation tool
- Thought cascading
- The ideas compass.

Bisociation

Bisociation techniques involve bringing together two previously unconnected ideas and are the brainchild of Arthur Koestler. They can be an effective way of finding a solution.

The approach

1   Give yourself time to relax, away from distractions.

2   Write the issue/challenge you have in the box below:

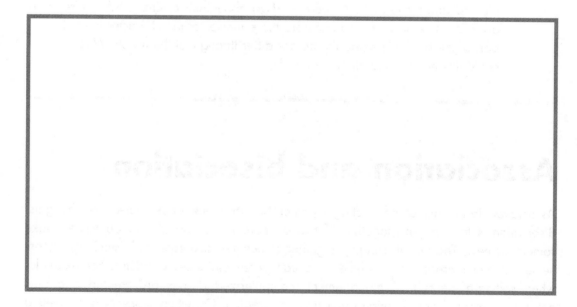

'The ability to learn is probably the most powerful visa you can have stamped in any passport to success.' *Tom Barwood*

3 Now in the box below write what you would rather have – your preferred outcome.

4 In the centre box in the grid below, write a key word or phrase that sums up your preferred outcome.

5 In the grid boxes around it, generate random words, ideas, pictures (you can ask others to help you or use the words in the analogy explorer tool to support you).

6 Now consider each random idea alongside the key issue and see what new ideas trigger in your mind. Write them in the 'new ideas' box overleaf.

'What the learner does is more important than what the teacher does.' *Geoff Petty*

New ideas

Reproduced with permission from Thomas, W (2005) *Coaching Solutions Resource Book,* London: Network Education Press.

'A teacher needs to have at their disposal a buffet of resources that can be accessed to feed the learning needs of different students at different moments in time.'

Thought cascading

Rules for thought cascading:

1 Write a key word that represents the problem, challenge or focus in the centre of the page and draw something to visually represent it.

2 Draw lines out from the central theme and begin to write any thoughts or ideas down which you naturally associate with the theme.

Thought cascading can also be referred to as brain storming or mind showering. The approach involves the rapid recording of every idea an individual or group can come up with associated with a problem, issue or topic. It is a raw process, where any idea is valid with an important principle of operation being that every idea is potentially valuable. Even the most outrageous or impractical offering is accepted as it may lead to further productive ideas. Approaches to thought cascading vary. It can be done in groups where all contribute to one central cascade page in turn, or alternatively as a simultaneous activity, each contributor holding a pen. In LogoVisual Thinking (see page 55) each person writes ideas onto sticky note in a timed 'dump' and then shares the ideas alternately as they stick them to a piece of flipchart paper. The outcome of all of these activities is a large collection of ideas relating to the central challenge or issue.

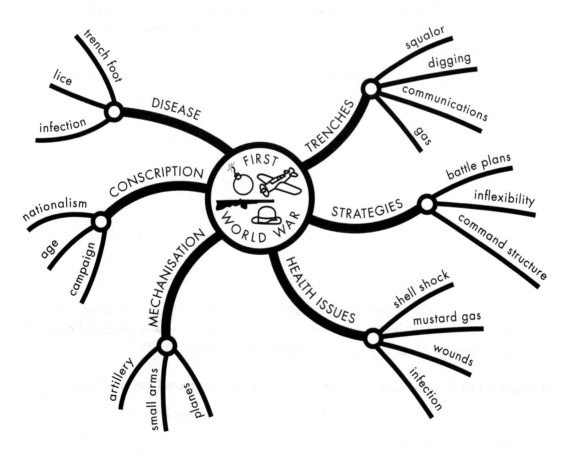

Figure 4.1: Example of a thought cascade

'In a time of drastic change it is the learners who inherit future. The learned usually find themselves equipped to live in a world that no longer exists.' *Eric Hoffer*

Ideas compass

In this activity, we combine good ideas to make more good ideas. Follow these instructions to generate new ideas.

1   Write down the preferred outcome (what you would like instead of the current situation you have):

2   There can be thoughts that seem to stop you getting this outcome. Listening to phrases we say to ourselves, in our head and out loud, gives us ideas about the things that are stopping us. Phrases such as 'That's OK but ...', 'The problem is ...', 'That's all very well. However, ...', 'If it wasn't for ... then I would ...'. What are you blaming for stopping you achieving the outcome you want? Write them down:

3   Now, ask yourself the following questions, taking the problems you identified as stopping you and placing them into the questions below where [problem] appears; for example, 'What might you do, if [time] were not a factor?'.

If a question doesn't seem to make sense, leave it and go on to another.

- What could you do if you didn't have to live with the consequences?

- What might you do if [problem] were not a factor?

- What could you do if [problem] were not a limitation?

'I am still learning.' *Michaelangelo*

- What would you do if you didn't have to consider [problem]?

- What could you do if you thought you were worth it?

4 For each idea you come up with, write it down and ask yourself: 'What else?' Now pick four ideas you think are most promising as solutions.

5 Using the ideas compass on the next page:

   a) Write each of the four ideas you have chosen into the N, E, S, W option boxes.

   b) Next combine the options, two at a time, and think about the possible outcomes here too. Write the combined options in the boxes provided.

6 What new options have you come up with?

7 Consider also:
- Combining options 1 and 3.
- Combining options 2 and 4.

Do it now and write down your ideas.

What about combining all options?

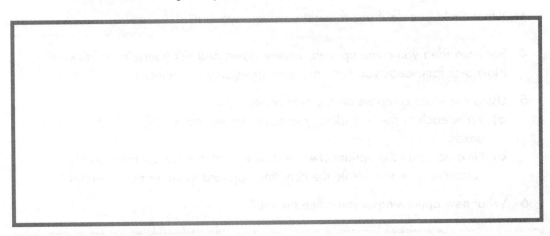

8 Now answer these questions:
- What new options have appeared as a result of this activity?
- Are there options that combine smaller parts of the options you have identified?
- Are there options that you have previously dismissed that might now be useful?

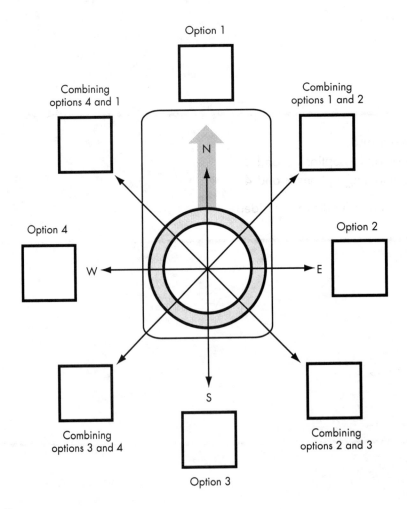

The Ideas Compass

Reproduced with permission from Thomas, W (2005) *Coaching Solutions Resource Book*, London: Network Educational Press.

'One learns through the heart, not the eyes or the intellect.' *Mark Twain*

Planning a science investigation into the effect of light on maggot behaviour using LVT.

The advantage of approaches like thought cascading, bisociation and LVT is that the recording of ideas in an unfettered way frees the mind to concentrate on generating associations.

Box 4.5: Association in the school setting

- Use thought mapping to review the skeletal system in the body.

- Plan a charity event by freely associating around the key word 'Fundraising'.

- Develop creative solutions for a problem by firstly future-basing the problem: 'When the problem is solved, what will you have as outcomes'? Next use either LVT or thought cascading on a page to dump ideas which might support the outcome you desire.

- Map all of the vocabulary you know in French which is the same or almost the same in English.

'It's never enough to just tell people about some new insight. Rather, you have to get them to experience it in a way that evokes its power and possibility. Instead of pouring knowledge into people's heads, you need to help them grind a new set of eyeglasses so they can see the world in a new way.' *John Seely Brown*

Chunking

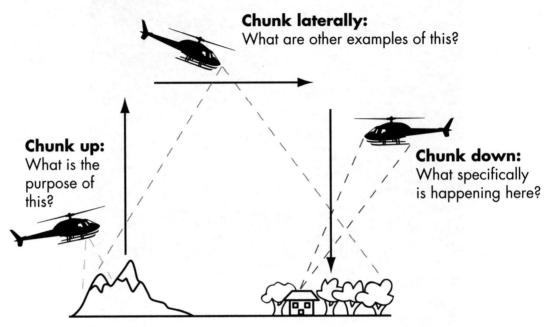

Chunk laterally:
What are other examples of this?

Chunk up:
What is the purpose of this?

Chunk down:
What specifically is happening here?

Figure 4.2: Chunking

Another approach to generating new creative ideas comes from changing the chunk size that we look at when we're considering a problem. What this means is changing between viewing the whole of a situation to the details or vice versa. An analogy which works well to explain this is to consider flying in a helicopter. If you fly down low and close to the issue you get lots of detail. If, on the other hand, you rise several thousand feet over the issue you see much more of the overview, and the way the issue is interconnected with its wider landscape. So we can *chunk down* into detail and *chunk up* to an overview. We can also chunk laterally, which means looking for other similar issues on the landscape, by having your helicopter fly across the landscape. Chunking shifts the viewpoint on an issue or problem and encourages the search for alternative ideas.

Figure 4.2 shows chunking up, chunking down and chunking laterally. To assist us to chunk in these ways we can use some helpful questions:

- To chunk down ask: 'What specifically is happening here?'

- To chunk up ask: 'What is the purpose of this?' Or 'What is this an example of?'

- To chunk laterally ask: 'What are other examples of this?'

'It is a miracle that curiosity survives formal education.' *Albert Einstein*

Box 4.6: Example of chunking

In a garden design project, a student decided to focus his design on a central fountain which was to be a lively centrepiece and would have a water stream of some two metres high. Having spent some time conceiving the design, he realized that there might be a problem getting water to the fountain, as it was to be located some considerable distance from the house and the nearest water supply. Other existing and well-established garden features meant it was not feasible to have the fountain anywhere nearer the house.

Using chunking questions he asked himself: 'What is the purpose of the fountain?'. He considered this with the garden owner and the conclusion was reached that the fountain's purpose was to draw the eye to towards the bottom of the garden as you looked at it from the house. Additionally, the owner wanted the feature to have some movement in it, to assist the drawing of the eye to the end of the garden. From this point he asked the question, 'What are other examples of features that would be visible from the top of the garden and also add movement?'. Now chunking laterally, they dumped a series of ideas on paper, including a rock stack which had water trickling over it, and a self contained pump, which would give height and movement but work on a small water volume. The possibility of a solar-powered pump was mooted. The other was to place a sculptural plant like an acer, silver birch or a pampas grass which would have natural movement, through being caught by the wind. The third idea they came up with was to buy or design and build a sculptural piece which was at least 2.5 metres tall, that would have moving parts which were caught by the wind.

The owner was inspired by the latter idea, particularly if the piece were an original design. The designer came up with an idea for a sculptural piece made from scrap steel and copper, with articulated moving parts designed to catch the wind.

In the example in Box 4.6, chunking up and then chunking laterally produced a range of new options which had the same purpose as the original unworkable idea.

Box 4.7: Classroom applications of chunking

In the classroom setting this process could be used as follows:

1 **Maths**: to determine a range of different ways of calculating the area of tiles in square metres needed to cover a bathroom.

2 **Food technology**: to determine a range of ingredients for a pasta recipe which have an appropriate shelf life.

3 **History**: to make links between historical events in different parts of the world across a given year.

Building metaphors

Metaphors are powerful symbols which demand that our subconscious finds meaning. These can be in the form of simple analogies or more complex stories. There are a number of ways of using them and stimulating them. Since the subconscious mind to likes work in symbols (evidenced by our dreams, which are seldom straightforward, and richly coded in metaphor), it provides a rich source of creative capacity.

The unconscious or subconscious mind is a hidden facet of the brain we use each day. It deals with our unconscious actions, like driving to work when your mind is focused on anything but driving. It rescues us from unexpected danger, by launching our fight or flight mechanisms and runs our emotional systems. The existence of the unconscious has been hinted at for centuries, beginning with the ancient Egyptians and the Mayans.

There is a series of rules about the unconscious mind and its functions which come from Neuro-Linguistic Programming. These are known as the *Prime Directives* of the unconscious mind. We include the principal ones here. The unconscious mind:

- Holds positive purposes for you in all that it does.

- Runs your mind and your body.

- Remembers everything that happens to you and around you.

- Searches for meaning and solves problems.

- Works with symbols and metaphors.

The unconscious mind plays a key role in problem solving and may be responsible for our intuition. There's emerging evidence that the unconscious mind processes far more bits of information per second than the conscious brain, and does so some 100,000 times quicker. This, coupled with its hunger for symbolically representing the world around it, means that metaphor is an ideal medium through which to present challenges for resolution.

'Creative minds have always been known to survive any kind of bad training.' *Anna Freud*

Stimulating young people to create metaphors

We draw analogies in teaching all of the time to assist students in understanding ideas. The science teacher who says that neurones in the nervous system are like electrical wires and that nerve impulses are like electricity travelling down a wire, provides a working metaphor for her students to understand nervous transmission. If she then describes the transmission between the dendrite of one neurone and the next as chemical messengers 'swimming like oxen across a river from one bank to the next', she further provides an analogy for neurotransmitter communication. But you don't have to create metaphors for young people, they can do it themselves and then use the metaphors to further develop their understanding.

The language required to take people into thinking metaphorically is very simple and comes from work done on symbolic modelling by Lawley and Tomkins (2000). The question, 'What is that like?' or 'If that was like something else, what would it be like?' creates the metaphorical comparison. In the classroom setting we might promote metaphor:

- When a student is struggling with a concept.

- To encourage learners to view concepts differently.

- To enable students to extend their thinking further.

- To help solve a problem.

As an example using nerve transmission, to extend students thinking further they can consider, 'How else is nerve transmission like an electrical circuit and how is it different? What might be a better likeness?'

Making stories with creativity and for creativity

Creating stories to embed learning is another use of the creative potential of metaphor. Teachers who use stories captivate students and there are a variety of story telling tricks and tips which add to the impact of a story, as shown in Case Study 4.1. Delivering content or process messages through a story are powerful ways of getting across key ideas memorably, and promoting further thinking.

'Live as if you were to die tomorrow. Learn as if you were to live forever.' *Mahatma Gandhi*

Case study 4.1: Using a story to promote learning

A simple story about a bear in a zoo was used by a teacher to reinforce his message to students about the importance of asking for support when they don't understand straight away, rather than letting the confusion continue through to the exam period.

The bear

A visitor to a zoo remarked to the bear keeper how sad a solitary brown bear looked, as it sat hunched in the corner of the bear enclosure. 'Why is the bear so sad looking? Is it because it is cooped up in the enclosure? Has it lost a cub? Is it unwell?' asked the visitor.

'No' said the bear keeper. 'He is perfectly well, and he has many healthy cubs inside the bear house over there, and the other bears are perfectly happy in this enclosure.'

'Aren't you worried that he is so unhappy?' said the visitor.

'No' said the bear keeper. 'I know exactly why he's unhappy.'

Looking quizzical, the visitor replied, 'Really, why?'

'Because he's sitting on a nail' said the zoo keeper in a quite matter-of-fact tone.

'That's bizarre, if it hurts him, why doesn't he get off the nail then?' asked the visitor.

'That's simple, because it isn't hurting enough!'

A simple process for creating functional metaphors for content and process is enshrined in the StoryBlender Process. StoryBlender has two formats, one for promoting problem-solving and one for content-based delivery through metaphor (see Box 4.8). There is also a third way to use the StoryBlender process and this is to provoke creative thoughts by asking open questions to promote divergent thinking.

'Thank goodness I was never sent to school; it would have rubbed off some of the originality.' *Beatrix Potter*

Box 4.8: Creating a transformational metaphor with StoryBlender

This process creates double symbolic dissociation from the original situation and consequently promotes more directed searching by the unconscious mind for solutions.

3: Theme

1 Actual situation	2. Random symbols	4. Themed symbols
Present reality/state		
Desired reality/state		
Blocks		
Resources/beliefs/ attitudes needed to move forward/key messages		

Steps:

1 Identify the features of the actual situation/problem.

2 For each feature, think of random symbols and list for the actual situation.

3 Decide on a theme – something of interest to the individual or group, either a contemporary interest the group might have (e.g. music, skateboarding, etc.) or a universal experience like receiving a gift, going to the zoo, visiting a theme park, Eid or other appropriate religious festival.

4 Cover up column one and then consider in the context of the theme: what is a symbol for the symbol in column 2? Record in the themed symbol column.

5 Weave a story using the symbols in column 4. Develop the losing of the blocks and the use of the resources in the story.

This process is adapted from an idea by David Shepherd (2005) called Dreamweaver for creating Transformational Hypnotic Metaphors.

Worked example

The situation:
A teacher wants students who are preparing for exams to feel calmer and more relaxed about them. He also wants them to get the work done that is necessary for them to perform well.

The planning:

3. Theme:

MP3 Players and music

'Since we are destined to live out our lives in the prison of our minds, our one duty is to furnish it well.' *Peter Ustinov*

1. Actual situation	2. Random Symbols	4. Themed symbols
Present reality/state Students tense	Coiled spring	A battery that has been over charged and is thus lacking in power
Desired reality/state Relaxed and enjoying working hard	Water skiing	Listening to your favourite tunes and learning the words easily
Blocks Lack of organization Lack of belief in themselves	A compost heap A withered prune	The music software has randomly jumbled the words of the tracks on your MP3 Ted has lost faith in his MP3 player
Resources/ beliefs/ attitudes needed to move forward/ key messages Self-belief Organization A little often is better than leaving it to the last minute	A full juicy plum A filing cabinet full of neat dividers A tap dripping into a bucket	Ted loves his MP3 player – it rocks! The music software is perfectly ordered with every track in its place and a place for every track Loading music on to the MP3 a little at a time because otherwise it is all left to one moment and it just won't get loaded

'The mediocre teacher tells; the good teacher explains; the superior teacher demonstrates; the great teacher inspires.' *William Arthur Ward*

The blended story:

Ted's new toy

Ted was proud of his new MP3 player. So proud was he that he couldn't wait to get it home to listen to it. As he travelled back from town he unwrapped it on the bus and marvelled at the neat design and played with the earphones, placing them in his ears, even though he couldn't listen to anything yet. Once at home he set about charging the battery and setting up a bunch of tunes on his computer. Ted didn't bother with instructions. Oh they were in the box, but he liked to get on and do it his way. Mum called him down for tea, and tea led on to a phone call to his friend, and then to going out for some footy.

Before long it was dusk and as he got back to the house he suddenly remembered his MP3. 'Oh no' he shouted to himself, 'I've been charging the battery all this time ... hours!'. Running upstairs he unplugged the player and pressed the start button. The screen lit up and a cheery welcoming symbol appeared, leaving a list of the options. Then without warning, and in a kind of silent death, the lights went out and the player was dead. 'I've overcharged the damn thing' he muttered to himself. He decided to give it a rest, because <u>resting something that's overcharged is good, isn't it?</u>

He daydreamed for a while, getting ready for bedtime. His daydream was brilliant. He had all his tunes stacked onto his MP3. There was his whole collection. He was selecting his favourite songs and listening to them, and learning the words to all those songs he'd longed to know. That night he slept really well, confident his MP3 was resting. Tomorrow he could really get to work on getting it set up.

Next morning, he woke up really early and he got out the instruction manual for his player, <u>because it's good to get advice sometimes</u>. He charged it for just the right amount of time; not too long and not too short. The battery was just right. Before he went to school he had decided to load his music onto his PC and put it onto his player. An easy job you might think. Not so. Firstly he had to put the software onto the computer, then restart it and then get his CDs together. By the time he had finished all of this, it was almost time to go to school and he wasn't even dressed! He thought about being ill, but he'd tried that one before and his mum still sent him to school anyway. He managed to get one CD onto the player before he left, but it wasn't right. The tracks were all in the wrong order, some had copied and some hadn't: what a hassle.

His enthusiasm dented, his head down, he was beginning to think it was impossible to make it work. Then he got a grip of himself, 'I've got to get properly organized' he said to himself as he marched down the road to the bus stop. And so he resolved to <u>get properly organized this week</u>. As he travelled home from school, thinking about the player, he realized he couldn't get all his tracks on in one day. This was

'The whole theory of modern education is radically unsound. Fortunately ... education produces no effect whatsoever. If it did, it would prove a serious danger to the upper classes, and probably lead to acts of violence in Grosvenor Square.' *Oscar Wilde*

a long term job and so he decided that <u>a little each day is the best way forward</u>. That meant <u>in six weeks you can have the whole collection easily</u>.

And do you know, that's exactly what he did, a little bit of copying here and there, steadily each day, and before long, his MP3 was stacked with music, <u>all ordered and organized</u>, <u>all under control</u> and do you know, <u>soon enough by taking action he knew the words to all the songs off by heart</u>.

Advice for maximum impact:

- Be sure to cover over the first column when creating your themed symbols. This creates subtle dissociations away from the original idea. This seems to increase the power of a metaphor (David Shepard 2005).

- Adding detailed descriptions of the characters and environment in your story enriches the experience, and draws the listener in. Additionally it pre-occupies the conscious mind and allows the story to be considered more unconsciously.

- Sleep on the story-making process overnight between step two and step three, to allow it to mature in your unconscious mind.

- Splitting a story in two and telling one half at the beginning of a lesson, topic, task or half-term and then closing the story at the end of the block creates engagement and a searching mindset. Delivering literal content/providing activities to stimulate thinking in-between the two parts of the story helps to embed the key messages in straight language.

- For creating even greater levels of curiosity among students, across a module or half-term create three to five short stories, divide them into two and open up all the stories in the first lesson of the block, and either close them all at the end of the block or gradually close one at a time.

- Emphasize key messages in the story with your voice. For example in the example above, the <u>get properly organized this week</u> is underlined because the teacher wants students to make those decisions imminently. These are known as *embedded commands*, and there is some evidence through studies into hypnotic phenomena that they're received more effectively in a story than when literally presented.

- If you wish to, use your talents in story-telling by giving characters different voices and mannerisms.

'Education is not filling a bucket but lighting a fire.' *William Butler Yeats*

Focused relaxation – the creativity state

A state of relaxed alertness is the ideal for learning and for creativity – characterized by the alpha brain state (see page 86). Students may not be as relaxed as we would like them to be, however. *Peripheral relaxation* is a quick and effective way of promoting calmness in your class. The technique originates from yoga and is used in a range of guises to promote a meditative state. The process involves staring at a black dot on the wall ahead of you and whilst still looking towards the dot, spreading your visual awareness to your periphery. Doing this in the manner prescribed below stimulates your parasympathetic nervous system which is the system which calms and quietens your body. It is an ideal activity to do before one of the other creative techniques outlined in this chapter.

Box 4.9: Peripheral relaxation script

The following is a suggested process for achieving the relaxed state of alertness in your students:

- Stand up and face the black dot on the wall (place above eye height where all can see it).

- As you stare at the dot on the wall take 10 deep breaths in and out.

- Now as you stare at the dot on the wall, allow your vision to spread out to the side of you on each side. Notice as you do this, whilst still staring ahead of you, how you can see much more around you now.

- As you widen your vision to the sides of you, notice how you can hear things you didn't notice before. Sounds around you and above you. And you might notice just how relaxed you feel?

- Now I know that you can't see behind you, but it feels like you almost can though, doesn't it? (ask this question with a *command* intonation not a question intonation, as if to get their agreement).

- As you become aware of even more of the room you notice how you double your relaxation now.

- As you become even more aware of every sound and sight around you, bring your awareness up above the back of your head, imagine you have an apple floating above your head and focus your attention there.

- You are now ready to be really creative!

'All that a man achieves and all that he fails to achieve is the direct result of his own thoughts.' *James Allen*

Jamming

Jamming is the process of keeping your logical conscious mind occupied whilst you think about an idea you want to develop creatively. There are lots of ways to jam your conscious mind and here we give a few practical approaches you can use in the classroom. In each case you should decide upon the area you'd like some creative insight into and then whilst you focus on it, carry out the activity shown.

Box 4.10: Classroom strategies for jamming

1   Write with the other hand or write with both hands – review what you've written or drawn after 2–3 minutes.

2   Put two pens on a piece of paper, one in each hand, and play a piece of music (one of the authors' favourite pieces for this is Beethoven's Symphony No.5). Whilst thinking about your area of focus allow your hands to respond to the music by drawing on a large sheet of paper in front of you. At the end of the music note down any insights that came into your head during the piece, or any insights or questions raised by the forms you have drawn on the paper.

3   Finger touches – simultaneously touch your thumb and forefinger together on both hands. Then your thumb and middle finger, then thumb and ring fingers and then thumb and little finger on both hands. Then go in reverse order, little finger to index finger etc. Repeat this backwards and forwards with both hands at the same time and ask a friend to read out a series of questions about the area you are focusing on. These questions should be based around open ended question styles: 'What?, When?, Where?, Who?, How?'. For example 'When is this needed?', 'How could you do it differently?', 'Who could help you?', 'Where else could inspiration come from?'. As ideas emerge your friend jots them down for you. The rule is that all ideas that come forth are potentially useful.

4   Counting backwards from a hundred, whilst you write or draw on the subject.

5   Press your tongue up hard on the roof of your mouth and concentrate on keeping it there as you think about the idea you want to develop.

'The soul never thinks without a picture.' *Aristotle*

Teaching and learning strategies

In the next part of this chapter we move from techniques for creative thinking to a range of ready-made creative ideas you could use in your classroom. They are organized into a series of themes to reflect a range of ways to provide variety, feed learning preferences and address functional issues within teaching and learning:

- Strategies to engage the eyes (visual).

- Strategies to engage the ears (auditory).

- Strategies to engage the body (kinesthetic).

- Strategies to stretch thinking.

- Strategies for coaching and problem solving.

- Strategies for assessment for learning.

Your role as a professional educator is to analyse the learning experience you're planning (considering such things as individuals' learning preferences, the intended learning outcomes, the resources and time available etc.) and to select the strategies which best fit your needs. This is where your creative judgement comes in. The strategies that have been included are all designed to stimulate creativity to a greater or lesser extent, and are intended to be adapted to the specific context you'll be using them in – in other words they're flexible, as the best techniques always are.

In recent years there has been an overemphasis on the concept of learning preferences based on Grinder and Bandler's work on internal filters. In their work, which comes under the umbrella of Neuro-Linguistic Programming (NLP), they point to so-called visual, auditory and kinesthetic (VAK) filters within our mind. The suggestion is that we have sensory preferences for experiencing the world around us. Latterly, this concept has been stretched into a pseudo-science which at its worst has sought to label children with a sensory learning label. Thankfully, the educational world appears to be moving into more enlightened thinking on the use of sensory preference concepts. Schools are recognizing that sensory preference is a useful way of thinking about learner needs, although not necessarily a valid way to label children. VAK can, therefore, can be helpful as a way of thinking about building *variety* into teaching to create multi-sensory experiences over time and to intrinsically motivate young people. The authors believe this is a more appropriate concept. In a bid to encourage a more holistic view of VAK we present strategies which predominantly provide for a particular sense, but which may feed more than one preference. Our belief here is that students need a variety of stimulus type over time – not least to widen their repertoire of learning styles.

Box 4.11: Teaching strategies to engage the eyes (visual)

1 **Uncover the truth**

   The teacher covers up a picture and slowly uncovers it throughout the lesson. The students have to guess what the picture is and how it relates to their learning that day. This can be done on the OHP with pieces of card covering the image, on the wall with the pieces of paper stuck on with Blu-Tack or on a PowerPoint slide with coloured squares or other shapes obscuring the view.

2 **Objects of interest**

   This involves using artifacts in the classroom that stimulate thinking and discussion. One approach is to have a designated place in a classroom where objects are placed with a standard question attached: 'What is it and how does it relate to our learning today?' This could be a once-a-week event or perhaps at the start of a topic.

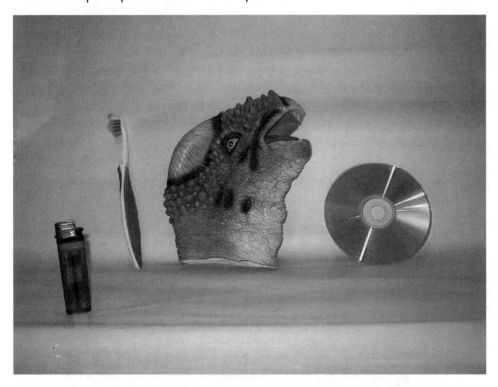

3 **It's all in the translation**

   Students take a piece of text and turn it into a drawing to explain what is meant. This can be done in a number of fun ways (e.g. using both hands to write, or their non-writing hand). They could also do it blindfolded while a friend reads the text.

'Some things have to be believed to be seen.'

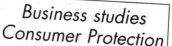

> ## Business studies
> ## Consumer Protection
>
> **Consumer Credit Act 1984** provides protection when you borrow money or buy items on credit. It is not permitted for under 18s to buy on credit. Businesses have to state an Annual Percentage Rate when they offer credit facilities and must have licences to give credit.
>
> **The Sale and Supply of Goods Act 1994** states that all products have to be of a 'satisfactory quality'. This means that they have to:
> - be safe
> - fit to last
> - be fit for their intended purpose
> - be in good working order when sold

4   Electric whiteboard heaven

A scrolling PowerPoint show of powerful images relating to the topic. Or model building with shapes to create a theoretical model to explain the relationships between ideas or wide screen cinema.

6   Cardboard theatre

Create a cardboard theatre from a box, placing curtains on the front. Devise or encourage students to devise a show making characters to explain ideas, tell a story etc.

The photograph here shows *Prawnography*, a theatre show highlighting the taxonomic features of the major animal groups as part of a science lesson. Here the teacher used real prawns, fish and model frogs and furry toys to highlight the features of the groups. A fun and highly memorable learning experience! Another show was a student group presenting a puppet show in geography on the theme of Hurricane Andrew. The aim was to devise a piece of theatre which would put across the devastating impacts of this natural disaster, which was shown to the rest of the class.

'Ten things children should experience …'

7 Ball and stick diagrams

'Ball and stick' allows students to show the relationships between ideas and structures. For example the stages in getting a product to market are represented by the ball and stick diagram below.

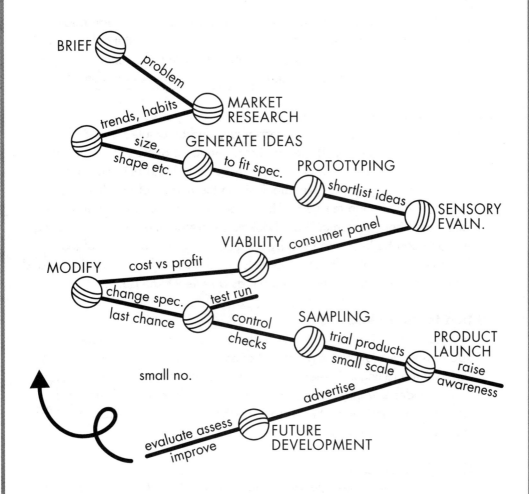

8 Video

Showing video clips which trigger thinking about the topic. Excerpts from the latest high-profile comedy show are good captivators. Freeze-frames can be a good way to analyse a particular sequence – and can sometimes be a way of injecting humour into the lesson if students are challenged to think up creative captions. Additionally, videoing students' work and playing it back on the whiteboard is a great review exercise for the next lesson.

9 Text your learning

Students are asked to write or type what they have learned or questions they have about the topic in text message format. They can then send their text by passing it or emailing it to other students.

10 Cartoon conversion

Convert your learning into a five frame cartoon strip. This could be a cartoon of a demonstration by the teacher, other students' presentations or key ideas from a video, poem or article.

11 Poster stations

With the advent of affordable colour printing and copying, high quality images from the internet can be blown up and put up at stations around the room with provocative questions to develop knowledge of content, engage and develop arguments and encourage the expression of opinions.

12 Key word mats

An A3 size mat which displays vocabulary and associated images for a whole topic or lesson. These can have one topic on each face and be laminated to make them a permanent resource to hand out and collect in. The students' paper or workbook sits in the middle of the sheet, so the vocabulary is around the edge. These can also contain key equations or reminders about the topic. Topic bookmarks are another way of achieving this, and can be kept and used by the students for the duration of the topic, then stuck in their files/books. Students could also make key word mats and topic bookmarks at the end of a topic as a review exercise.

13 Tied to the railings

In these times of global genocide and refugee movements, a more appropriate version of the game of hangman. A stick person is gradually tied to some railings. Agree the rules and number of railings before you begin! Students work in groups or pairs to provide key words from the topic and partners guess the words and then together they share what they know about the key word/idea.

14 Thought cascades

Students map their understanding using key words and radiating branches (see page 121 for more information).

15 Unmuddle and map

Give students anagrams of words for the topic and get them to unscramble them. Once unscrambled they write them onto card and produce a map on the desk with bits of string to link the words and relationships between them to form a concept map.

16 Newspaper

Students translate information given in the form of video, internet search, written material or presentation into a newspaper headline.

Box 4.12: Teaching strategies to engage the ears (auditory)

1 **Jingles**

Students invent an advertisement-style jingle to sell a concept to the class. Could be written, sung, videoed and played back, or recorded as sound only.

2 **Context concert**

Play music that fits the topic, either the teacher does the research or the students do. The fit could be related to the content of lyrics or the mood of the piece, connected to a pertinent film and so on. Running it as an MP3 top ten listing works well in this digital music era or, 'What are the top five Napster buys for this topic?' is a motivating web search activity. At the end of a lesson or topic, music can be used – in combination with visual images projected onto a screen – as a 'concert review' to embed key messages about learning. This works well with the lights turned down and curtains closed.

3 **Rap it up**

Students devise a rap to convey their understanding. It can be performed to the beat from an electric piano/organ or to sounds the students make themselves.

4 **Mnemonics**

Students devise a mnemonic, i.e. a saying or abbreviation which summarizes a list of key ideas (such as 'Richard of York gave battle in vain', which holds the first letters of the colours of the spectrum in it). Encouraging silly and rude mnemonics makes them even more memorable and enjoyable. A rule that the teacher doesn't get to hear the rudest ones – or that students' can only read them out if their grannies wouldn't be offended to hear them – is wise!

5 **Monking around**

This is a really 'out of the box' activity which, in our experience, students love if you have a really good relationship with a group. One of the authors remembers this being a great test of the good relationship if he could encourage students to buy into this activity. It involves getting students to sing what they have learned to one another in a group in the style of a Gregorian chant. Hilarious and unforgettable both in invention and on the receiving end. The task has a serious side too of course: students have later talked about running the chant in their heads in their exams to remember key concepts in their exams.

6 **Tall stories**

Students invent stories to make their learning stick – they can be imaginative, funny, outrageous – whatever works! Some of the advice above about devising stories could be used to help students.

7 Rummaging reporter

One student in each pair has a plastic or imaginary microphone and pretends to be a reporter. He or she interviews their partner on a topic, but they're only allowed to ask open style questions (e.g. questions that generally start with: 'What', 'When', 'Where', 'How' and 'Who' prefixes).

8 Expert in our midst

A teacher or student acts as the expert and is hot-seated in the room. The students, seated around, ask questions of the expert. This can be especially effective if a student is knowledgeable about a topic that's being studied. In one lesson taught by one of the authors on the effect of farming on the environment, a student from a hill-farming family provided counter arguments to the class when sweeping statements were made about the negative effects of farming. This made the learning much more real, as well as helping the expert student to be feel empowered, personally involved and valued by the teacher. This encouraged other students to become experts later in the term.

9 Varied groupings

To keep a variety of discussions going in the class change groups regularly. Regroup in a variety of ways by getting students in a line according to various features, for example, birthdays or birth signs, height, hand size etc. Alternatively, create cards with different animals on them, get students to pick an animal and then make a noise like the animal to find other members of their team. You could do a similar exercise with coloured pieces of card.

10 Changing your voice

Vary your accent, tone and pitch as you speak to add variety to the sounds students receive. Some teachers feel comfortable acting out scenes or scenarios using comic voices or accents. Such variety in teaching style can be stimulating for students. Role plays also allow the opportunity for the subtleties of the voice to be explored.

Box 4.13: Teaching strategies to engage the body (kinesthetic)

1 Three station nation

Create three learning stations around the room. Each one has resources to cover a different aspect of the topic, with appropriate questions for students to answer or tasks to do (any of the tasks included here in this chapter could be used). Students have a set time at each station and then move around clockwise. This is also referred to as a 'carousel' and is the subject of Case Study 4.1, in modern foreign languages.

2 Game show

Set up a game show situation to win credits or 'money'. Popular formats are *Who Wants to be a Millionaire?* and *The Weakest Link*, but new ones are being invented all the time. *Blind Date* still has some followers too. In the latter, suitors have information to give to the date to help them solve a problem.

3 Walk the talk

Turn the entire room into a system or process. For example in science, chalk or mark out the parts of the Haber process for ammonia production, or the tectonic plates in geography, or the family tree of a famous ruler in history. Make it big enough for students to walk around.

4 Rove and retrieve

After a period of group work, students retain one or two members of the group and send out the remainder to other groups to collect ideas, which they write on sticky notes and then return to their own group with the ideas. They then share what they've found.

5 Run and write

Students are organized into teams of four to six and have a piece of flipchart paper or similar on the wall or lying flat on a table. They stand in a circle a few metres away from the paper and have a fat felt pen between them. The teacher puts on a piece of music with a strong beat and fast pace (popular dance tracks are recommended). Students take it in turns to go to the paper and add a key learning point. They then return to the group, pass the pen and the next person adds an idea. It is the group's responsibility to ensure that everyone who goes to the flipchart paper has something to add. This can be run as an implicit or explicit competition.

6 Role play

A variety of role play situations can be developed. For example, two or more characters can enact a script provided for them, or small groups could develop their own scenes or playlets. For a group that is especially fond of learning in this way, the role plays can be quite elaborate and could be performed to other groups or even the whole year in assembly. For example students can 'become' the water in the water cycle set to music; take two sides of a controversial issue in citizenship or humanities; act out subtraction or other maths formulae.

7 Candy and chocolate

It doesn't matter how old students are, the idea of modelling concepts with sweets is appealing. How characters are related in a set English play with candy laces works a treat, as does organic chemistry with liquorice allsorts and cocktail sticks. Maths with smarties could really liven up the investigation of fractions or equations! You can even build a scale model of an iron age fort out of different types of sweets. Taking a digital picture of the end result really makes it a lasting memory when it's stuck in their books. Then of course, students get to eat the fruits of their learning – engaging the 'gustatory' learning channel, which is concerned with taste.

8 Design and make

Get students making things using plasticine, junk, straws, paper, card etc.

'… creativity' …

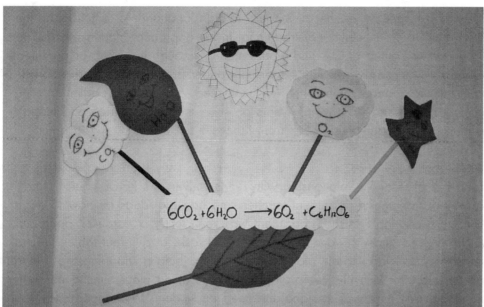

This need not be time-consuming – giving them a tight timescale to build a rough representation of what they're learning is still engaging, memorable and active. (e.g. building model temples in RE using cardboard boxes, finger puppets for a performances in English and geography).

9 Surveying the public

Getting students to generate a set of survey questions and then asking them to carry out the survey can be very engaging. It works especially well in real life projects or investigations in subjects like business studies, geography and maths.

10 Timelines

Marking out timelines on the floor and encouraging students to walk along them and add dates and labels can be an engaging way to learn historical events in sequence or remember a series of steps in a process. This can be done in groups, with individuals or even with a whole class.

Case study 4.2: Changing a traditional teacher's outlook

Tom was a respected teacher of modern foreign languages at a school on the outskirts of Bradford – but very traditional in his approach. Students tended to sit obediently in their places and work carefully through tasks set, or participate constructively in oral work. Tom began to wonder if a less traditional approach might help to engage some of the less motivated students in a particular Year 10 French class. But twenty years of 'success' using his tried and tested techniques was holding him back from innovating. He was happy to admit this himself.

As part of his school's relationship with Leeds University's PGCE course, Tom welcomed an enthusiastic student teacher who had big ideas for how to excite youngsters learning French. The student was keen to try a 'carousel' approach, which involved students working on a series of tasks at different tables around the room. Oral work, a role play, a puzzle, describing a shopping trip – these and other diverse activities were all going to be taking place simultaneously in the lesson. A whistle was to signal the need for students to change tables. It all seemed pretty wacky, but to his credit Tom he agreed to the experiment – it can do no long-term harm giving it a try he thought. And he would have his class back when the student's teaching practise came to an end.

The results were surprising for both the students and Tom. Though the students found it all a little unsettling after years of being taught in the same way, some students who had not been excited by French before started to smile, and several positive comments were made. There was a buzz in the classroom that Tom had not experienced for a while. One student even thanked the student teacher at the end of the lesson – that had not happened for ages. Tom recognized that, despite his reservations, the approach did have some merit and he committed to trying it out again in the future to see how this method might be incorporated into his teaching repertoire.

Box 4.14: Strategies to stretch students' thinking

1 It's an order

Give students seven factors important in an issue (e.g. the Gaza Strip feud, global warming, how to win Olympic medals). Ask them to put the factors into priority order with the most important at 1 and the least important at number 7. They must justify the priority they choose by saying why they have ordered them as they have.

2 Venn diagrams

These are great for comparing and contrasting information, aspects of an issue, weighing up the appropriateness of material, looking at two sides of an argument and so on. They can be made even more powerful by 'going large'. Provide students with three loops of string (or rope for a bigger scale of working). On pieces of card provide the key ideas (or you can just give them blank cards for them to create their own lists). Invite students to position the factors in the hoops or in the overlap between the hops. They must justify their decision. This idea is adapted from Rocket and Percival (2001).

3 Piggy in the middle

Great for encouraging students to distinguish differences between things, or comparing the usefulness of an idea. Provide students with lists of three to five factors to consider. Ask them to pick out the 'piggy in the middle'. This is the factor in the list that doesn't fit with the others.

4 Thinking about your learning

This can be turned into a great classroom poster of questions to encourage learners to further probe their ideas and those they research or are presented with.

Ten great questions to boost your learning:

- How did you do that?

- How did I do that?

- What was happening in my head whilst I was being successful?

- How did I check out my ideas?

- What risks did I take? What was the outcome?

- What influenced my thinking?

- Did I take this a step at a time or did I leap in big chunks?

- How did I reach a conclusion?

- What went well this time?

- How could I further improve what I have done?

'… empathy …'

5 Thinking prompts

This can be another great classroom poster that can be used to prompt learners to think critically about their work, and the concepts they're learning about.

Eleven thought provokers:

- I felt strongly. . .

- I got good ideas from. . .

- There is strong evidence for. . .

- There is weak evidence for. . .

- There is no evidence for. . .

- The way I see it. . .

- Someone else might see it as. . .

- We agreed about. . .

- We disagreed with. . .

- What puzzles me is. . .

- I'm still to be convinced about. . .

6 Five level feedback

Use this as a convenient way to gauge feedback in the classroom by getting a show of fingers. You'll find a poster version of this on the CD-ROM, so you can print it off and put it up on the wall in your classroom.

How am I feeling about my learning?

- 5 fingers: I totally understand and need something new to do.

- 4 fingers: I am feeling happy about this now.

- 3 fingers: I am pretty happy about this and would like to have some more practise.

- 2 fingers: I have some questions to ask before I can move on.

- 1 finger: I am really stuck, it's not making any sense.

7 Feedback formula

Drawing on research in the field of NLP, it seems that focusing on mistakes only serves to reinforce the mistake and focus the individual on the inappropriate behaviour. Consequently, feedback seems to be more effective if it reinforces what went well and then provides or prompts the more appropriate behaviour or outcome. Below, we make a suggestion for a feedback formula and provide it on the CD-ROM as a wall poster you can put up in your classroom.

Feedback that works

When we're in the trusted position of giving others feedback it's important to do it well. Research shows that the following way of giving feedback works. After the event:

1 Ask the person: 'What went well?' Listen to their responses.

2 Add up to three more things that you noticed they did well.

3 Ask the person: 'What could you do next time to make it even better?'

4 Add one thing you noticed that they could do to make it even better next time.

5 Then ask: 'When exactly will you do this?'

6 End by asking: 'How will you know you've done it better next time?'

Box 4.15: First aid for teachers

Ever run out of time to plan? Need ideas to use spontaneously in a lesson? Had a crisis and need to change direction?

Why not put the following posters up in your room with ideas for activities for different senses? (pages 152–154) These posters are available in A4 versions on the CD-ROM.

Why not put this bookmark of activities for starts and end of lesson reviews in your planner so it's always there? (page 155) This bookmark is available on the CD-ROM ready to cut out, laminate and hole-punch.

10 + Learning strategies FOR THE EYES

Peripheral display
Key word wall displays
Learning mats
Visualization techniques
Video
Demonstrations
OHP/projection
Memory mapping
Collage
Flipchart/sticky notes
Storyboards
Lively visual text
Posters
Using visual language
Artefacts
Characters

© Will Thomas 2003

10 + Learning strategies
FOR THE EARS

Discussion
Pair work
Active listening
Debate
Presentation
Music (to relax/energize/carry content)
Raps, rhymes and **rhythms**
Varied groupings
Dramatic readings
Stories
Vary accent, dialect, tone
Being the expert
Using auditory language
Characterization
Teacher instruction

© Will Thomas 2003

10 + Learning strategies
FOR THE BODY

Design and make
Walking time lines
Body positioning
Trips
Adding actions to learning
Mime
Regular state breaks
Role play
Games (with movement of self or objects)
Emotional stimulus
Public surveys
Sequencing (objects, cards, pictures)
Using kinesthetic language

© Will Thomas 2003

BOOKMARK
22 GREAT LESSON STARTER AND REVIEW ACTIVITIES

This resource can be printed, cut out and folded to make a handy bookmark for reference in your planner

Designed for use at the start of the lesson and at the end of the lesson, the activities here are useful for review of key words, ideas, understanding of those ideas and connections with other lessons and topics.

- Group discussion

- Students invent questions, and try them out on partner

- Teacher gives answers, students make up questions

- Make a flowchart for the content/process

- List three–five words/phrases related to a topic – discuss which is the odd one out and why

- Make a five question quiz for later revision use

- Slip tests – slip 10 question quizzes into the lesson

- Sketch a cartoon strip to summarize your learning

- Make or use a word search – key words from lesson, then explain what you understand by the word once partner has guessed it

- Hangman game with key words

- Use mime to summarize the lesson

- Cloze procedure

- Monastic chant

- Charades

- Use plasticine and build your learning

- Match questions to statements on cards

- Summarize in the style of your favourite celebrity

- Make a rap

- Write a poem

- Draft a radio script

- Draw it

- Mnemonics

- Record your learning in text message format

- Students ask teacher questions about the topic

© Will Thomas 2003

Strategies for coaching and problem-solving $1\rightarrow2\rightarrow3$

Coaching is a term that refers to a way of working with people that empowers them to make changes in the way that they work. Coaches believe that we all hold the solutions to our challenges within us, or that we can work out how to resolve issues ourselves.

Coaching:

- Is non-judgemental.

- Is non-critical.

- Maintains the coachee in a positive, solutions-focused mindset.

- Uses the skills of listening, questioning, reflecting and clarifying.

- Encourages individuals to break goals into manageable steps.

- Works through open questioning rather than telling.

- Is concerned with motivation.

- Helps individuals to overcome self-limiting thoughts and behaviours.

- Leads individuals to commit to change.

When someone has a problem or wants to improve their skill level or understanding, asking them questions about how they see the problem, what the blocks are to resolving it and what the solutions are, is empowering for them. They also learn how to process the learning so they can use it and transfer it in the future. It also prevents the person coaching having to carry the burden of solving the problems of others on top of those they already have. In classroom practice coaching is a very useful way to encourage children to work towards resolving their own challenges, and helps develops a sense of responsibility for their learning. Teachers' interest in the value of coaching in the classroom is gathering pace, as the benefits become clear.

More about coaching

Coaching exists in a variety of forms. Non-directive coaching is one of the most powerful forms. It revolves around a sequence of questioning:

- 'What is the situation right now with this?'

- 'What do you want to achieve?'

- 'What are the possible ways you have to move toward this goal?'

- 'Which way forward is best?'

- 'When will you take the steps needed to achieve the goal?'

'... what it's like to be in other people's shoes ...'

These are trigger questions for further explorations, which will maximize motivation and overcome barriers to success.

Coaching involves using an 'open-curious' questioning approach which seeks to encourage the learner to understand more about the situation they're in. In coaching we use a range of questions and language patterns to enable people to see their situation from different points of view. Coaching is not a separate process to teaching but a skill set which is integral to it. The development of an understanding of concepts in any subject involves learners resolving conflicts between their current levels of understanding and the new ideas. By encouraging them to think through these conflicts and resolve them for themselves, we're helping them to understand, to build bridges in their own understanding. We're also enabling them to be better learners too.

In Chapter 5, which deals with the reflection process, we introduce one coaching model, known as the STRIDE model. This model is useful for adults and students alike. You can use it to both support learners yourself, and also encourage them to use it with another student or alone, to resolve difficulties. We include at this stage a bank of useful questions for promoting greater learner insight into a problem, using coaching.

Box 4.16: Question bank for coaching

There are lots of clever questions around. Here are a few to help you or your students to unlock their potential:

- 'What strengths do you have that could help you here?'

- 'What do you <u>really</u> want?'

- 'What are the problems this is causing?'

- 'What might you do if you could move yourself a step forward now?'

- 'What could you do if you didn't have to explain it to anyone else?. How would that feel?'

- 'What could you do if you did not have to live with the consequences?'

- 'If you secretly knew what the answer was, what would it be?'

- 'What's next?'

- 'Who says that's true?'

- 'How will you know when you have been successful?'

'... how to admit you screwed up and move on ...'

Strategies for assessment for learning

AFL

Assessment for learning has become an important element of effective teaching and learning, especially since the publication of Black and Wiliam's research (1998). The research produced compelling evidence to support the extended use of *formative assessment* processes to enhance learners' performance. These are processes which are focused on providing information that will help the learner to improve their performance, rather than simply find out what they've learnt (summative assessment). In this part of the chapter we present a selection of strategies for improving the interactivity between learners and between learner and teacher in pursuit of improving performance, as opposed to proving performance. The best teachers have, of course, always used formative assessment methods, which are nothing new in themselves.

The strategies are organized into the following sets (Box 4.17):

- Questioning
- Feedback and marking
- Peer and self-assessment
- Sharing criteria.

Box 4.17: Assessment for learning strategies **AFL**

Questioning to promote reflection and self assessment:

1 Create the climate for questioning by discussing, modelling and reinforcing the ideas of: 'There are no mistakes, only learning', 'The only dumb question is the one you didn't ask' and 'Feedback is the breakfast of champions'.

2 Ask students to articulate what they need from you: 'What else can I do to help your understanding here?'

3 Use language that opens up thinking by emphasizing a possibility: 'What *might* be the <u>possible</u> answers to the question...?'

4 Build in thinking time with pre-processing of questions through paired or group discussion before a class question and answer session.

5 Use a greater proportion of open questions.

6 Use Bloom's taxonomy to build challenge into classroom activities.

7 Focus on what children say and try developing it, e.g. 'What do you think of that idea?', 'How could we build on that thinking?', rather than moving away from a student response.

8 Reduce anxiety around question and answer sessions; you could try a 'no

---

'... how to celebrate everyday ...'

hands up' session and just use a mini whiteboard – students write their answers on the boards and hold them up on your signal.

9 Providing a range of possible answers for students to pick from and say *why* they chose the answer.

10 Promote speculative thinking; 'What if…?' questioning – 'What if Mozart had not written his music?'

Feedback and marking – making it effective and smart:

1 Provide clear success criteria for the piece of work before commencement.

2 Be clear about how the work will be assessed at the outset.

3 Express marking comments as a view, e.g. 'My view is…'

4 Use specific comments more often than grades.

5 Write comments on work which:
- focus on the success criteria
- have an overall positive tone
- are personalized, i.e. use the student's name.

6 Consider providing feedback loosely in a 4:1 ratio of strengths:strategy for further improvement.

7 Suggest specific actions in comments. Have a sheet in the back of students' books for them to record when and where they've done corrections (for ease of checking). Also helps ongoing understanding of patterns of error and tracking and celebrating achievement.

8 Ask questions to encourage reflection on process and content-related learning. For example, 'What might make this piece more descriptive?', 'How did you go about developing this answer?', 'What can you take forward from your approach this time and use again in the future?'

9 Consider identifying mistakes by dots and nothing more – students are expected to reflect/make correction.

10 Try some trial marking: students mark good practice scripts for themselves using criteria. The more advanced the students, the more rigorous this kind of self-assessment can be. If you keep a portfolio of work at different levels and pin up items on the walls from time to time, students are able to refer to high quality work when they need to.

Peer and self-assessment:

1 Examiner for a day: Students have the opportunity to be an examiner and mark anonymous exemplar work using a mark scheme.

2 Teacher for a day: Students use learner-friendly criteria to find the strengths and development points in a piece of their work or another's.

3 4:1 Feedback: Students can be taught the feedback formula and asked to use it to give feedback on others' work in pairs.

4 Critical friendship: In pairs, using prompt questions, the person who produced the work is asked to explain what they've done and why. Questions are asked but nothing is written and the person who produced the work can redraft it.

5 Share the criteria in student-friendly language for every piece of work/module.

6 Make time for feedback in lessons.

7 Hot seating in pairs or singly, based in small groups.

8 Ninety-second bus journey: Students are between stops on a bus and have that time to tell another student everything they know about topic, then the partner gives feedback/adds to the knowledge.

9 Write your own exam! – students devise their own exam questions.

10 Pictionary – use the Pictionary concept to communicate to your partner what you like about their work and what might make it even better.

Sharing criteria:

1 Post-It note party: Invite students to write their own outcomes for the lesson once you've shared the outcomes you intend and the content and process of the lesson. Get them to identify success criteria: e.g. how will they know they're successful? Collect them at end of lesson or have the students write a question/response for teacher to read/respond to during the lesson.

2 Provide student-speak criteria for assessment at the start of modules.

3 Get students to devise criteria for a piece of work.

4 Take on the role of teacher/assessor/examiner/fly on the wall and use criteria to feedback to others.

5 Provide a test at the start of a module and then give the same test at the end – allow students to mark it and compare results. Pull out the successes and next steps.

6 Provide exemplar work and get students to create the criteria, share in groups and pool ideas.

7 Card swap: Future-base with students, get them to write down their success criteria on cards and swap cards with others, so they can notice when their friend is successful.

8 Picture it: Draw a picture of what success looks like, draw a picture of where you are now. Compare the two and identify the steps to reach the desired picture.

9 Panels of experts: give different aspects of the criteria for a project **AFL** or extended piece of work to 'away' groups and allow students to visit the panel of experts they need and get feedback on their progress – also works with geographical positioning of criteria around the classroom or on an intranet.

10 Virtual advice: Write criteria and then present it in the style of your favourite celebrity.

Task 4.2: Making sense of the plethora of techniques

This chapter has presented hundreds of teaching and learning techniques for bringing your lessons to life. Some will be new to you, others will be familiar friends and others still might strike you as far too wacky to try out with your current Year 9 group! It's important to try to make sense of this wide range of techniques, so that you're equipped to plan for the future. The table overleaf (repeated on the CD-ROM) provides a space for you to record the techniques that you've already tried successfully, plus those that you'd like to try in the future. Scan through all the techniques in this chapter and summarize your key thoughts about them in the table. Once you've tried a new technique make a point of reviewing how it went and evaluating how you might continue to use it in the future. At some point, do try to go beyond your comfort zone and do something really different – you never know, it may just become a valued part of your toolkit.

Creative strategies

Insert examples here:

	Strategies	Tried successfully already	Want to try soon	Want to try later	Notes
Strategies to engage the eyes (visual)					
Strategies to engage the ears (auditory)					
Strategies to engage the body (kinesthetic)					
Strategies to stretch thinking					
Strategies for coaching and problem solving					
Strategies for assessment for learning					

'… to know themselves …'

Using students' innate creativity

Young people, in our experience, are instinctively creative and respond well to being given the opportunity to use this creativity as they learn. Some of the techniques outlined above will really allow your students' creative juices to flow, so be brave and allow their creative wings to be unclipped – at least for a few lessons. We all know the pressures that the content-heavy curriculum brings with it, and we understand that it can seem like there's very little time to let students' imagination fly. However, we challenge you to take some risks, trust your students and just see what happens!

A word about Information and Communication Technology

Information and Communication Technology (ICT) is an extremely valuable tool for designing interesting and effective teaching and learning experiences, but it should be seen as precisely that – a *tool* for learning. The authors are both passionate advocates of using ICT – and have taught some of their best lessons using such technology – but we would like to warn against seeing ICT as a modern saviour of education. While it's true that most students do find ICT engaging, including some of those hard-to-reach disaffected learners that we're all desperate to engage, it's also true that ICT can easily be misused, and used simply as a way of keeping students busy.

When used effectively ICT – both hardware, including lesser-known items such as data recorders and a range of other specialist equipment, and software – has the potential to enrich the teaching of every subject area. However, space does not permit us here to enter into a detailed appraisal of teaching and learning approaches using ICT. It should, nevertheless, be borne in mind that ICT can be integrated into many of the learning approaches recommended above.

We encourage you to find ways to integrate it into your lessons, so that it forms a seamless part of the learning experience for your students. We also encourage you to build on your students' existing knowledge of ICT, which is many cases outstrips that of their teachers'. The challenge, appropriately for this book, is to find creative ways to use ICT to add value to learning. The termly professional file *ICT Across the Curriculum* is recommended as providing invaluable information on how to get the best from ICT across the full spectrum of subjects in secondary schools (see www.pfp-publishing.com for details).

'… learn to be themselves.'

Learning cycles in the classroom

The previous part of this chapter has focused on a wide range of creative teaching strategies designed to engage your students in their learning. But lessons are not just random collections of teaching techniques thrown together in the hope that students connect with some of them – they're carefully structured learning experiences. We end the chapter by considering how you might go about structuring teaching and learning in your own classroom.

There's been a great deal of emphasis in recent years on the use of *learning cycles* to structure teaching. A basic literature search reveals no less than 18 different types of learning cycles. Cycles come in five, four or three stage versions. The Key Stage 3 strategy in England recommends a three stage learning cycle – starter, main lesson and plenary.

In this book, we're strongly advocating a climate which supports and encourages professional judgement. The Five Domains of Effective Teaching and the Creative Teaching Framework are provided to enable teachers to think about their practice in a structured way. They do not prescribe practice. To this end, we present the benefits of using learning cycles to structure the planning and delivery of lessons. We also offer a range of learning cycles for you to consider, but we leave you to decide what's likely to work for you (Box 4.18).

Remember too that we learn a lot from trial and error – there's nothing wrong in using a variety of different learning cycles (as you would the teaching techniques that form part of them) and seeing what results you get. You'll come across teachers (and many consultants) who are passionate about a particular learning cycle, teaching approach or educational paradigm, but **remember that there is no one universally accepted way which is proven to be the *best* way to teach**. Teaching is such a complex activity that maybe there never will be – in every classroom there are literally *thousands* of interactions taking place every day which can affect learning. However, surely it is the teachers themselves who are at the forefront of finding out what really *is* effective.

Widespread benefits

Some of the benefits of structuring learning using a cycle include:

- It provides a convenient way to plan lessons.

- It promotes natural breaks and transitions within lessons which aids student concentration.

- It can support the writing of consistent schemes of work across a department.

- It promotes a consistent experience for students across a department or school.

- It can assist students and parents in understanding their learning process.

- It can provide a common language for discussing teaching and learning in collaborative reflection and planning.

'The luck factor advice: maximize your chance opportunities, listen to your lucky hunches, expect good fortune, turn your bad luck into good.' *Richard Wiseman*

Many variations

With so many variations on a theme, it begins to call into question whether there's really any one way of defining the steps of learning in a cyclical way. It may be over simplifying things to tie them into a single cycle. The following cycles, however, represent in our opinion a selection of the more robust versions.

Box 4.18: Three robust learning cycles

Juch's Four Stage Learning Cycle (1983)

This theoretical cycle attempts to distil some 17 other four stage cycles:

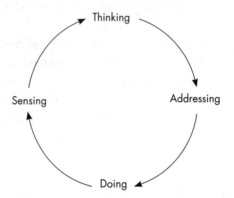

This cycle is more suited to problem solving and developing solutions in project work and collaborative learning with its focus on thinking about the issue, planning to address it, taking action (doing) and observing the outcomes of the activity (sensing), before thinking once more.

For more information see:
Juch, A (1983) *Personal Development: theory and practice in management training*. Wiley: Shell International.

Kolb's Experiential Learning Cycle (1984)

A four stage model which suggests within it learning preferences:

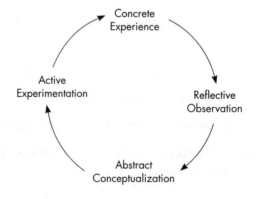

'True intelligence operates silently. Stillness is where creativity and solutions to problems are found.' *Eckhart Tolle*

A practical experience (Concrete Experience) is followed by thinking about the experience personally (Reflective Observation). Abstract Conceptualization describes the application of existing theory or the development of new theory to explain what's been observed. The next experience is then modified based on the previous steps and active experimentation occurs. Refining is then carried out again with the next concrete experience. This may occur over a matter of a few minutes, or up to many months or years.

For more information:

Kolb, D A (1984) *Experiential Learning: experience as the source of learning and development.* New Jersey: Prentice-Hall

Alistair Smith's Accelerated Learning Cycle (2004)

This is a four stage model which provides a clear structure for planning, structuring and delivering learning experiences:

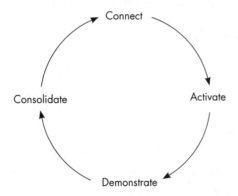

This is a model welcomed by the authors because it not only describes a set of stages that learners go through to learn, but it also has implicitly within it the key aspects of building the right learning climate. It also seems to closely fit the realities of classroom-based learning. 'Connect' relates to connecting to the learners themselves (building relationships), to the content and the processes of the lesson. 'Activate' involves learners being exposed to new ideas, thought-provoking demonstrations or other stimuli. The 'Demonstrate' stage involves learners having an opportunity to show what they've learned, to ask questions and to receive feedback for improvement. The 'Consolidate' phase provides opportunity for learners to commit their learning to long-term memory, and seek ways in which the learning can be used in other contexts.

For more information:

Smith, A, Lovatt M, and Wise, D (2004) *Accelerated Learning: a user's guide.* London: Network Educational Press.

Task 4.3: Exploring learning cycles

The learning cycles presented in this chapter represent just three examples of the many ways of structuring learning experiences. Reflect on the way you currently structure your lessons, whether you use any learning cycles or other planning frameworks, and your reasons for adopting these. Over the next half-term experiment with different ways of structuring learning experiences, using cycles and other means, so that you can become more critical about the broader context for the actual teaching methods you're using. Remember that the specific teaching and learning strategies included in this book need to sit within an overall framework for learning, which will help guide your students towards becoming lifelong learners themselves.

What about behaviour management?

Although this book is about promoting positive learning behaviours, we accept that many teachers are challenged on a day to day basis by student behaviour which is *not* supportive of learning. Indeed, behaviour management is fast becoming one of the key issues preoccupying schools as they try to improve opportunities for all young people. However, this is not a book on behaviour management, which is a highly complex topic in its own right. Rather than trying to treat it in a cursory way here, we instead point you in the direction of a text which we find extremely helpful in understanding how to manage behaviour for learning – Anne Copley's *Challenging Behaviour* (2006). Anne's ideas provide you with a first-class insight into the thinking, the strategies and tools you need to turn challenging situations around.

We would like to place on record, however, that in our experience – and that of numerous colleagues – when we take care of the climate and use creative teaching and learning methods, the behaviour tends to take care of itself. We believe that many learners are simply *choosing* to behave in inappropriate ways because it's more interesting than what else is going on their lessons. And we share Anne Copley's premise that if you get climate and learning right, students *will* be motivated and inspired to succeed. The many schools we've visited where the same students are behaving and learning well with one teacher, but not another, point to the fact that students are not simply 'good' or 'bad' learners.

Task 4.4: Does it all have to be new?

One of the key principles enshrined in this book is that by changing the way we do things we can get powerful results. Creativity is,

'What we must want to run from we'll end up running towards and drawing to us, the way sharks are attracted to thrashing bodies.' *Greg Levey*

after all, essentially about a quest for new ways of thinking and doing. However, we want to warn against trying too many new things all of the time – there *is* a place for the tried-and-tested, trusted techniques that you know engage learners. As we reflected on the importance of this constancy, we began to think about what other thoughts and ideas retain their potency over time. At the back of the book you'll find our author profiles, together with a list for each of us showing five things we knew when we were seven that are still true today – essentially some of our most deep-seated beliefs. Have a look at this page, then ask yourself the following questions, noting the answers in a reflection journal:

1   What did you know when you were seven that's still true today?

2   What did you know about teaching when you began your training course that is still true today?

3   Identify five 'old favourites' of your teaching repertoire that you cherish and use time and time again – why do these techniques work?

4   To what extent do you balance the new with the tried and tested in your classroom? What about three contrasting colleagues at your school? What's your vision for how you'd like to alter this balance in the future? What can this book do to help you make that transition?

Summing up

In this chapter we've outlined over 100 creative teaching strategies. Our hope is that over time you can provide a wide range of learning experiences that will invite the natural curiosity and engagement of your students. These activities are examples of creative approaches for engaging learners; there are *many* more which are possible too. We urge you to use the creative process to continue developing your own as well – much as you have invented or adapted teaching approaches throughout your career to date. The creative tools contained in this chapter are provided as further stimulus to help you to heighten your level of inspiration and innovation for lesson planning. As you move forward, remember some of the fundamentals about being more creative, and the need to involve students and parents in the process (Box 4.19). Remember also that within your school there will be many rich examples of creative teaching, including some from *outside* your usual teaching areas. Paying due attention to the techniques that other subject specialists use can be an enriching and creative step in its own right.

'Begin with the end in mind.' *Stephen R. Covey*

Box 4.19: Essential classroom creativity tips for teachers, learners and parents

For teachers and learners:

1 Ask 'What if' questions to encourage speculative thinking.

2 Provide a few minutes each week for children to think of good ideas to improve their learning experience.

3 Put the thinking prompts and questions posters on your classroom wall (they're included on the CD-ROM with this book).

4 Tell stories and anecdotes that illustrate learning points.

5 Encourage children to create their own memorable stories to remember what they've learned (they could use fables as a stimulus).

6 Allow students to record their work in novel and interesting ways.

7 Have 'blue sky thinking' slots in your week, when all ideas, no matter how outrageous, are considered.

8 Make up creativity boxes with a range of materials for students to use during review periods in lessons, and give free-range review time, so they can choose how to recall and memorize ideas at the end of a lesson.

9 Keep it light and fun – as much as is possible.

For parents:

1 Children with creative thinking skills can solve problems for themselves in life.

2 A cardboard box, some scissors and some sticky tape, a creative child and some time and – who needs to shell out on an X-Box?

3 Children who can get into creative flow are absorbed, contented and learning.

4 Encourage children to ask 'Why?', 'How?', 'What?', 'When?', 'Where?', 'Who?' and 'If…, then what?' questions. And ask a few yourself too!

5 Model creative thinking yourself by talking out loud, asking yourself questions and showing them 'try it and see' approaches.

6 Create times for your children to make things and to deconstruct things.

7 Encourage your children to adopt the attitude that there's no such thing as a mistake, just learning. Show them how you use that principle yourself to stay resourceful.

8 Encourage children to listen to the unconscious voice that gives them good ideas.

9 Read fantasy fiction to your children and encourage them to read it for themselves.

'At last, a moment to ponder, then next.' *Tim Billingsley*

There is no script or recommendation as to when you should use particular activities, or how you should blend them. You're a highly trained professional and you know your students better than anyone. We encourage you to use your knowledge of the students you teach to define the kinds of learning experiences you offer them. We urge you to be experimental and pick strategies across the senses and across the range of purposes included here – but importantly also to make time to *critically reflect* on the outcomes. We also urge you to involve your students wherever possible in the process of selecting learning activities, and to respect their differences as learners.

The need for creativity

Teachers need to be *creative* in selecting and utilizing teaching and learning strategies, because the context in which they're working is continually changing. New students, a revised curriculum, the latest government initiatives, exciting findings from the world of education research – these and other factors all combine to create a rapidly evolving *learning landscape* in schools. If we were to use the same set of techniques with every group, every lesson, we would soon see our students become disengaged from their learning. Learners crave variety, but they also need a careful *combination* of approaches that can help them to reach their own goals. This is where your professional judgement as a teacher is vital. Teaching is not, therefore, about learning a set of *rules* for teaching that are dogmatically followed. Instead it's about understanding what's in the teaching toolkit and having the knowledge and skills to use the most appropriate combination of tools for the learners and the learning experience at hand. It's also about experimenting to find new ways of doing things.

The Creative Teaching Framework resembles a flower. This is not an accident, as it helps us to see that the framework does not prescribe a set way of teaching that is fixed, but demands us to continually adapt what we do. Individual flowers wither over time, and need to be renewed; in a similar way teaching can become stale too. We wish to encourage you to think in terms of the wide range of teaching approaches available to you – which can be likened to a meadow or ecosystem rather than an individual flower – and challenge you to select the most appropriate blend of techniques for the particular learners you're working with at any moment in time. Only in this way will your teaching be in tune with the amazing complexity of the learning landscape in our schools.

'If you have only a hammer in your toolkit then you have to treat every job like it's a nail.'

Task 4.5: Reflecting on the big picture

A key tenet of this book is that you're a highly skilled professional, able to make decisions about why and how you teach. Moving on from that we maintain that step by step approaches to teaching that claim to be universal are not helpful, and oversimplify one of the most complex and demanding of activities. The key challenge facing teachers, therefore, is to be aware of the factors that contribute to effective teaching – especially the teaching and learning strategies that can be employed in lessons – but to make critical choices about when specific techniques are used and the overall framework in which they'll be presented to learners. This is where your professional judgement is vital.

How does this concept of the teacher as a discerning, skilled professional square with your own view of the profession? To what extent do decision-makers at the school, LEA or government level support this concept and allow teachers to make autonomous choices? Is it ever right for teachers to be told what to do and how to do it? Spend some time mulling over these major questions and discuss them with some colleagues. There are no easy answers but hopefully the exercise of thinking about them will be enriching in itself.

Review

This chapter has sought to emphasize the following key points:

- Classroom activities which are intrinsically fascinating rather than reward-focused motivational approaches promote creative flow and better learning.

- Students are more likely to engage with learning when they experience a *variety* of activity which stimulates flow.

- This chapter includes a selection of over 100 classroom strategies for promoting learning, enquiry and creativity, from which you're challenged to widen your own teaching repertoire.

- There are many learning cycles which can be used to understand and to structure learning. It's important for you to weigh up the benefits of using a cycle and decide which one best suits your needs – and to experiment with the cycles and the learning techniques that accompany them.

- Teachers need to be creative in applying teaching and learning techniques, in order to respond to the complex and evolving learning landscape in our schools.

'No one has yet realized the wealth of sympathy, the kindness and generosity hidden in the soul of a child. The effort of every true educator should be to unlock that treasure.' *Emma Goldman*

⇨ Action points

Consider the following action points in the light of this chapter and using the self-evaluation tool select those which are most appropriate to your needs:

- Consider your current rationale for motivating learners. Is it intrinsic or extrinsic? What are the implications of your approach?

- Reflect on the current range of strategies in your classroom and identify how this range of strategies varies between groups you teach. Consider the impact on learners of any variation you identify.

- Decide whether a learning cycle is helpful to you and your students and investigate some of the models.

👁 Further reading

Bandura, A (1997) *Self efficacy: The exercise of control.* New York: Freeman.

- An in-depth examination of self-determination and locus of control.

Black, P, Harrison, C, Lee, C & Marshall, B (2004) *Working Inside the Black Box: assessment for learning in the classroom.* London: NferNelson.

- An easily-digestible and practical resumé of the research on formative assessment approaches.

Juch, A (1983) *Personal Development: theory and practice in management training.* Wiley: Shell International.

- An interesting management-based approach to the learning and development process.

Kolb, D A (1984) *Experiential Learning: experience as the source of learning and development.* New Jersey: Prentice-Hall.

- The definitive publication on the experiential learning process.

Smith, A, Lovatt, M & Wise, D (2004) *Accelerated Learning: a user's guide.* London: Network Educational Press.

- A practical and readable source of ideas for making accelerated learning happen in your classroom. Includes detail of the four stage accelerated learning cycle.

Persaud, R (2005) *The Motivated Mind.* London: Bantam Press.

- A scientifically robust exploration of human motivation.

Thomas, W & Smith, A (2004) Coaching Solutions: practical ways to improve performance in education. London: Network Educational Press.

- An in-depth exploration of the processes, principles and practices of coaching in the educational setting.

'There is nothing new under the sun, but there are lots of old things we don't know.' *Ambrose Bierce*

> **End of chapter metaphor:** Read the story and use the questions that follow to consider further aspects of the chapter content.

Robot 3216A

In the distant future, on a planet similar to earth but a long way away, robots are carrying out many of the day-to-day tasks that human-like people used to do there. Robots cook; they tidy people's homes and gardens; they mend machines. And they also train other robots.

Robots have been programmed with the information they need to train others. They know every piece of research that has been published on training robots. The robots train other robots with precision and with effectiveness.

There are programmed rules about what the robots should and shouldn't train, and indeed the methods they should use to train. The robots are not permitted to go outside these rules. Units that do are decommissioned.

However, something is wrong on this planet far from earth. Rulers and decision-makers are troubled by the lack of progress of some of the robots. An enquiry has been set up into the problem, and robots from across the planet are being interviewed and tested to find out more about their work.

Robot 3216A is the source of much interest from the researchers. This unit has higher than expected levels of robot training success, and her robo-students show a trait never seen in robots before: they are showing signs of an emotion. They have passion, and they enjoy what they learn. Robots aren't supposed to be emotional, they are just supposed to get on and do the work. In short, robot 3216A seems to have found a recipe for robo-training success.

The leading robo-scientists and designers of the day perform a wide range of tests and investigations into what makes this special robot so effective. A long interview takes place, where robot 3216A talks about her work, as if she had a heart with real feelings. The investigators think they hear her say 'experiment' in a quiet voice, as they close the door behind her.

During their investigations, they uncover a tiny flaw in the programming code for the robot. This is reported to the rulers, who demand that the flaw is rectified before the unit is put back into service. Despite protests that the flaw might be worthy of further investigation from the researchers, the reprogramming is carried out. The search goes on for what makes robot 3216A a special trainer, this time led by a senior administrator. Many weeks and months pass.

'Success is the ability to go from one failure to another with no loss of enthusiasm.' *Winston Churchill*

On that planet, light years from earth, the search continues for how robots can become better trainers. Robot 3216A is back with her robot students, her flaw corrected, and her results mediocre. Something is missing, something has been lost, and now robot 3216A is thinking, searching. She has started her own quest to re-find what has been taken from her. She knows she will find it if she looks long and hard enough. The very fact that she is looking means that not all the code has been rectified.

You might wish to consider:

1 What thoughts and questions does this story raise in you?

2 What are the emotional responses you have to the themes?

3 How could you use the thoughts and feelings that emerge for positive change?

'Life is more a matter of choosing than of knowing. You can never know the eventual destination of your push, but you can always choose in which direction to take the next step.' *Mike Stover*

173

Chapter 5

Reflection

'Something deeply hidden was behind things.'

Albert Einstein (1879–1955)

Message to the reader

This chapter is designed to help you think more deeply about your teaching through focused reflection. If you're not the kind of person who enjoys introspection bear with us — we have included some very practical exercises that should help you to think about the key issues more clearly. Remember that reflection is one of the key domains of the Creative Teaching Framework, and it is simply an extension of what we all do naturally when we think about how things went, and devise better ways of doing things next time.

'Few people think more than two or three times a year. I have made an international reputation for myself by thinking once or twice a week.' *George Bernard Shaw*

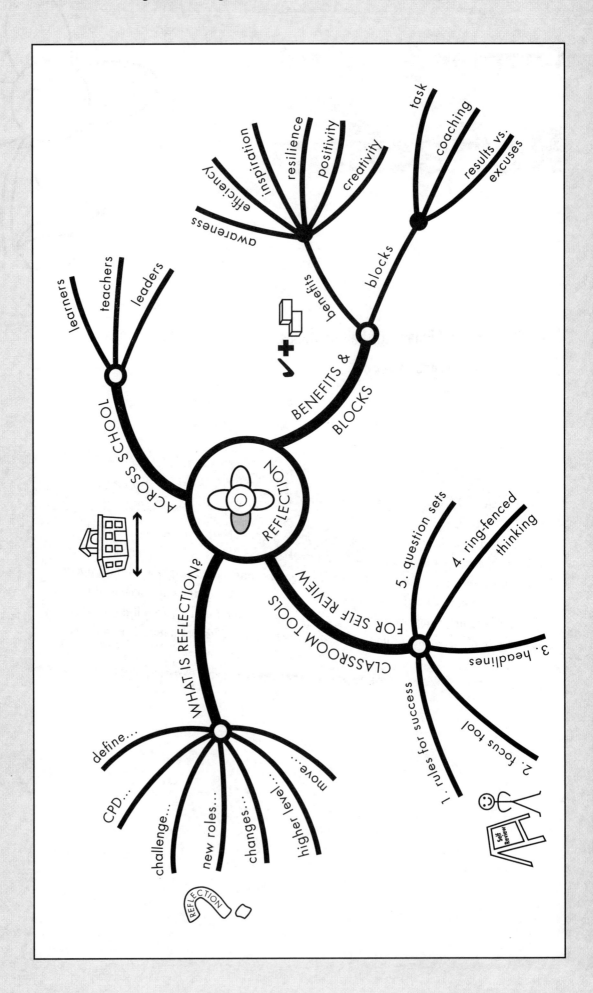

'If you think you can, you can. And if you think you can't, you're right.' *Mary Kay Ash*

Preview

This chapter explores the role of reflection in effective teaching and learning.

Key learning points:

▶ What is meant by the term 'reflection'.

▶ Approaches to reflection using the Creative Teaching Framework.

▶ Universal excuses for not reflecting and why it's vital to overcome them.

▶ Five tools to aid reflection.

Questions to ask yourself before reading this chapter:

1 What does professional reflection mean to you?

2 When do you currently take time to reflect?

3 How do you approach the process of professional reflection?

4 To what extent is the professional and the personal intertwined in the process of reflection?

5 To what extent do you reflect on the emotional impact of your role?

'The key to success is to risk thinking unconventional thoughts. Convention is the enemy of progress. If you go down just one corridor of thought you never get to see what's in the rooms leading off it.' *Trevor Baylis*

What is reflection?

The fourth facet of the Creative Teaching Framework is reflection. In this chapter we strongly advocate the taking of some structured time to consider the past, with a view to developing a future plan. There are a range of times when reflection might be particulary appropriate:

- As part of on-going professional development.
- When there's been a particularly challenging period of time.
- When you're undertaking new professional roles (for example following a promotion).
- When changes in your personal life impact on your professional life (for example when you form a long-term relationship, or have children of your own).
- When you want to move your practice to a higher level of competence.
- When you move school.

Reflection is something that can be done alone or with another person. There are differing benefits to each. On your own you have the flexibility to take reflection time to suit you and you can explore areas you might be reluctant to talk about with others. With another person it can be more difficult to find time together; the advantage however is that the other person may ask you more challenging questions and make suggestions which cross-fertilize ideas. Remember that asking incisive questions is often the key to making creative steps forward. But what exactly is reflection? The academics have a range of definitions.

Consider the following:

Dewey (1933) defined reflection as:

'An active, persistent and careful consideration of any belief or supposed form of knowledge in the light of the grounds that support it and the further conclusion to which it tends.'

Dewey believed that experience today shapes the quality of future experiences and was a strong advocate of experiential learning approaches.

Boud *et al.* (1985) consider it from the learner's point of view:

'A generic term for those intellectual and effective activities in which individuals engage to explore their experiences in order to lead to a new understanding and appreciation.'

Boud concludes that reflection is an integral part of a learning process.

Schön (1987) outlines two types of reflection.

'1. reflection in action (thinking on your feet) and 2. reflection on action (thinking retrospectively).'

'Never express yourself more clearly than you are able to think.' *Niels Bohr*

Schön suggests that people reflect when they meet new, unique situations which don't fit their current theoretical framework.

Kemmis (1985) argues that reflection is:

'A positive, active process that reviews, analyses and evaluates experiences, draws on theoretical concepts or previous learning and so provides an action plan for future experiences.'

Louden (1991) outlines reflection as:

'Serious and sober thought at some distance from action and has connotations similar to meditation and introspection. It is a mental process which takes place out of the stream of action, looking forward or (usually) back to actions that have taken place.'

Freeman (1991) argues that reflection must be to learn something wider and of more significance by 'making the tacit explicit'.

From this range of perspectives there are some key points to consider.

Reflection is:

- Serious, careful and sober thinking.
- Concerned with looking back at events.
- About using a range of thinking skills, including analysis and evaluation.
- Purposeful in searching for new understanding.
- A way of leading to an action plan for the future.
- An integral part of a learning process.
- Making 'the tacit explicit'.

We would also suggest that reflection is a necessary process to promote learning, and is about:

- **Starting** – planning to try new approaches.
- **Maintaining** – celebrating what's working and how to keep it going.
- **Developing consistency** – which includes capturing unexpected or occasional instances of effective practice and developing them to be consistent approaches.
- **Stopping** – breaking old patterns of behaviour which are unhelpful.

'Beyond all our actions stands the larger shadow: how are we to choose between what we have been taught to think right and something else which manifestly succeeds?' *Jacob Bronowski*

Task 5.1: Exploring your view of reflection

Reflection is considered so important by the authors that it's given its own component in the Creative Teaching Framework. But not everyone shares the same view on the importance of reflection. How important is reflection to you on a scale of 1–5 (5 = very important)? Many teachers feel that reflection is important, but there's very little time for it in the busy schedule of a teacher. To what extent does this reflect your view? What would the counter arguments be? Finally, consider in what ways you encourage your students to reflect on their work, and the benefits this brings. Is there room for more reflection here?

Reflection in the wider context of school

Evidence to support the value of reflection in the school context is growing. There is strong evidence that reflection brought about by a coaching process promotes learning and builds capacity for change in schools. In particular, two extensive studies (Cordingley, Bell *et al.* 2003, 2005) into effective continuing professional development point clearly to the importance of teachers entering into reflective, professional dialogue.

Some of the benefits of reflection brought about by a coaching approach are highlighted in a recent document *Leading Coaching in Schools* (2005):

- **For learners**: enhanced learning outcomes, motivation, organization, questioning skills; increased choice of learning strategies.

- **For teachers**: enhanced self-confidence, willingness and capacity to learn and change, knowledge and understanding; a wider repertoire of teaching and learning strategies; increased confidence in the power of teaching to make a difference.

- **For school leaders**: enhanced leadership of learning, all of the benefits for learners and teachers, together with enhanced organizational effectiveness.

Many schools are investing heavily in promoting reflection, either informally or more formally, to enhance its quality and frequency. In a study carried out by *Public Personnel* magazine the impact of structured reflection time was measured. Through a process of coaching, which we have previously described as 'a skilled facilitation', enticing statistics emerged. Two groups of public sector personnel were trained and then one group was returned unaided to the workplace and the other was returned with the support of a coach who worked with them, reflecting on their course content and relating it to their work. Using a series of job-specific productivity measures, changes in productivity in the two groups were measured. The unaided group saw a 22.4 per cent increase in productivity, whereas

'We are what we think.' *Gautama Buddha*

the group who were coached and therefore encouraged to reflect regularly saw an 88 per cent increase in productivity. We might add here that in this case the reflection of the latter group was mediated and supported by trained coaches, whose job it was to encourage reflective consideration to occur.

There are many examples of successful outcomes of coaching in schools (see case studies in this chapter). Whilst the Birmingham programme was a coach-mediated process, you don't need another person to promote reflection. What you do need to do is to *commit* to ensuring that it happens. Whether you do this alone or with another person, you will gain from the experience of taking time out to think.

Case study 5.1: Bournville school, Birmingham, West Midlands

In a study at Bournville School in Birmingham, middle leaders were invited to plan to spend about one hour once a month to reflect on their practice and generate forward planning. The outcomes of taking this time were elicited from them at the end of the programme.

The programme ran in total over an 18-month period. It began out of a perceived need to support a newly-appointed head of department and grew into a reflective coaching process which encouraged individuals to question their practice, capture successes and distil the behaviours, approaches and strategies from those successes that worked. The programme promoted reflection upon vision, climate and approaches to teaching, learning and personnel management, alongside the more personal and professional aspects of teaching and leading in schools.

The review of the programme yielded a number of key observations including:

- Colleagues reported feeling better about their roles.

- Improved exam results through more proactive planning and intervention.

- Improved awareness of teachers' own teaching approaches.

- Enhanced confidence in managing student and colleague personnel issues.

- Improved effectiveness in time management and life-work balance.

- Greater resilience in the face of stress, challenges and set-backs.

- Improved ability to keep a focus on their vision despite the daily demands which threatened to pull them off course.

- Enhanced so-called 'soft' skills such as assertiveness.

'The human mind prefers to be spoon-fed with the thoughts of others, but deprived of such nourishment it will, reluctantly, begin to think for itself – and such thinking, remember, is original thinking and may have valuable results.' *Agatha Christie*

The benefits and the blocks

Reflective processes take place in informal ways throughout each day, and these may occur on a number of levels:

- Your own professional practice.

- Your own personal domain.

- Your encouragement of reflection in young people.

- Supporting other colleagues to reflect on their practice.

Teachers whom we have talked to who have committed to regular reflection time cite the following benefits:

- Increased self awareness leading to better relationships.

- Improved efficiency, especially with routine administrative and planning tasks.

- More inspiring lessons with knock-on positive effects for children's motivation.

- Greater resilience and resourcefulness in the face of stress.

- More positive and engaging experience of the job.

- Enhanced personal creativity.

Conversations with colleagues who are not taking regular time out to consider their practice reveal a common set of reasons. Even though they understand the benefits, the reasons they cite still prevent reflection happening to any depth.

The following task is designed to provoke your thinking. The more honest you are with yourself about your responses, the more you will gain from the process.

Task 5.2: Thinking about your time

Consider this statement then respond to the questions below:

'Don't say you don't have enough time. You have exactly the same number of hours per day that were given to Helen Keller, Louis Pasteur, Michelangelo, Mother Teresa, Leonardo da Vinci, Thomas Jefferson and Albert Einstein.'

H. Jackson Brown

1 **What emotions are triggered in you when you read this statement?**

'Failure is instructive. The person who really thinks learns quite as much from his failures as from his successes.' *John Dewey*

2 **What is it supporting in you?**

3. **What is it challenging in you?**

The underlying idea here perhaps, is that it is the way we use our time which is important.

Results versus excuses

Thinking frames are alternative ways of perceiving challenging situations. A simple, yet very powerful thinking frame is referred to as 'Results versus excuses'. Interpreted, this means that if we want to get certain results, we need to eradicate excuses. We need to take action in order to make those results likely to happen. Excuses hold us back.

In many situations where we're not getting the results we want, there are excuses which *we* are creating which derail our efforts. Holding the Results versus excuses thinking frame enables us to challenge our perceived blocks or limitations more objectively – see Case Study 5.2.

Box 5.1: Example thinking frame

Derek wanted to develop ceramics in his school, but didn't have the budget to do this. He could say to himself, 'I don't have the budget, so I'll have to shelve this until I do'. Another teacher in the same situation said to himself, 'If I can't get the budget from school to do this, I'll get it some other way', and set about writing to parents asking for funds, materials and contacts, and slowly, by persisting, he gets what he needs from donations, sponsorship from local business etc. In short, he gets what he needs to get started and the programme is successful. Eventually, his headteacher finds the funding to further develop the project.

The first teacher was stopped not by his situation (i.e. lack of funds or lack of belief from the head in what he was doing), but by his *own* excuses. In other words, if you cut out the excuses, all you are left with is finding a way to make it happen. This can seem a little harsh as a mindset. It may not be very politically correct to take such a harsh position, but it does clear the mind. This frame does cut through lethargy and improve results. There is a presupposition within this that we create our own results, and that similarly we create our own blocks too. This isn't necessarily true the whole time, as there are occasionally insurmountable issues over which we have no control. However, thinking in this way gets us to push the boundaries of possibility further than we otherwise might and provokes creative solutions.

'The more you think, the more time you have.' *Henry Ford*

Case study 5.2: A North Worcestershire school

In one North Worcestershire high school, the headteacher operates a 'Results versus excuses' approach to the exam performance meetings with heads of departments each year. Subject leaders are required to present a succinct exam results review, focused not on the excuses for not achieving target grades, but on the ways in which the department will achieve them next time. Senior leaders within that meeting support the head of department to generate effective strategies for the coming year. The outcome is a time-bound meeting, full of useful outcomes for further improving performance. By focusing on the positive and 'what might be' rather than dwelling on the excuses, all sorts of possibilities are raised – along with staff aspirations.

Practical approaches

Let's use the idea of thinking frames to play devil's advocate with some of the common excuses for not taking time to reflect. In the following section we'll explore the excuse, look at the result of operating on that excuse and then make some practical suggestions to move beyond the excuse. Be warned, this may bring up some more powerful excuses! You may need to use the Results versus excuses thinking frame to move beyond your emotional response to some of these. You can treat this as a useful exercise in exploring the excuses that you create that might be holding you back.

Excuse 1: I don't have time.

Counter arguments and questions:

1 You do have time, you have 24 hours in every day.

2 How you *choose* to use the time is your choice.

3 You may not be using time as efficiently as you think – how much time do you spend doing the things you want to do compared with the things you need to do? Are you applying the 80 per cent rule enough of the time? (i.e. 80 per cent quality is good enough – be wary of the pitfalls of perfectionism; teaching does not allow it!).

4 How much time do you spend in a week telling other people how little time you have?

5 Are you doing things other people could do for you? What could be legitimately delegated to students (e.g. see Assessment for learning ideas, page 158).

6 How you prioritize tasks is your choice. Consider a range of approaches to prioritizing (see Box 5.2).

If you take up one or more of the above options, then it is likely to result in improved effectiveness and efficiency.

'If I look confused, it's because I'm thinking.' *Samuel Goldwyn*

Box 5.2: Prioritizing

A simple and very effective way to manage priorities is to use the URGENT-IMPORTANT grid. You can use the grid to identify the nature of a task:

Urgent and important (UI)	Non-urgent but important (NUI)
Crisis management Problems Some behaviour management issues Issues Other people's lack of planning	Communication Building teams Planning ahead Anticipating issues and preparing Learning and preparing to enhance it Rest and recuperation Providing feedback to learners
Urgent but not important (UNI)	**Non-urgent and not important (NUNI)**
Some interruptions Some email/snail mail Some other people's priorities	Quite a lot of email and snail mail Low level paperwork Bemoaning the teacher's lot Timewasters

Get into the habit of considering the urgency and importance of each task. If it isn't a UI or a NUI, then lower it in your priorities or strike it out altogether.

Excuse 2: I am too busy to stop and think about how to improve things...I've just got to keep going.

Counter arguments and questions:

In *The Seven Habits of Highly Effective People*, Stephen Covey tells the story of a man who is sawing logs. He is working so hard to saw back and forth, and the longer he saws for during the day, the harder the job seems to become. A friend walks up to him and says, 'Hey, how you doing?', to which the sawing guy replies, (with sweat pouring from his brow),'Oh this is so hard, I have been sawing, sawing all day and it's getting harder and harder, but I just have to get through these logs'. To which his friend pauses for thought and then replies, 'Why don't you sharpen the saw?'

This story serves as a reminder of the importance of taking time out to stop, and to consider how we might work more effectively. We need time to rest, as having time to rest renews

'A great many people think they are thinking when they are merely rearranging their prejudices.' *William James*

enthusiasm and builds resilience. But we also need time to reflect. If we take time out, we're fine-tuning our performance. What would happen if you did take a few minutes a week to review?

Excuse 3: But I have loads of stuff I have to do, it's never ending!

Counter arguments and questions:

You're right, it *is* never ending. And there's loads of stuff you *have* to do, but you can also consider this. Because it's never ending, you will never get to the 'take time to reflect' item on your To Do list. There will always be something else to do. In the authors' coaching work with teacher clients, what they frequently find is that a lack of pause for thought causes colleagues to continue patterns of behaviour which are time-wasting and inefficient. Where they commit to reflecting even once a month for an hour, they notice big improvements in their practice. Taking time out to reflect actually *saves* them time in the mid- to long-term, because they sharpen up their strategies. On the question of what we *have* to do, we may need to challenge that notion of 'have' to. Challenge what you have to do with these kinds of questions:

- Do I have to do this right now?

- Who could help me do this?

- How could students do this for themselves?

- Where can I cut corners safely?

- What is the worst thing that could happen if I don't do this task I am supposed to do right now? Now what is the likely, realistic outcome of not doing this?

One strategy that works particularly well in sorting out the 'have to do' tasks is to create a timeline. The timeline generates a realistic and visual pathway of deadlines.

Finally, remember that if the time you have available is less than the time it takes to do everything on your list, then something has to drop off the list. We urge you to experiment with making that something other than reflection time.

Excuse 4: If I don't dot all the i's and cross all of the t's then I will not being doing my job properly, and in the long term I might lose my job or fail my students if I don't get my head down and do the work.

Counter arguments:

You're right you do need to dot the i's and cross the t's on some things, but it's possible that, particularly if you pride yourself in doing a great job, there are things on your list for which 80 per cent would be good enough. In other words, you don't have to get everything perfect all of the time. If you treat your To Do list as a learning experience and experiment with seeing what is urgent and important and what is not, you will very soon work out what you can treat as an '80 per center'. Though it may need some practice, it's very liberating to realize that you do not have to give 100 per cent for *everything* you do – and you are

'The paradox is really the pathos of intellectual life and just as only great souls are exposed to passions it is only the great thinker who is exposed to what I call paradoxes.' *Søren Kierkegaard*

letting no-one down if you take this option. In truth, in a demanding job such as teaching, this is simply survival.

Excuse 5: That's all very well but you're talking about having a coach, i.e. having a skilled professional to help you find your way through, giving you advice.

Counter arguments and questions:

Coaches ask questions that provoke learning, they do not offer advice, but promote reflection. Whilst there is no doubt that having someone else to ask you challenging questions about your practice is really useful, there are questions you can ask yourself that will get you to think resourcefully. You can use the STRIDE model to promote reflective thinking and for coaching changes within yourself (Box 5.3).

Box 5.3: Coaching solutions using the stride model

STRIDE is a semi-sequential model for structuring change for yourself and others. It orders the process by which we define goals, overcome limiting beliefs and take manageable steps towards those goals.

The STRIDE model:

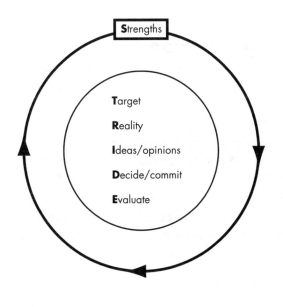

Strengths

Target

Reality

Ideas/opinions

Decide/commit

Evaluate

'I think like the species I am studying, whatever it is. If I am watching a lizard, I become the lizard. Gazing at the water at a pike, I become the pike.' *Desmond Morris*

Strengths: Paying attention to our strengths helps us to build and maintain positive, resourceful states of mind. This enables us to ask difficult and challenging questions and look at ourselves objectively.

Target: This is where we consider what we want to achieve and the outcome that's likely. The more precisely the target is defined, the easier it will be to examine the process of getting there and to overcome any barriers that we might encounter along the way. This calls for vision and creativity in imagining the outcomes we want.

Real situation: At this point in the model we explore the current situation in relation to the target. We explore what we've tried, what has worked so far and what hasn't worked. We find out here what's stopping progress.

Ideas: This part of the model focuses on opportunities and actions that might succeed in achieving the desired target. This section deals with the limiting beliefs that we hold and that may be holding back progress. It is a part of the success process where specialized questioning can be helpful to move through self-imposed barriers. We generate thinking about a range of possible solutions. This is the key creativity area in the coaching process.

Decision: At this point we consider the ideas in the previous stage and decide which is the best one for us to pursue. We remind ourselves of the target we're aiming for, as we make our decision. We define the timescale and precise actions we'll take.

Evaluation: In the evaluation phase a review happens at a time we set in the future. This is a time by when, the actions decided upon, are likely to have been carried out.

Key coaching questions

These are the questions that create turning points from one step in the STRIDE process to the next. They can be most useful for self-coaching or for coaching others:

Strengths: *Key question: What strengths do you have?*
Target: *Key question: What do you want?*
Real situation: *Key question: What's stopping you?*
Ideas: *Key questions: If the thing that is stopping you wasn't a problem what would you do then? What are the possible ways forward?*
Decision: *Key questions: What will you do? When will you do it?*
Evaluation: *Key question: How did it go?*

Taken from Thomas, W (2005a)

'With our thoughts we make the world.' *Gautama Buddha*

Excuse 6: Why would I want to think through all of the crap I have had this week? There's stuff in my mind I don't want to think about. And what if I find out something I don't like about myself?

Counter arguments and questions:
It's true that going over old ground and re-experiencing negative past emotions is unpleasant and often unproductive. Using the STRIDE process outlined above is a good way to avoid the trap of revisiting experiences in a negative way and replace it with a useful thought process. For really tricky experiences, have someone take you through STRIDE. That way you can gain insights that move your thinking forward.

Excuse 7: There's no point in thinking about things because they never change anyway.

Counter arguments and questions: All the time you think like that you will continue to find that nothing changes. 'Perception is projection' is another useful thinking frame. It means that what you expect is what you get, or what you perceive to be the truth, becomes the truth. For change to take place you must take action and see it through. Focusing attention on what you *can* make a difference with, however small, puts you back in control and is uplifting. Without this excuse you're empowered to influence your situation. Of course, in really tricky situations, your influence may not be enough. In these cases, you may need to change your attitude towards the situation in order to stay resourceful and maintain a degree of control. You may also need the help of others. Focus on changing the small things and above all challenge this excuse; instead consider: Who says there is no point? Who says things never change? Do you really mean *never*?

Excuse 8: My situation is so horrendous, I don't know which way to turn.

Counter arguments and questions:
'Catastrophizing' is a tendency to take difficult situations and turn them into disasters. This process is unhelpful and is usually triggered in people when they're working too hard. Teaching does indeed result in some very challenging situations, but are they really catastrophes? Consider this poem:

Survivor
Everyday,
I think about dying.
About disease, starvation,
Violence, terrorism, war,
And the end of the world.
It helps
keep my mind off things.

By Roger McGough (1937–)

'Thoughts give birth to a creative force that is neither elemental nor sideral. Thoughts create a new heaven, a new firmament, a new source of energy, from which new arts flow. When a man undertakes to create something, he establishes a new heaven, as it were and from it the work that he desires to create flows into him. For such is the immensity of man that he is greater than heaven and earth.' *Philippus Aureolus Paracelsus*

If you're having catastrophic thoughts on a regular basis it may be a sign that you need to cut back your workload. You might need to talk this situation over with a trusted colleague, as it can be a sign that your health may be at risk. Taking decisive action quickly will help you to get yourself back to a more manageable position.

Some questions which might help here are:

- What is *really* the problem here?

- If you knew deep down what you needed to commit to, to create change, what might it be?

In really challenging situations the support of another to listen, suggest, ask questions and provide a non-judgemental canvas to reflect on your situation, is invaluable.

Case study 5.3: South-west England, secondary school

Mary, a teacher of modern languages, had found herself seriously challenged by a group of what she described as 'rowdy' Year 9 students. Having just taken on the class halfway through a year, from a colleague who had gone off on long-term sick leave, she quickly became demoralized when the group did not respond to her usual repertoire of classroom management tools. She found herself describing the situation as 'ghastly', 'absolutely awful', 'desperate' and 'unbearable', and she noticed that the words were delivered with a sense of despair and force. She realized that she needed to have some support. She eventually approached a colleague she trusted, who advised her to seek support from her line manager. Although reluctant, the coaching support her head of department offered was excellent and she gradually became more positive about the group and her relationship with them improved.

Excuse 9: I keep hearing how I might solve things from consultants and other external people who have not taught for ages or do not understand my situation. Why should I believe what they say?

Counter arguments and questions:
You're right that no one can see your situation exactly as you do. You're also right that people who do not teach often get involved in coaching work. But there are many outstanding examples of coaching taking place within schools by fellow teachers and managers. It's also worth bearing in mind that people who do not work in your school can often step back from your immediate situation and ask helpful questions. Coaching is a different skill from teaching. Remember too that the purpose of coaching is not to provide advice, rather to enable you to explore various options for action to address a situation and select the one that seems right for you in order to create your 'preferred future'. The

'If everyone is thinking alike, then somebody isn't thinking.' *George S. Patton*

authors recognize that in their own teaching careers they would have benefited hugely from coaching, if it had been available on a regular basis. Tens of thousands of teachers are now discovering the benefits of coaching and it is they, above all, who are encouraging other teachers to engage with it.

To help reframe this question you might ask:

- What is holding me back from trying to engage in coaching?
- What have I got to lose – what is the worst thing that could happen?
- Who would I be happy opening up to in a coaching session?
- How might an external person help me to see things differently?
- What are the skills of a coach that could help me in my situation?

Task 5.3: Time to be honest with yourself

The previous section has tackled head-on nine 'excuses' for not engaging with reflection. Many of these are perfectly understandable in the context of the pressures teachers are under, and we've tried to help you to see how they might be reframed in a more positive light. Now is the time to be honest with yourself about whether there's still anything which is holding you back from using reflection to improve your teaching. Perhaps you have a concern that's not discussed above, which you'd like to have the opportunity to explore with someone?

We encourage you to take some bold steps forward in this key area, as we believe there's much you *can* gain from using reflection creatively to bring new insights. Remember too that practically every teacher reflects on their day-to-day lessons and how they went (though sometimes dwelling on the negative) and all we're suggesting is that some systematic reflection would really benefit you. Why not write a mini action plan right now that charts a more structured use of reflection over the next four weeks? On the pages that follow there's much help with the strategies that can be used to reflect.

In summary

In this section of the book we've sought to work with the Results versus excuses frame of thinking. It should be stressed again that this is just a way of thinking, and not necessarily true. It provides a way of challenging unhelpful thoughts and promoting positive reflection for change. It in no way detracts from the fact that teaching and leading learning is an incredibly difficult and demanding profession. It pushes us to the limits in terms of our time management skills, our subject knowledge, our emotional resourcefulness and at times our physical capabilities. There has been a tendency for teaching to be a solitary profession

'Change your thoughts and you change your world.' *Norman Vincent Peale*

which takes place behind closed doors with our classes, save for the occasional intrusive inspection. We would strongly advocate the sharing of practice and the use of paired or trio reflection wherever possible. Above all, reflection time is also a time for humour. One of the best antidotes to adversity is to laugh. We strongly recommend laughter as a stress-busting strategy!

A focus on classroom practice

Moving on from the Results versus excuses frame, we'll now consider reflection upon classroom practice. What follows is a series of self-review tools and a self-evaluation tool which you can use on your own or with others to track your progress.

Self review tools

When we do create the time for reflection it can be helpful to structure the time and the process. There are a number of helpful ways to structure our thinking, so that we can make 'the tacit explicit' (Freeman 1991) and make the most of the review, analysis and evaluation we discussed earlier in this chapter. We include here five useful review tools:

1 Rules for success

2 Professional Focus tool

3 Headlines

4 Ring-fenced thinking and wider reflection

5 Question sets.

1. *Rules for success*

Rules for success brings a conscious awareness to the beliefs and behaviours that have created successful outcomes for people. It enables you to understand what thoughts and strategies you have that create success. This is a really useful tool to use when evaluating year-end progress as well as shorter-term reviews. You decide upon the period over which the rules for success will be drawn. This tool promotes reflection on success strategies and reinforces their use in the future. It is highly motivating and builds self-esteem. It can be used by adults and youngsters alike.

Example

Colleen, a 17-year-old student is reviewing her term with her teacher. As part of the review process her teacher asked her to review her successes and draw out up to ten rules for success. These included: using creative and the logical thinking in balance, regularly reviewing progress, using her planner effectively, and so on.

'Real, constructive mental power lies in the creative thought that shapes your destiny, and your hour-by-hour mental conduct produces power for change in your life. Develop a train of thought on which to ride. The mobility of your life as well as your happiness depends upon the direction in which that train of thought is going.' *Lawrence J. Peter*

Box 5.4: Rules for success

Rules for success are a series of up to ten behaviours or thought processes that have brought us success when we have used them. This tool helps you identify these rules so you can readily use them when you meet challenges:

1 Think back over the past _____ weeks/months. What have been the successes and highlights? Plot them along the timeline below by writing the success at right-angles to the line.

2 Now reflect back over those successes again. For each success, what were the *rules* you used to create that success?

These further questions may help you:

- What did you do?

- How did you think?

- How did you respond?

- What sound choices did you make?

List the rules in the space below.

3 Now select from the list your top ten rules for success and prioritize them in the table below.

Priority	Rules for success
1	
2	
3	
4	
5	
6	
7	
8	
9	
10	

Adapted from Thomas, W (2005a)

'Discovery consists in seeing what everyone else has seen and thinking what no-one else has thought.' *Albert von Szent-Gyorgyi*

2. *Target focus tool*

This is a great way to review your current situation in a semi-quantitative way. It gives an overview of current levels of satisfaction in a range of areas of your professional role. It can be used equally effectively with students. The process is useful on a number of levels:

- Providing key information about what's important to you right now.

- It allows you to pull out your strengths as well as areas for development.

- It can boost self-esteem, when you choose easy areas to improve first and get quick results in those areas.

- It generates dialogue and helps to build rapport when you're working with another person.

- It can help you to highlight areas of concern and areas that you are avoiding addressing by adding the question at the end: 'What are you secretly avoiding putting onto this grid?'

Examples of use

It is particularly useful for:

- Self-evaluation to assist review of your whole role or parts of it.

- Assisting teachers experiencing stress to focus on key areas of concern and success.

- Students approaching key times, such as the build up to exams/SATs and so on.

- Leaders focusing on how best to develop their areas of responsibility.

- Anyone keen on improving their life-work balance.

- The start of a period of extended coaching or when it's time to review progress.

Box 5.5: Target focus tool

How to use this tool

Think of your whole life or your school life and divide it into eight parts, for example:

- Friends

- Family

- Learning

- Each subject you take/teach

- Hobbies

- Office

- Leadership roles

'As long as you're going to be thinking anyway, think BIG.' *Donald Trump*

- Finances

- Time management

1 Write each one along the base of the tool frame on the blank tool page.

2 Score each part between 1 and 10 where 1 = not satisfied and 10 = totally satisfied in this area. Make your decisions based on your 'gut feeling'.

3 Once you've done this, think about the questions printed beneath the blank tool.

An example of how to fill in the target focus frame is provided below.

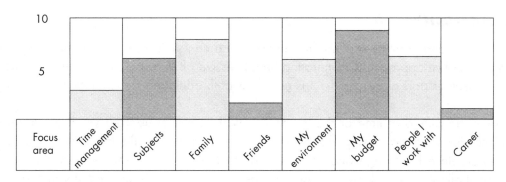

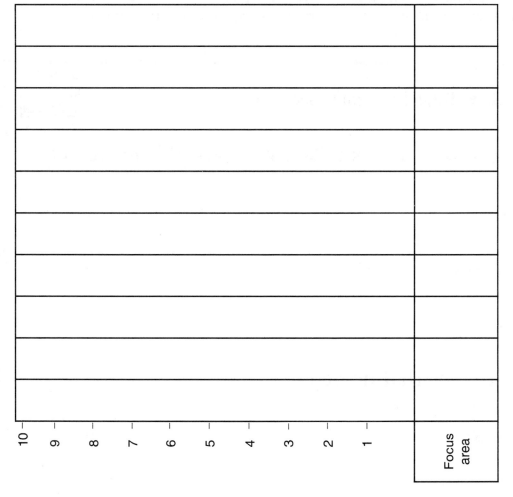

'Be a mirror to someone and show them how beautiful they are.'

Now think about these questions:

- What do you notice about the pattern of scores?
- What, if anything, surprises you about your scores?
- Which area would you change immediately if you could?
- What are you learning from this?

Adapted from Thomas, W (2005a)

3. *Headlines*

This is a fun and creative evaluation process which can yield some remarkable insights. Using a creative approach to generating headlines we often gain reflective thoughts from the unconscious part of our minds. It is useful for both adult and student reflection.

Consider the period of time or the lesson you wish to reflect upon. If you were to write headlines for your own newspaper, what would you write? Use the template below (Box 5.6) to create a front page and add some detail to each story. This technique is useful because it allows you to place some distance between what has happened to you and your immediate thoughts about this, so that you can try to see things objectively.

Box 5.6: The daily reflection

The best things today/this week/this term/etc:

Headline

Detail

A funny incident

Headline

Detail

Anyone that helped me

Headline

Detail

'Life is about expecting the unexpected, moving through the pain and striving for the rainbows.'

The challenges I met and faced

Headline

Detail

What I want in the future in this area

Headline

Detail

What I learned about myself

Headline

Detail

What I learned professionally

Headline

Detail

Hurdles still to overcome

Headline

Detail

What's next?

Headline

Detail

Adapted from Thomas, W (2005a)

4. *Ring-fenced thinking and wider reflection*

Reflecting on progress is important in terms of improving how to approach tasks and situations in the future. It's also vital to review and celebrate your successes, to create a resourceful state of mind so that you can tackle the key areas of difficulty and generate your next steps. Always do the ring-fenced thinking first, then the wider reflection.

'I will tell you there have been no failures in my life … there have been some tremendous lessons.' *Oprah Winfrey*

Box 5.7: Ring-fenced thinking

Ring-fenced thinking forces you to consider the *positives*:

1 Switch off the part of you that considers what didn't go so well.

2 Reflect on and list of all the successes – big and small – this week, term, year.

3 For each success identify the strengths you showed in achieving that success

Success	Strengths you showed

4 Take some time to reflect on your success and congratulate yourself.

5 File these and bring them out again when the going gets tough.

Adapted from Thomas, W (2005b)

Box 5.8: Wider reflection

1 Consider what things did not go so well.

2 What would you prefer to have in the future? Get really specific about what you want. Write it down.

3 What is stopping you from achieving that future goal?

4 What do you have influence over that you could do to make things run more smoothly in future?

5 What support might you need and how will you get it?

6 If you secretly knew what you needed to do next, what would it be?

'Every gift is exactly that ... a gift.' *Maya Angelou*

7 How will you move things on one step? What's next and when will you do it?

8 What did you learn about yourself in this situation?

9 When will you review this goal?

Adapted from Thomas, W (2005a)

5. Question sets

In this tool you're invited to ask a series of useful questions to help you review a situation/process/activity/performance. The first set of questions is designed to have you think about the situation you wish to review. Then there follows a set of questions which invites action. These questions are provided in boxes so you can copy them and cut them out. You begin by putting the questions into the order which you feel would be the most useful to ask yourself. Then you ask yourself the questions. Be aware that there may be some questions that you don't want to ask yourself. These are probably the ones that will give you most insight.

To begin with, ask yourself all of these questions:

- What's gone well over the period you're reviewing?

- What created the successes?

- What's not gone so well?

- What might make it go better next time?

Now cut out the questions in the boxes below. Put them into an order in which you feel would be helpful to ask yourself. Discard any questions that don't seem relevant. Be wary of discarding questions because you don't want to answer them, rather than them being irrelevant.

Box 5.9: Question sets

As a result of my recent experiences what will I start doing?

What will I have to do that I don't want to do if I take action to change the situation that is causing difficulty?

As a result of my recent experiences what will I do less of?

If I didn't have to live with the consequences of my actions what would I do next time?

What do I need to let go of that will allow me to move on?

'The ultimate creative act is to express what is most authentic and individual about you.' *Eileen M. Clegg*

What kind of outcomes am I now looking for?

As a result of my recent experiences what will I stop doing?

What do I need to accept that will allow me to move on?

What could move me one step closer to those outcomes?

What am I not taking responsibility for, which if I did take responsibility for, would cause a change?

As a result of my recent experiences what will I do more of?

What am I secretly enjoying about the situation that I am in, that if I took action to change it, I wouldn't be able to do any more?

Closing remarks on the tools

The tools that we've included in this section are designed to support celebration and to encourage breakthroughs in thinking. It's sometimes seen as unpopular or immodest to consider one's successes. We deliberately include it as a precursor to asking the more challenging questions associated with reflecting, so that you're in a good frame of mind to consider the more difficult questions. In our experience of evaluative work, people tend to be over-critical and hard on themselves. In dialogue there's someone there to help you manage your feelings and stay resourceful. If you're reflecting alone, you need to manage this yourself. So be kind to yourself and start with your strengths and successes! If coaching is especially interesting to you, there is a range of excellent books which will allow you to immerse yourself further in this very rewarding area – see page 202 for more details. On pages 235–242 we outline a more detailed self-evaluation tool that is designed to help you investigate in a structured way how you can improve your teaching.

Task 5.4: Time for some metacognition

Metacognition has also been called 'thinking about thinking' and is the ultimate big picture thinking which encourages you to consider the what, the why and the how of your thinking and subsequent actions. There's a growing appreciation of the value of metacognition as a tool for stretching students' thinking too, so as a teacher it's important that you have some experience of some 'metacognitive reflection'.

'There must be more to life than having everything.' *Maurice Senclak*

Think back over this chapter and try to record in sequence some of your main thoughts and feelings that came to you as you worked your way through it. They could include: interest, puzzlement, confusion, excitement, reluctance to engage, negative feelings, self-consciousness, empowerment and so on. Create a time-line with the appropriate words labeling particular moments in time. You could write them in larger text if the feeling became stronger. Be aware that some thoughts and feelings from the world outside the book may have 'invaded' your thinking too. Then try to sum up how the chapter left you thinking and feeling and what actions you've been left with to carry through.

Look back over your timeline and ask yourself: Why was I thinking that? What kind of thinking is that? What was I feeling at that time? How did that make me react? What did that lead on to?

When this exercise is complete, try to draw out some conclusions as to the value of the metacognition you just carried out, and what new insights it may have brought you. You may find that this is the first time you've thought so deeply about your own thoughts and feelings for quite a while.

⟳ Review

This chapter has sought to emphasize the following points:

- Reflection is a process which involves careful and sober thinking and which makes the tacit explicit.

- When leaders and teachers reflect and encourage students to do so, there are direct and indirect benefits to all.

- 'Results versus excuses' is a useful frame of thinking to assist in challenging limiting thoughts. It needs to be used with care and with due regard to the often difficult nature of work in schools, but it nonetheless can help to overcome blocks.

- There is a range of tools that can promote resourceful thinking and generate useful analytical and evaluative thinking. These are included in this chapter and are to be found as printable copies on the accompanying CD-ROM.

- A self-evaluation tool based around the Creative Teaching Framework is included at the end of the book and is also found on the CD-ROM.

⇨ Action points

Consider the following actions in the light of this chapter and using the self-evaluation tool select those that are most appropriate for your needs:

'What brings you energy? . . . Then follow it.' *Anon*

- Decide upon how much reflection time you would like to take in a day, a week, a month or half-term.

- Book out time *now* for reflection – include some flexibility in the planning so unexpected events do not completely derail your plans.

- Keep a reflection journal in which you record major observations about your teaching on a week by week basis – use it to note improvements, challenges, ideas, possibilities and the comments of others which shed light on your work.

- Experiment with bringing reflecting time up your priority list.

- Play with the '80 per cent good enough' concept and see where you can reduce any perfectionism and save time.

- Use the urgent/important grid to prioritize tasks.

- Experiment with the reflection tools.

- Carry out a self-evaluation using the tool and plan to repeat this in three months time.

👁 Further reading

Dewey, J (1933) *How We Think*. Chicago: Henrey Regney.

- An excellent introduction to the range of thinking processes and skills.

Godefrey, C & Clark, J (1990) *The Complete Time Management System*. London: Piatkus.

- Outlines a system for organizing your time. Informative and complete.

Louden, W (1991) *Understanding Teaching*. London: Cassell.

- An academic exploration of the key areas of teaching practice, with particular reference to reflective practice and the reflective practitioner.

Thomas, W (2005a) *Coaching Solutions Resource Book*. London: Network Educational Press

- Over 50 practical tools for each stage of the STRIDE coaching model talked about in this chapter. All tools are photocopiable for use with adults and children.

Thomas, W (2005b) *The Managing Workload Pocketbook*. Alresford: Teachers' Pocketbooks.

- An easily-assimilated education-specific look at tools and strategies for organization and time management.

'What happened to stopping and smelling the roses?' *Franklin Covey Company*

> **End of chapter metaphor:** Read the story and use the questions that follow to further consider aspects of the chapter content.

I just want to listen to my music

So you have this new MP3 player. It's a great piece of kit. You love its sleek and shiny exterior, its glassy cover and the exquisite feel of its operating buttons. You're excited, yes really excited about what it can do. But then as you unwrap it and discard the packaging you hit upon a problem. Where are the instructions? The manufacturer neglected to include them in the box. Presumably you'll need to install the software on the disk that came with it, so you do. You plug your MP3 into your PC and it springs to life. At least that's something. Reinvigorated, you install the package and begin to experiment with it.

You open the software and put the CD into the PC. Within seconds there it appears and you're ready to convert your first music files. This is great, at last you are going to join everyone else in the world who seems to have an MP3 player. You press the copy button and it all kicks in. 'Damn!' Now there's an error message. It reads: 'An error occurred in the installation of this software. It may not function fully or may close without warning'. It promptly does just that.

Your hopes raised, your excitement peaking and then dashed again. You try again and this time it works for a full half album. Then the error message again. Eventually you decide, deflated, but resolute, that it's time to remove the software and start again. So you do. An hour later you have three albums on your MP3 and you are really chuffed. But it wasn't easy, in all your excitement there was much disappointment and then back to hope and interest again.

> **You might wish to consider (as if you are the character in the story):**
>
> 1 What were you feeling throughout?
>
> 2 What strengths did you show in getting to a successful outcome?
>
> 3 What are the general rules for success with problem-solving in this story?

'Of all the judgements we pass in life, none is more important than the judgement we pass on ourselves.' *Nathaniel Brandon*

Chapter 6

Teachers' professional and personal domain

'When it comes to teaching, no-one is ever the finished article.'

Kitty Pollit

Message to the reader

This is the chapter that's missing from most handbooks for teachers! The assumption seems to be that these areas will 'take care of themselves'. The aim of the chapter is to explore in detail the professional and personal skills, knowledge and attributes needed in order to be a successful teacher. There's much to reflect on about your own circumstances, and true to the vision of the book, plenty of suggestions for practical things you can do in order to develop on a professional and personal level. This is also the place to go if you feel that issues from your personal domain — too much negative stress or frustration at all those initiatives, for example — are affecting your ability to perform in the classroom. The spirit of this chapter is that to continue to improve as a teacher you need to continually grow and develop — so we invite you to take up this challenge by thinking hard about your professional and personal domain. Who knows, this might be the key area that needs to be addressed in order for you to become an even more creative teacher.

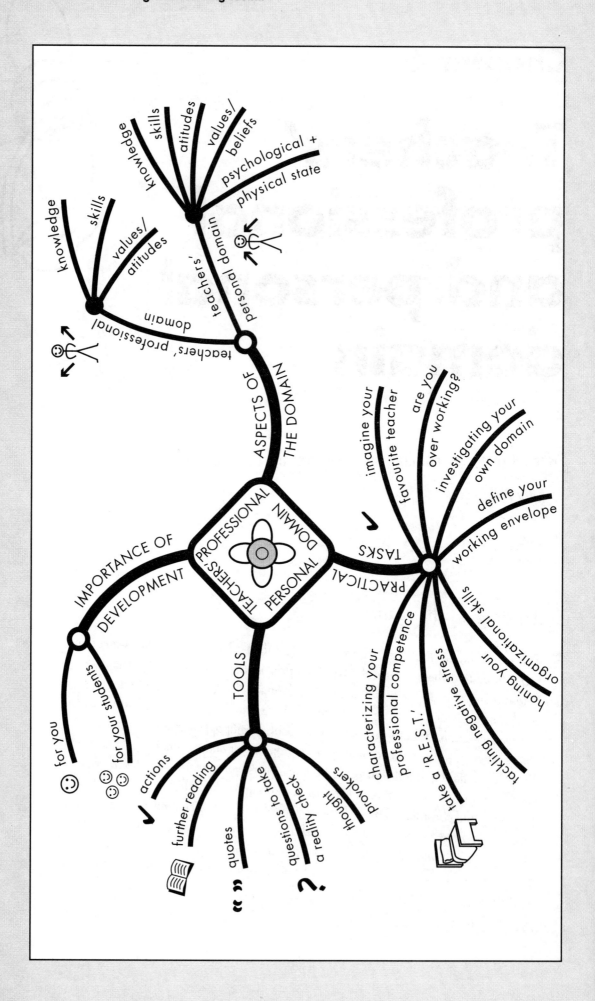

'Be patient and calm – for no one can catch fish in anger.' *Herbert Hoover*

Preview

In this chapter we focus on the teacher as an *individual* and explore the *professional and personal domain*. We consider the knowledge, attributes and skills that teachers need in order to be effective in the classroom; we also reflect on the role that values and beliefs play in shaping teachers. These factors need to be considered in the context of the other four Domains of Effective Teaching and the Creative Teaching Framework. Our view is that *every* teacher is capable of developing their professional and personal domain to benefit their teaching. Moreover, we maintain that teachers *must* continually develop as professionals if they are to continue to be effective practitioners.

We also acknowledge that teachers may possess the appropriate qualities to be a successful teacher, but there may be additional factors, some outside their control, that affect an individual's ability to perform at their highest level. In many cases these are things which affect the personal domain of the teacher, often profoundly so. For this reason the chapter considers in some detail this personal domain, which encompasses motivation, health and well-being. Unfortunately, this has tended to be overlooked in many books for teachers – the assumption seems to be that you'll turn up ready to teach in tip-top condition. We also explore the relationship between the professional and personal domains of the teacher, and how conflict between the two can create challenges.

Key learning points:

▶ What is meant by teachers' professional and personal domain.

▶ The various factors that constitute a teacher's professional and personal domain.

▶ How you can develop your professional competence as a teacher.

▶ Various strategies for enriching your professional and personal domain.

▶ The need to acknowledge your personal domain and take measures to enter a more resourceful state.

▶ The link between your professional competence, personal domain and the success of your students.

Key questions to ask yourself before reading this chapter:

1 What knowledge, attributes and skills do you feel teachers require in order to do their job properly?

2 Which of the above are most important? Why?

3 To what extent are *all* the facets of teachers' professional competence *learnable*? If some are not learnable why is that?

4 As a teacher progresses through his or her career, how does the mix of the competences they possess vary?

5 What would indicate that a teacher had acquired all the major competences needed to be successful in the classroom?

6 What personal qualities are required of effective teachers?

7 What factors can interfere with the performance of a teacher?

'The greatest discovery of my generation is that human beings, by changing the inner attitudes of their minds, can change the outer aspects of their lives.' *William James*

Getting back to basics

Students on teacher training courses spend much time musing on the qualities of effective teachers. At this early stage in their careers there is a recognition that there's a long way to go before they can be 'let loose' on a class, which results in considerable reflection on the knowledge, attributes and skills that they'll need to develop. This is often the point at which some trainee teachers begin to realize that they may simply not be cut out to be a teacher, which is soon confirmed on their first teaching practice!

However, for most teachers once they're qualified and are installed in their first post, this reflection on the professional competences of effective teachers tends to come to a halt – or at least is less prominent. Instead, teachers' day to day lives are dominated by lesson preparation, teaching and marking. Working life in schools is so intense and hectic that many established teachers would admit that it's many years – or even decades – since they last paused to think seriously about what really make teachers effective. It then often comes as something of a shock to the system when on a course or conference they're once again asked to muse on these factors. Once over this initial hurdle, however, many teachers rediscover the joy of thinking in detail about such a critical area of their practice, and they realize that there are many things that they're already doing – or could do – that will enable them to improve still further.

Continual development

We believe passionately that in order to maintain your effectiveness as a teacher, it's vital to reflect regularly on your own professional competence. But more than that, it's essential to continue *developing* your teaching competence through specific actions. If you don't do this, then you'll be in danger of stagnating as a teacher, with serious consequences for your students.

This chapter – and the self-evaluation tool that complements it (page 235) – will provide you with the opportunity to think more deeply about your professional competence, perhaps more so than ever before. It will also provide you with a wealth of practical ways to address any weaknesses that you identify. A key principle underpinning this chapter is that when it comes to any profession, nobody is ever the 'finished article'. Because teaching is such a complex and demanding profession, it's surely one of the most difficult to master.

We also wish to stress that your abilities as a teacher are strongly affected by your *personal* knowledge, attributes, skills and values – things which might have been developed outside your role as a teacher. In fact the two are inextricably linked, which is why they're placed centrally within the Creative Teaching Framework, one within the other. Although we often think in terms of the professional qualities needed of a teacher, in practice it's not really possible to rigidly divide the professional from the personal. They both influence each other profoundly. We explore these facets separately in this chapter not because we see them as operating independently, but to clarify and characterize the main features of the

'Make the most of you because that is all there is of you.' *Ralph Waldo Emerson*

professional and personal domain of the teacher to enable careful analysis. They combine to shape the overall professional competence of the teacher.

Task 6.1: Imagining your favourite teacher

Most people, during their school life, had a favourite teacher – somebody they looked up to and with whom looked forward to learning. Think back to your own education and identify one of your favourite teachers. Form a mental picture of that person now and notice when you do so the kind of feelings this invokes. Now begin to list all the things that made that person such a great teacher and the effects they had on you as a student. How did this teacher influence your life while you were a student? (and perhaps even now, if you think really deeply about it). How did they make you *feel* as a student?

By doing this exercise you'll be able to make concrete your views on what a really good teacher felt like to work with, as a student. This is an important insight for anyone who hopes to emulate a great teacher, who must above all connect emotionally with his or her students. Very little effective learning can take place without this basic human connection.

Box 6.1: 'We've heard it all before!'

We would be surprised if at some point over the last few weeks a teacher at your school has not uttered those familiar words, 'We've heard it all before!'. Some people can certainly be cynical. Unfortunately, the cyclical nature of education does offer some sort of strange justification for the disaffected, which can lure others into the path of discontentment.

It can be easy to slip into a path which is unfulfilling, particularly when the pervading school culture might be critical and stressful. We would urge you to think back into your past, to the time when you first began in the profession and reconnect with the earliest passion for teaching and learning. Ask yourself, what was it that brought you into the profession? What do you need to refocus your energy on?

Reconnecting in this way is both of benefit to you and your students. It can also support your colleagues to rekindle their interest and their energy. Lack of fulfilment and negative thoughts about your work can really drain your reserves and be detrimental to your well-being. It stifles creativity and your classroom performance can lack edge. The profession has been rough on many colleagues, but our experiences show that the spirit of great teaching and learning can return and this leads to a renewed fervour for professional development.

'There are two ways to live: you can live as if nothing is a miracle; you can live as if everything is a miracle.' *Albert Einstein*

For all those who find themselves thinking negatively about the demands of one of our country's most important professions, it's vital to remember that there is choice out there. We encourage you to use it to respond to 'We've heard it all before' with 'But let's look at it through fresh eyes, and maybe there are some things we haven't actually realized before, and maybe some of the old stuff is actually pretty good too'.

Teachers' professional and personal domain explored

We begin by explaining more fully what we mean by the professional and personal domain of a teacher, and then outline the many factors that are included in these domains (Box 6.2).

Teachers' professional domain encompasses the knowledge, skills and values/beliefs that a teacher uses on a day to day basis, which are closely linked to their professional role.

Teachers' personal domain includes the personal knowledge, life skills, attributes and values/beliefs a teacher brings with them to their teaching. It also encompasses a teacher's psychological and physical state – in other words their readiness to teach.

'We have to give ourselves the responsibility of constructing a vision of the world that is truly ours, not a colonised version. An independent liberated view of the world. If we paint a nightmare, we live in a nightmare.' *Alberto Baltazar Uritsa*

Box 6.2: Teachers' professional and personal domain

TEACHERS' PROFESSIONAL DOMAIN	EXAMPLES
Professional knowledge	– Subject-specific knowledge – Other school-specific knowledge (e.g. 'school culture') – Knowledge of learning theories and how the brain works
Professional skills	– Ability to plan and deliver effective teaching and learning experiences in the specific subject – Ability to manage behaviour of students positively – Ability to select an appropriate curriculum to provide a framework for learning – Ability to give helpful verbal and written feedback to students on their work (shown to have a very strong link to achievement in many research studies)
Professional values and beliefs VALUES & BELIEFS	– Acceptance of the need to be a positive role model for students – Belief in the importance of the curriculum – Belief in the importance of the school – Love of subject area and belief in its value
TEACHERS' PERSONAL DOMAIN	
Personal knowledge	– General knowledge about the world – Knowledge of people and how they behave

'Most people die before they are fully born. Creativeness means to be born before one dies.' *Erich Fromm*

Personal skills	– Written, verbal and gestural communication skills – Organizational skills – Creative skills – Skills of empathy – Ability to build rapport
Personal attributes	– Physical size – Interests and hobbies – Cultural background – Tendency towards optimism/pessimism – Daily cycle (i.e. morning or evening person) – Patience – Prevailing levels of commitment – Prevailing levels of determination – Sense of humour – Ability not to take oneself too seriously – Interest in children and learning
Personal values and beliefs	– Respect for young people – Belief in the value of education – Enjoyment of the company of young people – Pleasure in sharing skills/knowledge
Psychological and physical state	– Effects of physical or mental illness – Levels of negative stress – Motivation – Alertness – Fulfillment – Empowerment – Resourcefulness

'We must become the change we want to see in the world.' *Mahatma Gandhi*

Professional knowledge

In order to be effective teachers need to have appropriate *professional knowledge*. Most important, especially in the secondary phase, is their *knowledge of the subject(s)* they're teaching. Secondary teachers are, after all, subject specialists who bring with them a body of knowledge in a specific area or areas, gained through extensive study, both in formal institutions and informally (through personal research, reading etc.). This will form the foundation of the knowledge that their students will gain through their own study. Because knowledge is constantly evolving in every field, teachers need to work hard to stay up to date with the latest developments – knowledge is not finite.

No teacher can be truly effective if their subject knowledge is scanty, or if they're unable to expand on a topic when probed by students. In this sense teachers can be seen as experts in their subject, though being an expert in a subject is not in itself enough to mark a person out as an ideal teacher. We have surely all witnessed those impenetrable lectures from eccentric professors who, although clearly very eminent in their fields, were simply not able to communicate this knowledge effectively.

Teachers' knowledge, however, goes far beyond expertise in their subject specialism(s). Also important is their knowledge of what can be called the 'school culture'. This *school-specific knowledge* includes an appreciation of the context for the learning that takes place in schools, and includes the prevailing systems and protocols underpinning teaching. This school-specific knowledge often differs from country to country, sometimes from region to region and occasionally from school to school, but there are key principles that remain constant in all schools. An example is the way in which lessons tend to be structured to build on what has been learnt before, and that which will follow.

Psychology is the science underpinning teaching and as such teachers must also know about the relevant major theories on how people learn and keep up to date with research into the brain and learning. They need to have this theoretical understanding to ground their day to day work, and to benefit from new methods of teaching that are informed by research.

Teachers' professional knowledge tends to be developed through formal study, especially during teacher training courses and through teaching experiences. It is also developed through continuing professional development activities of a variety of types.

Personal knowledge

Teachers also possess knowledge that is not focused on their professional role, and instead stems from the life experience or interests of  the individual – their *personal knowledge*. This includes their *general knowledge*, which is easily overlooked. The teaching of a subject does not take place in isolation from the prevailing world events, or separated from what we know about related areas. Teachers, therefore, need to know about these matters, though precisely what and how much they need to know can vary from subject to subject, and in any one subject or field is open to question. Remember too that teachers need to be able to link the different types of knowledge and make bridges between them, so that learning experiences are enriched.

'If you would create something, you must be something.' *Johann Wolfgang von Goethe*

213

Also included in personal knowledge are the things we know about people and how they behave, as these can bring fascinating insights into the role of the teacher. For example, bringing up children, spending time with young people outside school brings with it important knowledge about how children think and behave. This can have a key bearing on how we interact with them in the classroom.

Professional skills

Teachers must be equipped with a range of *professional skills* that will enable them to be effective in the classroom. These include skills linked to the planning, preparation and teaching of lessons and the feedback given to students on work completed. A key element is the teacher's ability to promote positive behaviour in the classroom and how he or she manages classroom climate. Teachers also need to be able to relate learning to students' own worlds – to personalize and encourage connections. Such skills are initially gained during teacher training courses, but are mainly developed through classroom experience. They can be enhanced through attendance at courses or engagement with other forms of continuing professional development.

Teachers should also take an active *interest* in their subject area(s), by visiting places of interest, attending plays and other events, reading appropriate literature and practising the skills relevant to the subject (e.g. playing sports, musical instruments, reading maps, writing poetry and so on). This helps to develop both subject knowledge and skills, and reminds us that each field is constantly evolving.

Personal skills

Personal skills have a very considerable influence on a teacher's effectiveness. Such qualities as strong organizational skills, well-developed communication abilities and creativity are essential for effective teaching. They're listed here because they tend to stem from an individual's personal make-up, rather than being developed only in association with the role of a teacher. A teacher who is not creative outside school is not likely to suddenly discover creative skills for use in the classroom. However, it's probably true that some of these skills have a degree of context-specificity – meaning that being 'organized' or having good communication skills in the context of a school brings with it special conditions. This means that such skills need to be honed in the school too.

Personal attributes

There are, of course, a range of *personal attributes* which make some people naturally more suited to teaching than others. They include, patience, a tendency towards being committed and determined, being  good humoured and willing to laugh at oneself. Being interested in children and learning is also critically important. These are often the personal qualities that mark out future teachers before they begin their training courses. It could be argued that these attributes are the hardest element to *learn* – some people seem to be naturally blessed with them whereas others have them in short supply. However, we believe that most of these attributes *can* be developed to one degree or another. Some of the exercises in Chapter 4 are designed to address these personal attributes.

'Argue for your limitations and sure enough, they're yours.' *Richard Bach*

Professional and personal values and beliefs

Values and beliefs underpin everything we do. There are particular values and beliefs associated with being a teacher in a school, such as belief in the value of the particular school you've chosen to work in, or the curriculum or teaching method that you've selected. It could be argued that subject teachers also need to love the subject area that they're teaching, otherwise students cannot be expected have their inner fire for learning ignited.

On the personal level too, your values and beliefs determine your feelings and actions, so it's vital to consider how these affect what you do as a teacher. For example, you may have a passion for sharing what you know about a subject, or enjoy the company of young people. These personal values and beliefs are not strictly related to the role of the teacher, but have an important bearing upon it. The fact that you believe that formal education in institutions is worthwhile (not everyone does!) will have contributed to you finding a job in such an institution.

Ideally, professional and personal values and beliefs should be *congruent*. In other words they should complement each other, with no major mismatches. Sometimes we might find that there is a conflict between our personal and our professional values. For example, we might value very strongly on a personal level the importance of treating every person as an individual; yet when we write the end of term reports for our students, we use statement banks to save time, or because it's the school's policy. When such conflicts occur we can feel uneasy, or even become upset. Understanding the link between professional and personal values, and the need to identify conflicts, is very helpful in resolving these kind of issues (see also Box 2.4).

Psychological and physical state

Finally, within the personal domain we must not forget the vital importance of an individual's psychological and physical state. These have a most profound effect on your ability to teach, even if you have the rest of the knowledge and skills required of a teacher. Stress in particular is taking a heavy toll among teachers, to the detriment of learners. This is a key area to consider in addressing your teaching competence, but tends to be forgotten or dismissed in many schools. However, there *is* plenty you can do to address this aspect of the personal domain in order to be in a more resourceful state in which to teach. This chapter contains a range of ideas for consideration. Your prevailing school and departmental culture also affect your psychological and physical state, and this is where the leadership of your school managers is paramount. They can do much to create a climate that allows teachers to thrive. Task 6.2 explores a key aspect of a teacher's psychological state.

'He who laughs, lasts.' *Anonymous*

Task 6.2: Are you overworking?

A government work-life balance survey questioned teachers who worked more than 48 hours per week:

- 70 per cent of such teachers were too tired to hold a conversation at home.
- 43 per cent of these teachers' partners were fed up with having to shoulder domestic burdens.
- 29 per cent of these teachers' partners felt the long hours had a negative effect on their relationship with their children.
- 56 per cent of the teachers said they dedicated too much time to their work.

Ask yourself whether you are spending enough time with your family and friends. What impact is teaching having on your health and welfare?

Take time off when you're poorly!

When teachers get ill they often head in to work anyway, through fear that things will not run smoothly without them, or that it will be easier in the long run because absence will only lead to more work. This is another kind of overworking. Make of list of the worst things that could happen if you don't go in for a day or two. Then make a list of the worst things that could happen if you get seriously ill because you did not take the time off you needed. Which seems like the best course of action now? Remember that teachers are often not kind enough to *themselves*, because they think of their students and colleagues first. It's vital to look after yourself too!

Task 6.3: Investigating your personal and professional domain

The previous section has discussed at length the personal and professional values, beliefs, attributes, skills and knowledge that teachers possess. All these combine to influence the effectiveness of teachers. Pause to reflect on how your personal domain can affect your professional domain as a teacher. Think of instances when something from your personal domain *helped* your professional domain. Now think of times when something from your personal domain *hindered* your professional domain. What challenges do these examples suggest teachers must face? What lessons can we draw from this? Some teachers find that there is a lack of congruence between their personal values and their professional values as a teacher. Is this true for you? In what ways? What implications does this have for us all?

'Good judgement comes from experience, and experience comes from bad judgement.' *Barry LePatner*

Developing your professional and personal domain

This section gets down to practicalities by suggesting 35 ways in which you can develop your professional and personal domain. The central message is that there's lots you *can* do to enhance your performance as a teacher, including a wealth of practical strategies. By developing your toolkit of approaches you'll be better equipped to cope with whatever the profession throws at you. You'll also be able to harness your own and your students' creativity to get better results.

Bear in mind also as you read this next section that **without personal change there can be no professional change**. Although the strategies are separated into the professional and personal here, they're *all* about what *you* can do to develop as a teacher.

TEACHERS' PROFESSIONAL DOMAIN	STRATEGIES FOR DEVELOPMENT OR CHANGE
Professional knowledge	– Join a professional society, and read their web pages or magazine monthly/quarterly – Book out some of your free time periodically to focus on subject-specific updates – Set yourself the task of writing an article for the school newsletter/magazine on an issue relating to your subject – Look out for subject updates on the radio, get an MP3 player and download the podcasts: Radio 4 is particularly good for this www.bbc.co.uk/radio4 – Set homework for your students to research new areas of knowledge which are beneficial to you and them – Bring experts in from outside to update you and your students. Places to start for this: universities and colleges, local businesses, your local chamber of commerce and your school governors – Book some Continuing Professional Development (CPD) time to observe others teach and to learn about some of the whole-school monitoring and pastoral systems that underpin your work. This will improve your knowledge of the culture of your school – Attend a conference on education research which is designed for teachers

TEACHERS' PROFESSIONAL DOMAIN	STRATEGIES FOR DEVELOPMENT OR CHANGE
Professional skills	– Review your professional competencies using the self-evaluation tool in this book, and identify two immediate areas for action – Identify your strengths and set some goals to achieve to further your development areas – Watch others teach and ask them questions on the attitudes, behaviour and language they use – Demand that you go on a course to develop your professional skills each year – Buddy up with colleagues and develop coaching pairs or trios. Use the STRIDE model and principles of coaching in Chapter 4 to provide one another with some supportive coaching to explore and develop empowering beliefs and to swap useful strategies and ideas – Consider your life-work balance (notice it's this way round and not work-life) and set a working envelope: How much time do you want to spend each week working? (see Box 6.3) – Further improve your organization using specific strategies (see Box 6.4) – Keep a reflection journal in which you record significant observations about your lessons: what went well or otherwise; key points about topics taught; reminders about things to try next time; philosophical musings on education; or whatever else helps you to consider issues which impact on your professional skills as a teacher – Book in time to watch some of the excellent programmes on Teachers' TV (www.teachers.tv)
Professional values and beliefs	– Seek feedback from your students on how you come across to them. Anonymous feedback is usually the most genuine. Work alongside another colleague to help you process the feedback – Carry out the values exercise in Chapter 2 every 12 months to evaluate what's important to you. Make comparisons with the previous exercise each time and repeat the exercise after any period of intensive training or learning – Buddy up with colleagues and develop coaching pairs or trios. Use the STRIDE model and principles of coaching in Chapter 4, as outlined above

'In the creative state a man is taken out of himself. He lets down as it were a bucket in his subconscious, and draws up something which is normally beyond his reach. He mixes this thing with his normal experiences and out of the mixture he makes a work of art.' *E. M. Forster*

TEACHERS' PERSONAL DOMAIN	STRATEGIES FOR DEVELOPMENT OR CHANGE
Personal knowledge	– Never underestimate the personal experiences you have and try to bring them into the classroom; they make you even more interesting, relevant and human – Take up learning something new each year, something away from school, or develop something you already do to the next level – Experiment with using personal experiences as metaphors in your teaching
Personal skills	– Ask colleagues to identify your strengths in communicating with them. If you're feeling really brave, ask for their opinions on your development areas and for suggestions as to how you could further improve – At the end of each year review your progress. Identify all of the successes, large and small. Then produce a list of your rules for success in that previous year, e.g. if having a clear goal helped you achieve last year, then one of your rules for success might be set clear goals. You can use this to support you in planning the new year and also in times of challenge, by asking the question, what success rule might help me here? – Use the creative tools in Chapter 4 to develop your creativity and widen your toolkit for creative thinking. Continue your search for creative strategies in your readings in future
Personal attributes	– Earlier in the chapter we listed the personal attributes of a teacher. Some of these are fixed (e.g. physical size) but others are attitudinal and can be adapted. List your personal attributes, and for the purposes of this exercise, list attributes that you see as negative as well as those you see as positive. When your list is complete, challenge yourself (and get help from others if you need it) to turn your negative attributes into positive ones (e.g. 'I am very short, and I can't always see what's going on at the back,' turns to 'But I am much more on the same physical level as many of my students'.

'When your daemon is in charge, do not try to think consciously. Drift, wait and obey.' *Rudyard Kipling*

TEACHERS' PERSONAL DOMAIN	STRATEGIES FOR DEVELOPMENT OR CHANGE
	– Try to think about how someone else might approach the particular issue you're facing. How would they think about it or deal with it? This could be a famous person, someone you admire or respect, or just for fun, a pet! Try to ask yourself: What blinkers am I wearing by thinking about this situation in the way I am at moment? If I take the blinkers off, how can I see things differently?
Personal values and beliefs VALUES & BELIEFS	– Consider what you bring into the classroom of your own values and beliefs as distinct from those you might class as professional – Consider what you model or espouse in the classroom. Feedback on this can be very useful. Ask students and colleagues these questions: What do you see that I am prepared to: • Tolerate? • Encourage? • Stop? • Challenge? Invite others to do the same.
Psychological and physical state	– Be prepared to acknowledge that high levels of pressure and stress are NOT just 'part of the job' and to tackle others who think it is (see Box 6.5) – Look after your mental and physical health through: • Planning ahead for the long, medium and short-term • Blocking out planning and relaxation time each week and taking it • Being realistic with your plans, even if the targets you've been set are not! • Being flexible • Building in enough margin for coping with unexpected demands • Making lists – celebrate the ticks • Taking 'time out' during the day – even a few seconds • Eating and drinking healthily, especially water as irritability comes with dehydration

'When you make a mistake, don't look back at it long. Take the reason of the thing into your mind, and then look forward. Mistakes are lessons of wisdom. The past cannot be changed. The future is yet in your power.' *Phyllis Bottome*

TEACHERS' PERSONAL DOMAIN	STRATEGIES FOR DEVELOPMENT OR CHANGE
	• Creating time for exercise and mental space – no excuses
	• Doing something for YOU each week, something you enjoy and look forward to
	• Seeking help from others if you feel you are suffering from too much stress
	– Use a long-term 'R.E.S.T' prescription (see Box 6.6)
	– Be aware of what constitutes your ideal psychological and physical state for teaching: note the features of this state and make plans for how you can enter it more consistently. Note what the blocks are and discuss with a trusted colleague or loved one what you can do to overcome them

Box 6.3: Define your working envelope

This is a highly individual matter and depends on so many parameters in your life. You may have some unrealistic expectations! It may be important for you to set challenging targets for reducing your working envelope. It is vital, however, that you build in realistic timescales for reducing workload, if this is something that you'd like to do.

If your work is currently overwhelming you there may be a number of key areas to work on. These matters may take some time to address, so be kind to yourself and give yourself reasonable timescales for change. The result of setting unreasonable demands is often disappointment and consequently loss of resilience.

Defining your envelope:

1 Be clear about how much time you're contractually expected to work over a year.

2 How many hours do you typically work per week? (Include before work, after work, at home, at weekends and in the holidays).

3 Total up the hours you spent above this contractual obligation.

4 Consider how much time you are <u>really</u> satisfied to put in each week.

5 Decide on a working envelope for a week.

We'd like to stress that within the concept of 'life-work balance', we don't actually achieve 'balance' but achieve 'balan<u>cing</u>', as things are constantly changing. Many of us try and fail to juggle our priorities because when we achieve a success we allow ourselves to give up the strategies that got us there. The moment of balance is lost, and we quickly fall back to a position of imbalance.

When we commit to making a difference to our lives, then we commit to life-work balan<u>cing</u>. This involves setting very specific goals and cultivating the behaviours that bring personal and professional effectiveness. There is no endpoint; it is *ongoing* actions which keep us balancing over time.

Box 6.4: Honing your personal organization skills

Personal organization is key to maintaining a healthy life-work balance and getting things done.

The key principles to organization are:

- Know where you're going
- Plan your day, week, month and year
- Prioritize
- Take decisive action.

Know where you are going
Be absolutely clear what your goals are for the year, the term, the week and the day. Define how you'll know when you've achieved them, and what the benefits are of accomplishing them.

Plan your day, week, and month and year
Actually do this in reverse order. Decide what your goals are for the year. Spend a few minutes each week reflecting on these goals and what you need to do to keep moving towards them.

Prioritize
Once you've defined your goals it's then much easier to prioritize the things that come your way. Not everything that comes into our lives is a priority. When we

'We never reach a point of balance, but are constantly balancing. The sooner you accept this the sooner you'll realise you already have the answer.'

wrongly prioritize some things over others we can unbalance ourselves. Failing to prioritize causes us to become reactive rather than proactive and sometimes the trivial overrides the really important.

Take decisive action

This helps us to make progress and avoid procrastination. The following tips should be useful:

- Tackle first the thing on your task list you most want to avoid!

- Break down big tasks into a series of subtasks.

- Do high-level cognitively-challenging tasks when you have your highest energy levels in the day (e.g. understanding complex concepts and deciding how to teach them).

- Work on low-level repetitive tasks when you have low levels of energy. This can actually make these tasks more rewarding (e.g. simple marking or making resources).

- For emotionally challenging tasks, predict the likely challenges and plan a range of assertive ways to deal with them – ask others to help you think it through (e.g. planning how to deal with the behaviour of a challenging student).

- Above all, get started – do something, anything to get the ball rolling when you recognize yourself procrastinating (e.g. clear your desk of everything except one simple task and do it there and then).

- Avoid moaning – in schools there sometimes can be a culture of complaining about how bad things are. At a low level this can serve to acknowledge the strains of teaching, but if allowed to be the focus of interaction with others, it can lock you into a negative thinking cycle. Acknowledge the difficulties, then move on.

- Choose companions carefully for lunches and breaks, shift negative conversations to positive with a focus on humorous or successful events.

- Working with a professional coach can be useful to help you break the patterns of behaviour that lead to procrastination. Look for a coach who uses NLP coaching techniques. Visit www.visionforlearning.co.uk for more information.

'Nobody ever arrives at a very big idea through a conscious, rational thought process. It comes from your unconscious.' *David Ogilvy*

Box 6.5: Tackling negative stress

If negative stress is beginning to make your life especially difficult, then it's time to do something about it. If you try to ignore it, or bottle it all up, then it's possible that some time later it will surface again in a much more nasty form – a serious stress-related illness or breakdown. And if you're suffering from undue stress then your students will be suffering too: it's simply not possible to perform at your best when you're under this much pressure.

What is stress?

Stress is your body's response to potentially threatening situations. *'Positive stress'* refers to the fight or flight response or adrenalin rush which you get when something is exciting, exhilarating or requires an immediate response. It is not in itself damaging and can actually enhance performance in several areas. *'Negative stress'* on the other hand, is the result of sustained exposure to situations which sap your body's mental reserves. It can manifest itself through feelings of anxiety, panic attacks and sleep problems, and physical symptoms such as headaches, indigestion and heart palpitations. Some of the day-to-day indications that things are not right may be poor concentration, irritability and losing track when teaching.

How much stress is too much?

It's vital to assess accurately whether the stress levels you're suffering could be damaging in the long-term, but when you're under pressure it's often hard to make objective judgements of this sort. It's also important to recognize that we all suffer from frustrations, hassles and day to day anxieties in our work and private lives, but this is not the same as experiencing sustained negative stress. If you begin to feel that you've had enough of feeling the way you do, or that you're suffering several of the classic symptoms of stress, then it's time to do something about it. Do not just put up with it – there's *lots* you can do to start feeling better.

Try to identify the root cause

We experience negative stress from many quarters, including work, home-life, financial issues and relationships. Think about what it is that's really bugging you – it could, of course, be a combination of factors. If it's a school issue, try to be as specific as possible. For example, if it is a discipline problem is it with just one group, certain types of students or a specific issue across the board? If it's about a relationship issue, is it a personality clash with another colleague, or something that seems to be interfering with your relations with most people? If it's too much work, when are the times when you are working and you would rather be relaxing? Reorganization is a common source of stress, but which specific aspect is getting to you?

'Most striking at first is the appearance of sudden illumination, a manifest sign of long unconscious prior work.' *Henri Poincaré*

Discuss the issues

Talking about what's causing you stress can be helpful in itself. This could be with a loved one, a friend, colleague, mentor or coach – anybody whom you trust and feel comfortable talking to. Try to formulate an action plan that will seek to resolve the underlying issues causing the stress. Make a serious commitment to carrying the actions through.

Managing others

In some schools there's a culture of ignoring stress. Either it's classified as 'just part of the job', or ignored in the hope it will go away. This is actually a leadership failure, as schools should take the issue of stress extremely seriously. A common problem arises when a teacher suffering from stress identifies that they need to cut back on school work and other commitments, but this is simply not actively supported by the school. This is when things can get intolerable. Perhaps the best way to deal with this is to find out how other colleagues in your school are coping. It's likely that there will be *many* others who will feel like you, and together you can form a more powerful voice for change. The Teacher Support Network also offers a free and confidential helpline to help you explore the options (Tel. 08000 562 561 in England; 08000 855 088 in Wales; 0131 220 0872 in Scotland). The various strategies linked to the personal domain suggested elsewhere in this book may also help you.

Be prepared to seek further help

If you feel that you're not managing to reduce your stress level in a time-frame that seems reasonable, then be prepared to seek further professional help. This is often a difficult step to take, but it can be very helpful to discuss things with a trained health care professional, such as your GP or a specialist nurse or counsellor. This is *not* an admission of failure, rather a request for some external support to get you on the road to feeling better again. It's an extremely positive step to take.

Read more

It's not possible here to give full justice to the important and complex topic of stress management. We do not want to trivialize things by suggesting that there's a simple quick fix, or an easy step-by-step approach that works for everyone. Further, more detailed, advice about this critical area is contained in *The Managing Workload Pocketbook*, written by one of the authors (Thomas 2005b).

There's also an excellent free downloadable guide to managing stress available from www.mind.org.uk. The Teacher Support Network also contains some invaluable information on this topic and related issues, such as life-work balance (www.teachersupport.info).

'Give yourself plenty of new starts and remember that tomorrow can be the first day of the rest of your life – if you want it to be.'

Box 6.6: Taking a 'R. E. S. T'

R. E. S. T. stands for:

Refuel – eat and drink properly for maximum performance.
Exercise – take regular exercise for posture, health and stamina.
Stop – take stimulus-free time.
Time to reflect – use time to reflect on your successes and plan your next steps to aid life-work balance.

Tips on *Refuel*

We're hearing a great deal in the news about obesity and poor diet. The figures suggest a nation eating inappropriately. A balanced diet of unprocessed foods with plenty of fruit and vegetables is at the heart of good health. There's strong evidence now to link poor diet with life-threatening diseases like cancer and cardiovascular disease. It's also well known that we need a balanced diet for long-term health. We now also know that what we eat and drink affects our mental as well as our physical well-being in more immediate ways, as the following indicate:

Teacher's fix: Caffeinated drinks e.g. coffee, cola and tea, cause our nerves to misfire and create alertness hyper-states. This affects sleep, creates irregular heart rates and feelings of anxiety. Cut back for a couple of weeks and notice the benefits. Drink water instead, or herbal teas.

Teacher's famine: Going for long periods during the day without food leads our body to think it's facing famine. We develop low blood sugar levels leading to headaches and irritability, and feel low in energy. This can promote the deposition of fat when we next eat. Set some boundaries about eating well in school and stick to them – and eat away from your desk!

Teacher's rush: Eating high carbohydrate foods like chocolate and bread create high sugar loads in our bloodstream in very short time frames. Our body responds with high insulin release and over-zealous blood sugar reduction. A lack of energy follows the initial rush. We can feel extremely tired after sugary foods, and irritability and poor concentration follow. Avoid sugary foods like chocolate and replace with slow release carbohydrates balanced with fat and protein (e.g. oatcakes, wholegrain bread, rice, pasta, cereals).

Water and hydration: Water makes up 80 per cent of our body and surrounds every cell in our body. Our cells carry out all of the specialized functions in our body. Many work together to balance our internal chemistry. Cells suffer when there's insufficient water around.

When we're dehydrated:

- Cell energy production is compromised and headaches occur.

'In order to solve this differential equation you look at it until a solution occurs to you.' *George Polyá*

- Brain cells are sensitive to dehydration and learning is impaired.
- Prolonged low water levels in the body can compromise kidney function.

When you're well hydrated, you quite literally feel great! Get into the habit of drinking water during the day and remember that caffeine actually exacerbates water loss. The more caffeine you take, the more water you need to drink.

Tips on *Exercise*

Even moderate exercise is good for you. The British Heart Foundation (www.bhf. org.uk) recommend five sessions of exercise per week, each lasting around 30 minutes. Exercise should raise your heart rate and breathing rate and make you feel a little warm.

Here's why building-in exercise is so beneficial:

- It boosts feel-good chemical levels – endorphins and enkephalins.
- It enhances concentration and alertness.
- It encourages healthy functioning of the cardiovascular system.
- It improves muscle and lung performance.
- It supports healthier weight.
- It helps you look and feel better, enhancing self-esteem.

Endorphins help you feel resourceful and you don't have to go to a gym to benefit. Choose an exercise that you will enjoy. One of the finest exercises is just walking.

Tips on *Stop*

Really take time out and stop. Maybe we have forgotten how to *really* rest and provide ourselves with a low stimulus environment? Teachers may have in excess of 70 human interactions per hour in a typical day. That could mean as many as 500 interactions in one day!

When you finish your day make time to reduce the number of stimuli.

You could:

- Meditate and clear your mind through focusing on your breathing.
- Sit quietly and read the paper.
- Sit and listen to music.
- Close your eyes and think of being in your dream location.

'...those little people, my brownies, do one half of my work for me while I am fast asleep, and in all human likelihood do the rest for me as well, when I am wide awake and fondly suppose I do for myself.' *Robert Louis Stevenson*

- Spend some time with someone you care about.

- Spend some time with a pet.

- Take a walk or some other form of gentle exercise.

- Engage in a hobby.

- Watch some 'junk' TV.

- Have a bath or shower and change your clothes (move out of your 'uniform').

- Day dream.

During the day too you can stop thinking about school work by:

- Having lunch with a group who agree not to 'talk shop'.

- Going off the school premises once a week for a lunch or a summer picnic.

- Chatting to some students about their weekend and hobbies.

Tips on *Time* to reflect

Reflecting on progress is important in terms of improving how to approach tasks and situations in the future. It's also vital to review and celebrate your successes, and part of a process of rest and renewal. Using the ring-fenced reflection and wider reflection (pages 197–9) processes are helpful.

Warning!

Remember that poor life-work balance has detrimental short-term effects on our ability to meet deadlines, sustain relationships and even memorize. In the long-term it can have real consequences for our health, with a range of diseases being caused by, or intensified by, stress. They include cardiovascular disease, diabetes, asthma, migraines, psoriasis, immune problems, panic attacks, depression, ulcers and colitis. If you're beginning to show any preliminary signs of these, then it's time to take a 'R.E.S.T.'

'Sometimes I observe with curiosity that uninterrupted activity which, independent of the subject of any conversation I may be carrying on, continues its course in that department of my brain that is devoted to music.' *Pyotr Tchaikovsky*

Blending your professional competence

The previous sections have explored in detail the qualities of effective teachers. But at different points in your career it's likely that the particular blend of knowledge and skills you bring to the role of the teacher will be balanced differently. Newly-qualified teachers are likely to display quite a different profile to much more experienced teachers, or heads of department (Figure 6.1). The key point is to recognize how your own blend of competences has varied, and to carry out steps to develop those things that you wish to improve.

How teachers' competences can vary

The three diagrams show how the blend of competences required of a teacher may vary at different points in a career. In each diagram the professional knowledge, professional skills and personal attributes possessed by each teacher are indicated by proportional circles. The examples shown - for imaginary teachers - are provided to illustrate the range of knowledge, skills and attributes which are possible. They are not intended to imply that every teacher follows the same pattern.

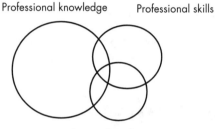

Professional knowledge   Professional skills

Personal attributes

Jake (23) Newly qualified teacher
Jake has good subject knowledge because he has recently completed a degree in his subject specialism. This gives rise to a large circle for professional competence. His professional skills as a teacher, however, are in their early stages of being developed. Likewise, although he displays some fine attributes of a potentially good teacher, there are aspects of his personal attributes that can he developed further in years to come. The circles for those latter two areas are correspondingly smaller.

Professional knowledge   Professional skills

Personal attributes

Sima (30) Head of department
Sima has developed a wide repertoire of professional teaching skills in the eight years she has been a teacher, and she has now progressed to head of department. Life at the chalkface has also allowed Sima to enhance her personal attributes in a way that has benefited her teaching. Both these circles are correspondingly larger than those for Jake. Although her subject knowledge is not as strong as Jake's, her overall professional knowledge remains proportional to his because she has gained additional knowledge of the education system and how schools work, which has compensated for slightly diminished subject knowledge.

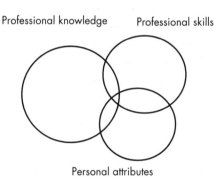

Professional knowledge   Professional skills

Personal attributes

Chris (43) Assistant head teacher
Chris has many management and leadership duties as well as being a classroom teacher. Her attendance at management courses has meant that the professional knowledge of her subject has tended to be neglected, with the result that she is rather rusty compared to new entrants to the profession. Her professional skills as a teacher, however, are at their peak, and have been honed by 20 years in the classroom: she is a very confident practitioner. Because she has to deal with a variety of stressful situations and is required to manage others in her school, Chris's day to day life in school is frenetic and as a result her personal attributes as a teacher have suffered. For example, she is finding it harder to relax in lessons, be creative and even laugh at herself occasionally.

Figure 6.1: How professional competence can vary

'We must walk consciously only part way toward our goal, and then leap in the dark to our success.' *Henry David Thoreau*

Task 6.4: Characterizing your own professional competence

Study Figure 6.1 showing three examples of teachers and their blend of professional competences. Reflect on your own competences as a teacher as they stand now – you might find it helpful to do this in collaboration with another colleague. Draw a Venn diagram similar to these that illustrates your three domains, making the size of the circles proportional to how well-developed your competence is in each area (e.g. if you're especially pleased with your teacher knowledge, make this larger etc.). You might find it useful to consider how your blend of competences has varied at different points in your career, and how it might develop in the future. What would the ideal blend that you're currently working towards look like? Finally consider how your personal competences affect the diagram?

The key role of creativity

This chapter has explained in detail the things that single out successful teachers. We believe that *the* most important attribute of a teacher is creativity. Teachers who are able to use this creativity will be much more likely to find appropriate ways to teach, or solutions to a whole raft of challenges which they face on a daily basis. The good news is that we can all develop our creativity through a range of practical approaches, as detailed in Chapter 4.

Creative approaches can also clearly be used to develop the knowledge, attributes and other skills of a teacher. Indeed, it could be argued that teaching is such a complex and multi-faceted profession that *unless* creative approaches are used, teachers can never keep up with the pace of change that may be required.

When it all gets too much

Finally, we'd like to address the difficult question, 'What should I do if I feel that I am no longer being effective as I would like in the classroom?' This is surely something we have all felt at some point in our teaching careers, but if this feeling becomes overwhelming it's time to do something about it. If it's causing you undue negative stress then study Box 6.6 first and take decisive measures before things get worse. Then ask yourself some fundamental questions (Box 6.7).

'To discover new oceans we must leave behind familiar shores.'

Box 6.7: Questions to take a reality check

At times the going gets tough, and it may help to take a reality check. Here are some useful reality check questions:

1 Am I being too hard on myself?

2 Am I being too hard on them?

3 Am I selling myself short?

4 How can I make this easier and still do it right?

5 Who is this really about, me or them?

6 How could taking a break help me here?

7 What's the plan? What's next?

8 Who else could do this for me?

9 What's really stopping this from being successful?

10 Do I need to make a major change for my *own* benefit?

11 Is it time to think of myself and my future?

12 What exciting alternatives are there and what do I see myself doing in three years?

Remember too that it's perfectly OK to give yourself lots of *fresh starts* as you try different strategies to make the breakthroughs that you want. Some things will not work out; others may take some time and a good deal of determination before they bear fruit. Be prepared to abandon what's really not working and try something else instead. Remember the saying 'tomorrow can be the first day of the rest of your life', but remember that you need to *choose* to act if things are going to change. Don't hold back, act now!

If things still look very gloomy, we strongly recommend a short career break for personal development and re-energizing. There are many roles related to teaching which can be very rewarding, and give you the chance to learn new skills, as well as taking stock of your current situation. These include secondments to education projects in your LEA, working in a support capacity with schools, and education roles outside classrooms (see Best and Dover 2006 for more details). Having the chance to work outside your current school can itself be exciting and invigorating, as you can escape the unique constraints and often entrenched politics of a single institution. Teachers tend not to move around that much in their careers, and a result can have a rather blinkered view of the world. If you take off your blinkers the world can be a much more exciting place. This can sometimes be achieved simply by changing schools.

'No one ever said on their deathbed: "I wish I'd spent more time at work".'

↻ Review

This chapter has aimed to demystify the important area of teachers' professional and personal domain. It has sought to emphasize the following key points:

- Teachers' professional and personal domain is the central element of the Creative Teaching Framework, and influences strongly all other domains of the framework.

- The professional competence of a teacher can be broken down in to knowledge, attributes and skills – each is also strongly influenced by the personal domain.

- Beliefs and values underpin much of the professional and personal domain, and by allowing these to surface we can learn much about ourselves and any conflicts which we're experiencing.

- Creativity can enable teachers to make the most of their professional and personal domain.

- Every teacher is capable of developing their professional competence, but need to *choose* to do so.

- There is a range of approaches to developing your professional competence as a teacher, for which a frank self-evaluation exercise (see page 235) can provide the launching pad.

- Due attention must be given to the personal domain of the teacher as it can affect profoundly an individual's ability to teach effectively – negative stress in particular is the enemy of effective teaching and of personal motivation.

⇨ Action points

Consider the following actions in the light of this chapter and using the self-evaluation tool select those that are most appropriate for you needs:

- Carry out the tasks outlined in this chapter in tandem with some other professional development activity in your school, seeing how one can enhance the other.

- Create your own action plan for developing your teaching competence under the headings 'knowledge', 'attributes' and 'skills'. Identify who can support you as you move forward with the action plan.

- Find other teachers in your school who are fully committed to developing their teaching competence. It's empowering to work with people who are similarly committed, and such collaboration can form the basis of a powerful learning community.

- Consider what more you can harvest from your personal domain to help you professionally.

'Your dreams can provide a window into your inner world ... if you allow yourself to daydream you sometimes get a sneak preview of what's inside.'

👁 Further reading

The Hay McBer model of teacher effectiveness is an interesting framework for effective teaching that includes teachers' professional competence. It can be downloaded from the DfES website.

Best, B & Dover, S (2006) *Teaching Uncovered*. Richmond: Trotman Publishing.

- An overview of the range of roles working with school-aged children in education settings.

Ginnis, P (2002) *The Teacher's Toolkit*. Bencyfelin: Crown House Publishing Ltd.

- This excellent book includes some thought-provoking content about the professional and personal domain.

'It's hard to get the best from your students if you've not committed ensuring you're at your best to teach them.'

233

> **End of chapter metaphor:** Read the story and use the questions that follow to consider further aspects of the chapter content.

Next to the A449 Kidderminster road, rush hour

'Hey rabbit!'

'Yeah, what is it squirrel?'

'What are you doing?'

'I'm playing chicken across the road'

'How do you play chicken'

'You wait for a car, then run across the road as it comes past'

'Really? How do you avoid getting squashed?'

'Easy, wait until the front of the car is level with you, then shout "ONE" out loud to yourself and then run as hard as you can. Rabbit waited for a car and as the front of the car approached his nose he screamed 'ONE' as loud as he could and launched himself forward. As the dust settled, squirrel dared to look; between the speeding cars he saw rabbit bouncing up and down, laughing on the other side of the road. 'You now,' shouted rabbit.

Squirrel stretched his legs, took a deep breath and waited for the next car. . . 'Oh. . .Not ready,' he said to himself as the first car passed. Then with all the courage he could muster, as the next car came level with his nose he shouted 'ONE!' and launched himself forward.

'DU-DUM,' went the car, squashing the squirrel.

'Oh *@!&!' screamed rabbit.

Alas, squirrels have shorter legs than rabbits.

> ## You might wish to consider:
> 1 What is the moral of this story?
> 2 Where are there examples of rabbit's way of supporting people in your workplace?
> 3 What is there to learn from the story?

'To dare is to lose one's footing momentarily. Not to dare is to lose oneself.' *Søren Kierkegaard*

The self-evaluation tool

As well as providing specific tools for reflection as detailed elsewhere in the book we wanted to include something much more substantial that would allow you to chart a structured path to improving your teaching. The comprehensive self-evaluation tool that follows is designed around the Five Domains of Effective Teaching and the general concepts around creativity. It helps you take a closer look at all of the key aspects of your role. The tool also serves to bring together the key themes of *The Creative Teaching and Learning Toolkit* into a highly practical self-development exercise. It provides a series of thought-provoking questions which stem from each of the chapters in the book.

The self-evaluation tool is designed to be flexible and is available electronically on the accompanying CD-ROM. Once you're familiar with how it works, you can adapt it more closely to your needs by adding sections or questions. By making it more personally relevant it will have greater appeal and impact.

The tool could be used alone or with colleagues. You could also invite trusted individuals to evaluate you against the questions and compare your views with theirs. Experience of doing this ourselves and with others suggests that this latter approach is an enlightening and uplifting experience. It is a good idea to set out some ground rules before doing this, particularly in the areas of honesty and approaches to feedback.

To use the self-evaluation framework, follow the steps below:

The self-evaluation tool

Guidance for completion

1   Work through it by reading the questions and score yourself by ticking the appropriate box according to the following key (work in pencil at this stage):

   0 = you feel you have not begun to address the question

   1 = you have started work, but it is in its early stages

   2 = you feel quite confident about the work you have done in this area

   3 = you feel the work you have done in this area represents excellent practice

2 As you do so note down any action points or issues that come to mind – this forms the basis of your action plan for improving your teaching.

3 Then add up the scores (and work out the percentages) for each section. This will give you a more quantitative assessment of which areas need further development. If you like you can draw charts and diagrams to bring the figures to life. You can work out your score for the self-evaluation as a whole, or use this figure to see what category you fall into (see page 242).

4 Take a photocopy of the self-evaluation framework so you can refer back to it in future. Repeat termly, or at other regular intervals to track your progress. Identify the steps to maintain or improve what you do.

5 Formulate your action plan for improving your practice, including timescales.

Self-evaluation tables

CREATIVITY	← Emerging		Advanced →	
	0	1	2	3
Do you understand the importance of creativity in learning experiences for young people?				
Do you plan using creative thinking?				
Do you plan to incorporate creative thinking opportunities for your students in lessons?				
Are you challenging any preconceptions you might have about your own creativity?				
Do you have clear arguments to challenge the limiting beliefs of others about their creativity?				
Do you understand the creative process (page 28)?				

CREATIVITY	← Emerging		Advanced →	
	0	1	2	3
Are you taking steps to further develop your students' understanding of creativity?				
Do you see creativity as an essential skill for students in solving problems?				

Creativity score: /24 = %

VISION	← Emerging		Advanced →	
	0	1	2	3
Do you have a clear vision for your teaching (or your department's or school's teaching) processes?				
Do you have that vision written down?				
Are you using a Vision Pyramid (page 51) or a similar tool to plan your future approach?				
Are your students involved in shaping that vision?				
Are you integrating your vision with that of others?				
Are you communicating that vision effectively to your students?				
Are you communicating that vision to other stakeholders?				
Do you understand the importance of values in relation to young people?				
Are you using the Values Clusters Model and values process (pages 69–72) to develop even stronger connections with students?				

VISION	← Emerging		Advanced →	
	0	1	2	3
Are you using values clusters to inform your collective vision?				
Over the last month did you work only in the time you allocated for work?				

Vision score: /33 =   %

CLIMATE	← Emerging		Advanced →	
	0	1	2	3
Do you actively consider and take steps to manage the physiological dimensions of classroom climate (page 84)?				
Do you actively consider and take steps to manage the psychological dimensions of classroom climate (page 85)?				
Do you actively consider and take steps to manage the teaching and learning strategies dimensions of classroom climate (page 89)?				
Do you ask your students regularly about what's working and what's not working in their classroom climate?				

Climate score: /12 =   %

TEACHING AND LEARNING STRATEGIES	← Emerging		Advanced →	
	0	1	2	3
Do you actively audit your lessons based on the eight factors vital for long term motivation?				
Are you confident in the use of the creative tools in Chapter 4?				
Have your students been introduced to the creative tools in Chapter 4?				
Are you taking steps to further develop your own competence in using the creative tools in Chapter 4?				
Do you build in opportunities over a half-term for students to use: visualization, association, dumping, chunking, metaphors, focused relaxation, and jamming in their work?				
Do you construct and use stories to convey content or process messages in your teaching?				
Do you use a range of strategies to engage the eyes over a week?				
Do you use a range of strategies to engage the ears over a week?				
Do you use a range of strategies to engage the body over a week?				
Do you audit your lesson planning to have a range of strategies for the eyes, ears, and body?				
Do you coach using open questions, rather than tell or ask closed questions?				

TEACHING AND LEARNING STRATEGIES	← Emerging		Advanced →	
	0	1	2	3
Do you plan for and deliver a range of assessment for learning opportunities, providing a genuine formative assessment process in your classroom?				
Do you use a lesson structure approach?				
Are you aware of the need to be creative in blending teaching and learning approaches to ensure that the methods you use do not become stale?				

Teaching and learning strategies score: /42 =   %

REFLECTION	← Emerging		Advanced →	
	0	1	2	3
Are you taking a few minutes each day to review your experiences constructively?				
Are you taking time out on a regular basis for longer reflection periods?				
Are you managing your own resource-fulness with a focus on your strengths and successes before moving to your areas for development?				
Do you take time out to challenge your excuses when you're feeling stuck?				
Do you use a system for prioritizing your tasks?				
Do you structure reflection for yourself and others by using a change process model like STRIDE (page 187)?				

REFLECTION	← Emerging		Advanced →	
	0	1	2	3
Do you regularly have the coaching support of another person to aid your reflective process?				
Do you utilize a reflective tool like 'Rules for Success' (page 192) or similar to assist your reviews?				
Do you teach and encourage colleagues and students to use a range of self-reflection tools?				
Do you use and encourage open curious questioning in your classroom, meetings and ad hoc discussions?				
Do you carry out a full professional review at least once per year with another colleague to support you?				

Reflection score: /33 =   %

TEACHERS' PROFESSIONAL AND PERSONAL DOMAIN	← Emerging		Advanced →	
	0	1	2	3
To what extent are you aware of the professional and personal qualities you bring to your teaching?				
Have you considered the professional knowledge, skills and values required of a teacher?				
To what extent are you continuing to develop your knowledge and skills?				
Have you considered how your personal knowledge, attributes, skills and values influence your teaching?				

TEACHERS' PROFESSIONAL AND PERSONAL DOMAIN	← Emerging		Advanced →	
	0	1	2	3
Have you reflected on the effect that your physical and psychological state has on your readiness to teach, or your professional performance?				
Are you taking steps to ensure you're in a more resourceful state, more of the time?				
Are you working with another person at your school to share your concerns and make plans for a better future?				
Are you engaging in coaching work on a personal level?				

Teachers' personal and professional domain score: /24 = %

Total of your raw scores for all sections

$$\frac{\rule{5cm}{0.4pt}}{168} \times \textbf{100} = \quad \%$$

Date evaluation was carried out: _____

You can use the key below to interpret the individual sections of the questionnaire as well as the overall result for your teaching.*

Key

0–30%	emerging teacher
30–59%	improving teacher
60–89%	effective teacher
90%+	advanced teacher

*Note that these categories are just intended to give you checkpoints to work towards and are not intended to be definitive assessments of different levels of teaching.

Concluding questions

To close the main chapters of the book, we'd like to offer some 'big picture' questions that will encourage deep reflection and metacognition:

- In your opinion what are the most creative acts that have ever taken place on the earth? In the context of education and learning, what creative leaps forward do you recognize as most significant?

- We included in the introduction our commentary on the 'curriculum versus creativity' debate, by stating that one of the major challenges facing schools is to design a 'curriculum of creativity'. What would such a curriculum look like?

- Throughout this book we have tried to stress the *changes* that need to take place in order for teaching to be more effective. Reflect on your own circumstances – what are the top three changes you would like to implement that will enable you to improve your teaching?

- We have endeavoured to tackle the difficult area of the teacher's personal domain as we believe it has a fundamental bearing on teacher effectiveness, yet has not been adequately considered in previous books for teachers. When you think about yourself, what are the main challenges that lie ahead when considering your personal domain?

- The book has included a range of strategies that you can implement to try to get better results in your classroom, coupled with an overall framework for thinking about teaching. As you think about your teaching in the weeks to come, what balance will you try to strike between using new approaches and those which you already find effective? Is there a point at which 'new' activities, week after week, just become tiresome for learners?

- One of the authors' key beliefs is that we can learn much about effective teaching from the world of education psychology. To what extent do you share this belief, and if so, how will you keep up with findings in this field?

- Students are singled out as a vital source of information to improve your teaching and their learning. How ready are you to embrace the views of students on your teaching? What prejudices will you or other people have to suspend in order to engage fully with students in this way?

- As a result of reading this book what will you:
  - Start doing?
  - Stop doing?

- Do more of?
- Do less of?

- If you had to explain your vision for your classroom/department/school right now to a stranger in an elevator and you only had one minute to do it, what would you say?
  - How will you know when you have achieved this vision? What will you see happening around you?
  - If you secretly knew what would make you unstoppable in achieving this vision what might that be?

- What did you know to be true at the age of seven that is still true now?

Concluding thought !

Throughout this book we have focused on the things that you can take control over, or can influence. We would suggest that most things are within our gift to influence. Some things we can control, but there are of course situations over which we have no control. It is these that allow our true professionalism to show through, for what we can change, we take action on, what we can influence gives us hope, and that which we have no control or influence over brings us humility, grace, and true emotional intelligence. It is these things that we must learn to accept or let go of. What we can accept often teaches us more than that which we have obvious choices over. In the words of Victor Frankl, concentration camp survivor:

'The last human freedom is the ability to choose one's attitude in any situation'.

Sometimes the actions we take are not outside of ourselves but within. Your attitude <u>always</u> belongs to you.

Good luck!

If you wish to take this ideas in the book further, training courses are available with the authors – for details see www.visionforlearning.co.uk

Glossary

Accelerated learning Learning which proceeds at a faster rate, and with deeper understanding, than that normally expected using conventional teaching methods. In the last few years a range of techniques and approaches have been developed, taking into account recent knowledge of how the brain works, that allow children to learn more effectively. These include mind mapping, multiple intelligences, knowledge of learning styles and use of thinking skills. Accelerated learning also includes the promotion of a positive learning environment, and ensures learners are in an appropriate physiological and psychological state to learn.

Action research Research concerned with the everyday practical problems of teachers, rather than educational theory. Action research is often carried out by teachers themselves.

Active learning Learning which stimulates children to play an active part in the learning process.

Affective learning Learning which deals with emotions, feelings and beliefs.

Assessment for Learning Assessment which focuses on providing information which will help a student learn more effectively in future, rather than simply establishing the level of knowledge and understanding they have reached. The government has recently championed the role of Assessment for Learning as part of its various national strategies, and a guidance document giving ten principles of Assessment for Learning is available. (www.qca.org.uk/3.html)

Attainment Achievement as measured by an individual's knowledge, skills and understanding in a particular area of learning.

Beliefs Rules we operate on at a subconscious level or of which we're barely conscious. They are ideas or constructs that we no longer question.

Cloze A technique used to develop literacy involving selected words being deleted from a text, and children being challenged to fill in the blanks.

Closed question A question only likely to lead to a yes or no answer.

Cognitive To do with the thinking part of the brain. Cognition is the act of thinking or the mental processing of information.

Cognitive Acceleration through Science Education (CASE) A programme of lessons in science to promote effective learning. It focuses heavily on using accelerated learning principles and developing thinking skills. Studies have shown beneficial effects in science examinations for children undertaking CASE lessons, together with improvements in English and maths results.

Didactic teaching   A traditional method of teaching involving whole class instruction.

Differentiation   The process of effectively matching the needs of learners to the tasks given. For example a teacher must ensure that appropriate levels of challenge are provided to all children, so that during a lesson no child find tasks too difficult or too easy.

Enrichment   Usually refers to the provision of extra activities out of school hours that enhance the core curriculum.

Fine motor skills   Skills, such as holding a pen correctly or moving the lips to eat food, which require the fine manipulation of hands, feet or other parts of the body.

Flow   A state of mind in which there is a feeling of being immersed in and carried by an activity. The state is characterized by a lack of self-consciousness and seamless experimentation.

Formative assessment   Assessment that provides feedback to improve teaching and learning, rather than for grading or putting in rank order.

Gifted   A gifted child is defined by the DfES as a child who achieves, or has the ability to achieve, significantly above their peers in their school. Gifted children are very able in one or more of the National Curriculum core subjects, or an 'all rounder'.

Gross motor skills   Skills involving larger movements of the limbs and body, such as running and jumping.

Higher order thinking skills   Thinking skills which require sustained effort for most students to achieve, such as evaluation.

ICT Across the Curriculum   A government initiative to promote the use of ICT in all subject areas. The principal aim is to ensure that ICT becomes embedded in subject teaching, rather than being a discrete skill to be developed only in ICT lessons.

Inclusion   The process through which a school seeks to recognize and encourage each individual, enabling them to access, participate and achieve fully.

Independent learning   Learning which is focused on the student rather than the teacher, and which involves a degree of self-regulation by the student.

Individual learning plan   A document which sets out the learning needs of an individual student, taking into account such things as learning style, prior knowledge and individual strengths and weaknesses.

Learning style   The particular method of learning preferred by a child. In recent years there has been a general acceptance that learning styles fall into three categories:

- Visual – through seeing
- Auditory – through hearing
- Kinesthetic – through doing.

As part of the accelerated learning approach teachers are now encouraged to vary their teaching styles to include all three types of learners. However, care is needed to avoid labelling students as one 'type of learner'.

Metacognition   Understanding of how you think and reason. Sometimes referred to as 'thinking about thinking'.

Modelling   The process whereby a teacher demonstrates how they perform a task themselves in order to help students see how it can be done effectively.

Multiple intelligences   The theory of intelligence that maintains that people are intelligent in many ways, not just in terms of their Intelligence Quotient. Put forward by Harvard professor Howard Gardner in the 1980s the theory suggests that people are intelligent in at least the following ways:

- Interpersonal
- Intrapersonal
- Linguistic
- Kinesthetic
- Mathematical/logical
- Musical
- Natural
- Visual-Spatial

It has been embraced by many educational professionals and is a popular element of accelerated learning programmes.

Open question   A question that promotes more sophisticated thinking and avoids a yes or no answer.

Oracy   Speaking skills.

Peer observation   The practice of teachers observing other teachers in the classroom for the purposes of professional development.

Pedagogy   The methods used to teach and the way the curriculum is put together.

Personalized learning   Learning which respects the individual personalities, learning preferences and differences of students.

Plenary   A part of a lesson during which the learning is reviewed, often through the extensive use of teacher questioning. During a plenary the teacher should refer to the learning objectives and allow the students to reflect on what they have learnt. Part of the DfES recommended lesson structure.

Prime directives   Main operating principles, e.g. the main principles that the unconscious part of our mind operates on.

Progression   Ensuring that children make progress in line with their previous achievements.

Qualitative   Relating to quality. Used mainly in the context of more subjective information gained on students' performance by teachers, which does not easily translate into numerical information or statistical data.

Quantitative   Relating to quantity. Used mainly to refer to information on students gained from hard data such as tests and examinations, which easily translates into numerical information or statistical data.

Rapport   The existence between two or more people of a mutual state of openness, trust, closeness and safety. It is characterized by a willingness to take risks, explore options and share thoughts and feelings.

Scaffolding   Support provided to enable children to complete more complex tasks, typically by breaking down the task into simpler ones, or providing prompts that enable children to make step-by-step progress.

Starter   An initial activity with which a teacher begins a lesson, and the first part of the recommended DfES lesson structure. Starters are designed to engage interest and arouse curiosity, providing an effective basis for the lesson to follow.

Streaming   A type of school organization where children are placed into groups according to their ability and stay in these groups for most of their lessons.

Summative assessment   Assessment taking place at the end of a course, which aims to identify the student's level of attainment.

Teaching style   The particular teaching method used by a teacher. Studies of the most effective teachers show that they vary their teaching style to appeal to different learning styles.

Talented   A child is defined by the DfES as talented if they're very able in art, music, physical education or performing arts. The word has also been used more generally in the past by teachers to refer to an able child. Talented children have come under the spotlight as part of the Gifted and Talented Strand of Excellence in Cities.

Thinking skills   Skills which promote effective thinking. The government has identified five thinking skills as part of the National Curriculum: information-processing skills, reasoning skills, enquiry skills, creative thinking skills and evaluation skills.

Values cluster   A convenient way of describing groups of values for an individual or group of people so that comparisons can be made. The cluster does not accurately represent the full detail or hierarchy of the individual or group values, but makes for a generic way of describing what is likely to be important to them. This is useful in planning interventions where there's conflict between individuals.

Values set   Collections of values in a hierarchy and which are unique to an individual.

Values   What's important to us. Values are constructed from complex interactions between our beliefs.

Writing frame   A printed framework to help children write more effectively, usually involving prompts and other devices to promote thinking and planning.

Bibliography

Adey, P & Shayer, M (1994) *Really raising standards: cognitive intervention and academic achievement.* London: Routledge.

Adey, P S, Shayer, M & Yates, C (1995) *Thinking Science: the curriculum materials of the CASE project.* Nashville: Thomas Nelson and Sons.

Amabile, T M (1996) *Creativity in Context.* Nashville: Westview.

Bandura, A (1997) *Self efficacy: the exercise of control.* New York: Freeman.

Baird, D (2004) *A Thousand Paths to Creativity.* London: MQ Publications.

Baron, J B & Sternberg, R J (Eds.) (1987) *Teaching Thinking Skills: theory and practice.* New York: Freeman.

Best, B (2002) *The LVT Classroom Guide: using Logovisual Technology to infuse thinking skills into key stages 3 and 4.* Settle: Centre for Management Creativity.

Best, B (2003) *The Accelerated Learning Pocketbook.* Alresford: Teachers' Pocketbooks.

Best, B, Blake, A & Varney, J (2005) *Making Meaning: learning through logovisual thinking.* London: Chris Kington Publishing.

Best, B, Craven, S & West, J (2006) *The Gifted & Talented Coordinator's Handbook: practical strategies for supporting more able students in secondary schools.* London: Optimus Publishing.

Best, B & Dover, S (2006) *Teaching Uncovered.* Richmond: Trotman Publishing.

Black, P, Harrison, C, Lee, C & Marshall, B (2004) *Working Inside the Black Box: assessment for learning in the classroom.* London: NferNelson.

Boud, D, Keough, R & Walker, D (1985) *Reflection: turning experience into learning.* London: Kogan Page.

Bowkett, S (2005) *100 Ideas for Teaching Creativity.* London: Continuum.

Buzan, T (2003) *The Mind Map Book: how to use radiant thinking to maximize your brain's untapped potential.* London: BBC Books.

Cavilglioli, O & Harris, I (2000) *Mapwise: accelerated learning through visible thinking.* London: Network Educational Press Ltd.

Cavilglioli, O, Harris, I & Tindall, B (2002) *Thinking Skills and Eye Q: visual tools for raising intelligence.* London: Network Educational Press Ltd.

Claxton, G (1997) *Hare Brain, Tortoise Mind.* London: Fourth Estate.

Claxton, G & Lucas, B (2004) *Be Creative: essential steps to revitalize your work and life.* London: BBC Books.

Coles, M J & Robinson, W (1989) *Teaching Thinking.* Bristol: Bristol Press.

Copley, A (2006) *Challenging Behaviour: a fresh look at promoting positive learning behaviours.* London: Network Continuum Press.

Cordingley, P, Bell, M, Thomason, S & Firth, A (2005). *The impact of collaborative continuing professional development (CPD) on classroom teaching and learning: how do collaborative and sustained CPD and sustained but not collaborative CPD affect teaching and learning?* London: EPPI.

Cordingley, P, Bell, M, Rundell, B & Evans, D (2003). *The impact of collaborative CPD on classroom teaching and learning: how does collaborative Continuing Professional Development (CPD) for teachers of the 5–16 age range affect teaching and learning?* London: EPPI.

Corrie C (2003) *The Emotionally Intelligent Child.* London: Network Educational Press.

Covey, S R (1989) *The Seven Habits of Highly Effective People.* London: Simon and Schuster.

Craft, A, Jeffrey, B & Leibling, M (2001) *Creativity in Education.* London: Continuum.

Creasy, J & Paterson, F (2005) *Leading Coaching in Schools.* Nottingham: National College for School Leadership.

De Bono, E (1990) *Lateral Thinking: a textbook of creativity.* London: Penguin

Dewey, J (1933) *How we Think.* Chicago: Henrey Regney.

Dilts, R (1999) *Sleight of Mouth: the magic of conversational belief change.* Capitola: Meta Publications Ltd.

Fisher, R (1998) *Teaching Thinking: philosophical enquiry in the classroom.* London: Continuum.

Fisher, R & Williams, M (eds) (2004) *Unlocking Creativity: teaching creativity across the curriculum.* Abingdon: David Fulton Publishers.

Freeman, D (1991) To Make the Tacit Explicit: teacher education, emerging discourse and conceptions of teaching. *Teacher and Teacher education 7*: 5–6.

Gardner, H (1993) *Frames of Mind: the theory of multiple intelligences.* London: Fontana.

Godefrey, C & Clark, J (1990) *The Complete Time Management System.* London: Piatkus.

Goleman D (1995) *Emotional Intelligence.* New York: Bantam.

Ginnis, P (2002) *The Teacher's Toolkit: raise classroom achievement with strategies for every learner.* Bancyfelin: Crown House Publishing Ltd.

Horn, R (1988) *Visual Language: global communication for the 21st century.* Washington: MacroVU Press.

Hughes M (2001) *Closing the Learning Gap.* London: Network Educational Press.

Jensen, E (1995) *Super Teaching.* San Diego: The Brain Store Inc.

Juch, A (1983) *Personal Development: theory and practice in management training.* Wiley: Shell International.

Kolb, D A (1984) *Experiential Learning: experience as the source of learning and development.* New Jersey: Prentice-Hall.

Knight, S (1995) *NLP at Work.* London: Nicholas Brealey Publishing.

Leat, D (ed.) (1998) *Thinking Through Geography.* London: Chris Kington Publishing.

Lawley, J & Tomkins, P (2000) *Metaphors in Mind.* Lisburn: The Developing Company Press.

Lewis, B & Pucelik, F (1990) *Magic of NLP Demystified.* Portland: Metamorphous Press.

Lovatt, M & Wise, D (2001) *Creating an Accelerated Learning School.* London: Network Educational Press.

Louden, W (1991) *Understanding Teaching.* London: Cassell.

McDermott, I & Jago, W (2003) *The NLP Coach.* London: Piatkus.

McGuinness, C (1999) *From Thinking Skills to thinking classrooms: a review and evaluation of approaches for developing pupils' thinking.* London: DfEE, (Research Report RR115)

McLeod A (2003) *Performance Coaching.* Bancyfelin: Crown House Publishing

Oldfather, P & West, J (1999) *Learning Through Children's Eyes: social constructivism and the desire to learn psychology in the classroom.* American Psychological Association.

Persaud, R (2005) *The Motivated Mind.* London: Bantam Press.

Petty, G (2004) *Teaching Today.* Cheltenham: Nelson Thornes.

Robbins, A (2001) *Unlimited Power.* New York: Pocket Books.

Rockett, M & Percival, S (2001) *Thinking for Learning.* London: Network Educational Press.

Sternberg, R (ed.) (1999) *Handbook of Creativity.* Cambridge: Cambridge University Press.

Sternberg, R J & Lubart, T I (1999) In: Sternberg, R (ed) (1999) *Handbook of Creativity.* Cambridge: Cambridge University Press.

Straessens, K & Vandenberghe, R (1994) Vision as a core component in school culture. *Curriculum Studies* 26:187–200.

Schön, D (1987) *Educating the Reflective Practitioner.* San Fransisco: Jossey Bass.

Shephard, D (2005) *NLP Master Practitioner Training Manual.* London: The Performance Partnership.

Shephard, D (2001) *Presenting Magically.* Bancyfelin: Crown House Publishing.

Smith, A (2000) *Accelerated Learning in Practice.* London: Network Educational Press.

Smith, A, Lovatt, M & Wise, D (2004) *Accelerated Learning: a user's guide.* London: Network Educational Press.

Talbert, M (1996) *The Holographic Universe.* London: Harper Collins.

Thomas, W & Smith, A (2004) *Coaching Solutions: practical ways to improve performance in education.* London: Network Educational Press.

Thomas, W (2005a) *Coaching Solutions Resource Book.* London: Network Educational Press.

Thomas, W (2005b) *The Managing Workload Pocketbook.* Alresford: Teachers' Pocketbooks.

Tsigilis, N & Theodosiou, A (2003) Temporal stability of the Intrinsic Motivation Inventory. *Perceptual and Motor Skills* 97: 271–280.

Wallace, R (1996) *Vision for Practice.* London: SAGE.

Wallace, B (2004) *Thinking Skills and Problem-solving: an inclusive approach.* Abingdon: NACE and David Fulton Publishers.

Wallace B, Adams H B, Maltby, F & Mathfield, J (1993) *TASC: Thinking actively in a social context.* Bicester: AB Academic Publishers.

Zeus, P & Skiffington, S (2002) *The Coaching at Work Toolkit.* Maidenhead: McGraw-Hill.

Materials to promote LogoVisual Thinking can be obtained from www.logovisual.com/education

Index

About the authors

Brin Best

Brin worked as a teacher, head of department and LEA adviser before forming Innovation *for* Education Ltd in 2002. His company works with teachers and school managers to secure a better future for our young people. Brin's main professional interest now centres on effective teaching and learning, which is also the focus of his doctoral studies in education at the University of Leeds. He writes and speaks widely on a variety of topics, is the author of twelve previous books on education and is the series consultant for the award-winning Teachers' Pocketbooks. Brin still teaches part-time, mainly in further education, and is a very active as a volunteer in the charity sector. His company runs the School Innovation Awards, which encourage and fund creative approaches to education. Brin has a passion for nature, wilderness areas and exploration and is a Fellow of the Royal Geographical Society.

Things Brin knew when he was seven that are still true today

- Always try your best – it's more important than being the Best

- Birds are brill, especially toucans and parrots

- Say what you think, but say it kindly

- Respect older people – we can learn a lot from them

- Never trust strangers.

Will Thomas

Will is an experienced trainer, consultant and performance coach. His career began in personnel management with Marks and Spencer plc, and was followed by successful roles in teaching, educational leadership and advisory work. Since he formed Vision for Learning Ltd, he has passionately developed tools for young people, teachers and managers. Will holds a Masters Degree in mentoring, counselling and guidance and a Certificate in Performance Coaching. He is an Accredited Performance Coach, Master Practitioner of Neuro-Linguistic Programming and a Registered Hypnotherapist. He has worked extensively in UK schools and with British and American schools overseas. He has written five books in the education field, including the award-winning *Head of Department's Pocketbook* with Brin Best. He is also a consultant to Alistair Smith's company ALITE. He loves mountain environments and is involved with the Duke of Edinburgh's Award Scheme and other charitable organizations.

Things Will knew when he was seven that are still true today

- Being honest makes you happy

- Your real mates hang around, whatever happens

- People who are unkind to you are usually even more unkind to themselves

- Stag beetles are fab, but you don't see them much anymore

- Learning new stuff is 'well good'.

Turn to page 167 for a task linked to this page.